Karen Brown's
California
Charming Inns & Itineraries

Written by
KAREN BROWN, JUNE BROWN, and CLARE BROWN

Illustrations by Barbara Tapp
Cover Painting by Jann Pollard

Karen Brown's Guides, San Mateo, California

Karen Brown Titles

Austria: Charming Inns & Itineraries

California: Charming Inns & Itineraries

England: Charming Bed & Breakfasts

England, Wales & Scotland: Charming Hotels & Itineraries

France: Charming Bed & Breakfasts

France: Charming Inns & Itineraries

Germany: Charming Inns & Itineraries

Ireland: Charming Inns & Itineraries

Italy: Charming Bed & Breakfasts

Italy: Charming Inns & Itineraries

Mid-Atlantic: Charming Inns & Itineraries

New England: Charming Inns & Itineraries

Portugal: Charming Inns & Itineraries

Spain: Charming Inns & Itineraries

Switzerland: Charming Inns & Itineraries

To Our Outstanding Webmistress Lynn Upthagrove
And Her Constant Canine Companion, Bob

Editors: Clare Brown, June Brown, Karen Brown, Iris Sandilands, Lorena Aburto.

Web designer: Lynn Upthagrove.

Illustrations: Barbara Tapp, Vanessa Kale page 66.

Maps: Chrismar Mapping Services Inc.; Inside cover photo: W. Russell Ohlson.

Copyright © 2002 by Karen Brown's Guides.

This book or parts thereof may not be reproduced in any form without obtaining written permission from the publisher: Karen Brown's Guides, P.O. Box 70, San Mateo, CA 94401, USA, email: karen@karenbrown.com.

Distributed by Fodor's Travel Publications, Inc., 280 Park Avenue, New York, NY 10017, USA.

Distributed in Canada by Random House Canada, 2775 Matheson Boulevard. East, Mississanga, Ontario L4W 4P7, Canada, phone: (905) 624 0672, fax: (905) 624 6217.

Distributed in the United Kingdom, Ireland, and Europe by Random House UK, 20 Vauxhall Bridge Road, London, SW1V 2SA, England, phone: 44 20 7840 4000, fax: 44 20 7840 8406.

Distributed in Australia by Random House Australia, 20 Alfred Street, Milsons Point, Sydney NSW 2061, Australia, phone: 61 2 9954 9966, fax: 61 2 9954 4562.

Distributed in New Zealand by Random House New Zealand, 18 Poland Road, Glenfield, Auckland, New Zealand, phone: 64 9 444 7197, fax: 64 9 444 7524.

Distributed in South Africa by Random House South Africa, Endulani, East Wing, 5A Jubilee Road, Parktown 2193, South Africa, phone: 27 11 484 3538, fax: 27 11 484 6180.

A catalog record for this book is available from the British Library.

ISSN 1535-4032

Contents

Introduction

San Francisco Cable Car

California, the Golden State, is fascinating with its diverse regions, dramatic scenery, exciting places to visit, and appealing places to stay. There is almost too much—it can be confusing to decide the most important sights to see and the most special inns to choose. This book is written to help you through the maze: we have done your homework for you. The first section of the book presents five detailed driving itineraries that spider-web across the state. The second section features our personal recommendations of places to stay, written with the sincere belief that where you lay your head each night makes the difference between a good and a great vacation.

About Itineraries

Five driving itineraries map and describe a route through the various regions of California so that you can choose one that includes the area you have your heart set on visiting. These itineraries are outlined on the maps at the back of the book. Each routing can easily be tailored to meet your own specific needs by leaving out some sightseeing if time is limited, or linking several itineraries together if you wish to enjoy a longer vacation.

CAR RENTAL

The itineraries are designed for travel by car. If you are staying in San Francisco at the beginning of your trip, it is not necessary to pick up a rental car until you leave the city since the public transportation system is so convenient and this is a wonderful town for walking. However, if your vacation begins in Los Angeles, you will need a car within the city to get from place to place and should pick it up on arrival at the airport.

DRIVING TIMES

California is a large state, approximately 1,000 miles from tip to toe. If you stay on the freeways, you can quickly cover large areas of territory, but if you choose to savor the beauty of the coast along California's sensational Highway 1 or dip into the countryside along scenic back roads, plan on traveling about 30 miles in an hour and remember to allow extra time for stopping to enjoy countryside vistas.

MAPS

The colored map section at the back of the book shows the driving itineraries' routings and all the towns in which we have a recommended place to stay. For detailed trip planning it is essential to supplement these with comprehensive commercial maps. Rand McNally maps are available on our website, *www.karenbrown.com.*

PACING

At the beginning of each itinerary we suggest our recommended pacing to help you decide the amount of time to allocate to each one. The suggested time frame reflects how much there is to see and do. Use our recommendation as a guideline only, and choreograph your own itinerary based on how much leisure time you have and whether your preference is to move on to a new destination each day or settle in and use a particular inn as base.

WEATHER

At the beginning of each itinerary a brief note is given on what you can expect to encounter weather-wise in the various regions. In California a whole new climate emerges in just a short distance. The idea that the entire state is sunny and warm year-round can all too quickly be dispelled when the summer fog rolls into San Francisco or 3 feet of winter snow falls in the High Sierras.

About Inn Travel

We use the term "inn" to cover everything from a simple bed and breakfast to a sophisticated resort. A wide range of inns is included in this guide: some are great bargains, others very costly; some are in cities, others in remote locations; some are quite sophisticated, others extremely simple; some are decorated with opulent antiques, others with furniture from grandma's attic; some are large hotels, others have only a few rooms. The common denominator is that each place has some special quality that makes it appealing. The descriptions are intended to give you an honest appraisal of each property so that you can select accommodation based on personal preferences. The following pointers will help you appreciate and understand what to expect when traveling the "inn way."

BATHROOMS

Not every inn recommended in this book has a connecting bathroom for each bedroom. Some inns will offer guestrooms that share a bath with other guestrooms, or rooms that have private baths down the hall. We make a note in the bottom details of the inn description if each guestroom does NOT have an en-suite bathroom. We do not specify whether the bathroom is equipped with shower, tub-shower, tub, or Jacuzzi.

BREAKFAST

A trademark of many inns is their morning repast—many cookbooks have been authored by innkeepers. Breakfast is almost always included in the room rate, but we definitely mention if it is NOT. Although innkeepers take great pride in their delectable morning offerings, know that breakfast can range from a gourmet "waddle away" feast to muffins and coffee. Sometimes breakfast is Continental in the privacy of your room or a hot breakfast with others in the dining room. Breakfast times vary—some innkeepers serve a hot breakfast at a specified time, while others replenish a buffet on a more leisurely schedule. Breakfasts are as individual as the inns themselves.

CANCELLATION POLICIES

Although policies vary, inns, by necessity, are usually more stringent than large chain hotels in their cancellation policies: understand their terms when securing a reservation.

CHARM

It is very important to us that an inn has charm—ideally an inn should be appealing, perhaps a historic building, beautifully decorated, lovingly managed, and in a wonderful location. Few inns meet every criterion, but all our selections have something that makes them special and are situated in enjoyable surroundings—we have had to reject several lovely inns because of a poor location. Many are in historic buildings, but remember that California is a relatively young state, so anything over 50 years in age is considered old—few inns date back further than the mid-19th century and many are new or reproduction-old buildings. Small inns are usually our favorites, but size alone did not dictate whether or not a hostelry was chosen. Most are small (a few have only three guestrooms), but because California offers some splendid larger establishments of great character and charm (one has 681 guestrooms!), a few of these are also included.

CHECK-IN

Inns are usually very specific about check-in time—generally between 3 and 6 pm. Let the inn know if you are going to arrive late and the innkeeper will make special arrangements for you, such as leaving you a door key under a potted plant along with a note on how to find your room. Also, for those who might arrive early, note that some inns close their doors between check-out and check-in times. Inns are often staffed only by the owners themselves and that window of time between check-out and check-in is often the one opportunity to shop for those wonderful breakfasts they prepare in addition to running their own personal errands.

CHILDREN

Many places in this guide do not welcome children. They cannot legally refuse accommodation to children, but, as parents, we really want to know and want to stay where our children are genuinely welcome. Under each description we have indicated the general policy of each inn, i.e., whether children are welcome or whether the inn is not appropriate for children—but these are only guidelines. Many places will accept children with certain stipulations such as if they have the proper room available, if the children are of a certain age, if other families are going to be in residence, or if it is a slow period.

COMFORT

Comfort plays a deciding role in the selection of inns recommended. Firm mattresses, a quiet setting, good lighting, fresh towels, scrubbed bathrooms—we do our best to remember the basics when considering inns. The decor and innkeeper will soon be forgotten if you do not enjoy a good night's sleep. Note that parts of California can be hot during the summer and several inns in older buildings do not have air conditioning.

CREDIT CARDS

Whether or not an establishment accepts credit cards is indicated at the bottom of each description—AX (American Express), MC (MasterCard), VS (Visa), all major, or none. Even if an inn does not accept credit cards it may take them as a guarantee of arrival.

FOOD

The majority of places featured in this guide do not have restaurants but usually there are restaurants close by. Almost all of the inns include breakfast in the tariff: quite often a sumptuous one. Frequently, in addition to breakfast, tea or wine and hors d'oeuvres are served in the afternoon. Sometimes, if you request in advance, a picnic lunch can also be prepared. If you have any special dietary requirements, most innkeepers will gladly try to accommodate your needs. It is best to mention any special requests at the time of making your reservation, both as a courtesy and from a practical point of view so that the innkeeper can have on hand any out-of-the-ordinary items that you might need.

PROFESSIONALISM

The inns we have selected are run by professional innkeepers. There are many homes that rent out extra bedrooms to paying guests but this was not what we were looking for and they are not included in our guide. We have recommended only inns that have privacy for the guests and where you do not have to climb over family clutter to reach the bathroom.

RESERVATIONS

The best way to make a reservation is to pick up your phone and call. It is very satisfactory to be able to discuss the various differences in available accommodation. Please try not to call during breakfast hours. Also, inns are often homes, so late-night calls are not appreciated. A convenient way to request a reservation is by fax: if the inn has a fax, we have noted the number. Another excellent way to make reservations is by email and we have included the email addresses of inns that feature on the Karen Brown website (*www.karenbrown.com*). Be aware that the majority of inns in this guide require a two-night stay on weekends and over holidays.

RESPONSIBILITY

Our goal is to outline itineraries in regions that we consider of prime interest to our readers and to recommend inns that we think are outstanding. All of the inns featured have been visited and selected solely on their merits. Our judgments are made on the charm of the inn, its setting, cleanliness, and, above all, the warmth of welcome. Each property has its own appeal, and we try to present you with a very honest appraisal. However, no matter how careful we are, sometimes we misjudge an inn's merits, or the ownership changes, or unfortunately sometimes inns just do not maintain their standards. If you find an inn is not as we have indicated, please let us know, and accept our sincere apologies.

ROOM RATES

It seems that many inns play musical rates, with high-season, low-season, midweek, weekend, and holiday rates. We have quoted the 2002 high-season, general range of rates from the lowest-priced bedroom for two people (singles usually receive a very small discount) to the most expensive suite, including breakfast. The rates given are those quoted to us by the inn. Please use these figures as a guideline and be certain to ask at the time of booking what the rates are and what they include.

We have not given prices for "special" rooms such as those that can accommodate three people traveling together. Discuss with the innkeeper rooms and rates available before making your selection. Of course, several inns are exceptions to our guidelines and whenever this is the case we mention the special situation (such as breakfast not being included in the rate). Please be aware that taxes are not included in the rates quoted and usually inn taxes are very high—frequently around 10%.

SMOKING

In addition to California's law that prohibits smoking in any public places, most inns have always had extremely strict non-smoking policies. A few inns permit smoking in restricted public areas or outside, but in general it is best to assume that smoking is not appropriate. If smoking is of great concern to you, be sure to ask the hotel specifically as to their policy about smoking in the garden, on the deck, or in a specially designated public area.

SOCIALIZING

Inns usually offer a conviviality rarely found in a "standard" hotel. The gamut runs all the way from playing "cozy family" around the kitchen table to sharing a sophisticated, elegant cocktail hour in the parlor. Breakfast may be a formal meal served at a set hour when the guests gather around the dining-room table, or it may be served buffet-style over several hours where guests have the option of either sitting down to eat alone or joining other guests at a larger table. Then again, some inns will bring a breakfast tray to your room, or perhaps breakfast in the room is the only option.

After check-in, many inns offer an afternoon refreshment, such as tea and cakes or wine and hors d'oeuvres, which may be seen as another social opportunity. Some inns set out the refreshments buffet-style where guests are invited to meander in and out mixing or not mixing with other guests as they choose, while others orchestrate a more structured gathering, often a social hour, with the innkeeper presiding. Choose the inn that seems to offer the degree of togetherness or privacy that you desire.

WEBSITE

Please supplement this book by looking at the information provided on our Karen Brown website (*www.karenbrown.com*), which serves as an added dimension to our guides. Most of our favorite inns are featured on the site and on their web pages you can usually link to their email so that making a reservation is a breeze. Also featured on our site are comments, feedback, and discoveries from you, our readers, information on our latest finds, post-press updates, special offers, and features such hotel specials.

WHEELCHAIR ACCESSIBILITY

If an inn has *at least* one guestroom that is accessible by wheelchair, it is noted as being wheelchair friendly in the details listed at the end of the description. Because the term is vague, depending on your own needs, be sure to question the hotel, inn, or B&B in more detail as to the type and specifics of accessibility they offer.

San Francisco to Los Angeles via the Coast

Golden Gate Bridge

You can drive between San Francisco and Los Angeles in a day or fly in an hour. But rather than rushing down the freeway or hopping aboard an airplane, drive leisurely along the coast between these two metropolises and enjoy the quaintness of Carmel, the charm of Santa Barbara, the splendor of the Big Sur coastline, the opulence of William Randolph Hearst's hilltop castle, and the fun of experiencing a bit of Denmark in Solvang. Also intertwined in this itinerary are stops to appreciate a piece of California's colorful heritage—her Spanish missions. This routing roughly follows the footsteps of the Spanish padres who, in the 1700s, built a string of missions (about a day's journey on horseback apart) along the coast of California from the Mexican border to just north of San Francisco. Today many of these beautiful adobe churches and their surrounding settlements have been reconstructed and are open as museums, capturing a glimpse of life as it was lived by the Spaniards and the Indians in the early days of colonization.

Recommended Pacing: We recommend a minimum stay of two or three nights in San Francisco, affording two full days for a quick introduction to the city, and definitely more time if your schedule allows. San Francisco is a beautiful city and there is much to explore and enjoy. From San Francisco, if you take the direct route, you can easily drive to Carmel in about three hours. However, located just south of San Francisco is the Año Nuevo Reserve, where you can observe the enormous elephant seals in their natural habitat. It takes several hours to walk around the secluded beaches where the seals congregate, so if you want to visit the reserve en route to Carmel, we recommend an early start from the city—or use Karen's own Seal Cove Inn, located just south of San Francisco, as a more leisurely stopping point. Plan on at least two to three nights (or again, if possible, more) in the Carmel, Pacific Grove, or Monterey area. One day can easily be devoured exploring the Monterey Bay Aquarium, Cannery Row, and the wharf. Another full day is needed to drive the gorgeous Seventeen-Mile Drive, walk the spectacular Point Lobos State Park, visit the beautiful Carmel Mission—and we have yet to even discuss shopping in downtown Carmel! From Carmel, you can drive the dramatic coastline of Big Sur and on to Santa Barbara in four to five hours, but plan to overnight in Cambria if you want to include even just one of the tours of Hearst Castle and visit the cute artists' town of Cambria—it's too much to do in one day. From Cambria we recommend you head inland through gorgeous pastoral scenery in order to discover a relatively new, beautiful wine region around Paso Robles, then spend a night or two in this region before angling back to the coast in the direction of Santa Barbara. Santa Barbara is a beautiful, charming city with an expanse of lovely beach. You'd be disappointed if you didn't plan at least two nights in the area before continuing on to Los Angeles.

Weather Wise: San Francisco and the coast are often foggy during June, July, and August. The farther south you go, the earlier in the day the fog burns off. The northern California coast is cool and rainy during the winter. In southern California the weather is warmer year-round and traditionally less rain falls during the winter. Smog is a problem in certain parts of the Los Angeles area during the summer.

When you ask travelers around the world, "What is your favorite city?" many times the answer is "San Francisco." And it is no wonder: **San Francisco** really is special, a magical town of unsurpassed beauty—spectacular when glistening in the sunlight, equally enchanting when wrapped in fog. But the beauty is more than skin deep: San Francisco offers a wealth of sightseeing, fabulous restaurants, splendid shopping, and a refreshing climate.

There are many large, super-deluxe hotels in San Francisco and we recommend a marvelous selection of small, intimate inns. Study our various recommendations to see what most fits your personality and pocketbook. Be advised that hotel space is frequently tight, so make reservations as far in advance as possible.

A good way to orient yourself in San Francisco is to take a half-day city sightseeing tour (brochures on these tours should be available at your hotel) and then return to the destinations that most catch your fancy. If you like to study before you arrive, there are entire guidebooks devoted to San Francisco and the Visitors Bureau will send you an information packet on what to see and do (San Francisco Convention and Visitors Bureau, P.O. Box 6977, San Francisco, CA 94101, 415-391-2000, *www.sfvisitor.org*). To keep you on the right track the following is an alphabetical listing of some of our favorite sights.

Alcatraz: Wreathed in mystery, the often fog-shrouded island of Alcatraz lies in the heart of San Francisco Bay, a scant mile and a quarter from the sights and sounds of downtown. The site of the first lighthouse on the west coast, in operation since 1854, "The Rock" has since been used as an army fortress and a jail. The latter, supposedly escape-proofed by the icy-cold waters and dangerous currents of the Bay, was home to criminals deemed "incorrigible" by the Federal penal system. Numbered among its inmates were Al Capone and Robert Stroud, the infamous "Birdman of Alcatraz." Access is by ferry from the San Francisco waterfront. Trips run daily but are extremely popular and should be booked well in advance (for more information and to purchase tickets, contact TeleSails, 415-705-5555, *www.telesails.com*). The island is now under the control of the National Park Service and ranger-guided and audio-assisted tours provide a fascinating insight into the island's history, as well as affording spectacular views of San Francisco and its bridges. Be sure to wear sturdy, comfortable shoes and warm clothing.

Cable Cars: You cannot leave San Francisco without riding one of the colorful little trolleys that make their way up and down the breathtakingly steep city hills. Rather than touring by cab or bus, plan your sightseeing around hopping on and off cable cars. You can travel easily from the shopping district of Union Square past Chinatown and the "crookedest street in the world"—Lombard, and on to the Ghiradelli Square-Fisherman's Wharf area. For a behind-the-scenes look at this charmingly antiquated transit system visit the Cable Car Museum at the corner of Washington and Mason Streets. Here you can view the huge cables that pull the cars from below the streets and a historical display that includes the very first cable car.

California Palace of the Legion of Honor: Without a doubt, this is our favorite museum in San Francisco—we just love the exhibits and the spectacular setting on a bluff in Lincoln Park overlooking the ocean. The original of Rodin's famous *Thinker* welcomes you to the San Francisco replica of the Palais de la Légion d'Honneur in Paris where Napoleon first established his new government. A self-guided audio tour is available to steer you through the galleries, which include one devoted to medieval art (there's a ceiling from a 15th-century Spanish palace), a British gallery with paintings by Gainsborough and Constable, and 19th- and 20th-century galleries with their popular works by Monet, Renoir, and Picasso. Located at 34th Avenue and Clement Street. For more information call 415-750-3600, or visit their website at *www.thinker.org*.

Chinatown: Just a few short blocks from Union Square you enter beneath the dragon arch (at the corner of Bush Street and Grant Avenue) into another world with street signs in Chinese characters, tiny grocery stores displaying Chinese vegetables and delicacies, apothecary shops selling unusual remedies, spicy aromas drifting from colorful restaurants, older women bustling about in traditional dress, and the surrounding hum of unfamiliar phrases. Of course the streets are jammed with tourists and locals and there is a plethora of rather tacky, but fun-to-explore souvenir shops. Don't limit your exploration of Chinatown to the main thoroughfare of Grant Avenue: poke down the intriguing little alleys and side streets. Plan a visit to 56 Ross Alley, the Golden Gate Fortune Cookie Factory. Down another alley, at 17 Adler Place, is the Chinese Historical Society of America—a small museum portraying the story of the Chinese immigration. The Chinese Cultural Center, housed in the Holiday Inn at Kearny and Washington streets, offers fascinating docent-led heritage and culinary walks affording a glimpse of the "real Chinatown." For information call 415-986-1822, or visit their website at *www.c-c-c.org*. The Cultural Center also has a wonderful small museum offering an ever-changing schedule of exhibits.

Coit Tower: Coit Tower, located at the top of Telegraph Hill, is a relic of old San Francisco and fun to visit—not only because of the great view, but because its story is so very "San Francisco." The money to construct the watch tower, which resembles the nozzle of a fire hose, was willed to the city by the wealthy Lillie Hitchcock Coit, a volunteer fireman (or should we say firewoman) who dearly loved to rush to every blaze wearing her diamond-encrusted fire badge. A mural on the ground floor provides a vivid depiction of early California life.

Fisherman's Wharf to Ghiradelli Square: This portion of the waterfront is very popular with tourists. **Pier 39** is lined with New England-style shops; nothing authentic, but a popular shopping and restaurant arcade complete with street performers and a beautiful two-tier carousel. Pier 39 is also home to a new aquarium and some very boisterous and amusing sea lions (415-981-7437, *www.pier39.com*). Pier 41 is where you purchase tickets for the popular excursion to Alcatraz (see listing). **Fisherman's Wharf**, where fishermen haul in their daily catch, has long been a favorite with tourists. It is difficult to find even the heart of Fisherman's Wharf behind all the trinket-filled souvenir shops and tourist arcades, but look carefully and sure enough, you will see the colorful fishing boats bobbing about in the water at the waterfront between Jones and Taylor Streets. Nearby, Fish Alley, a small pier extending out into the harbor, affords a good view of the fishing fleet and the aroma of fresh fish mingling with the salty air. At the corner of Leavenworth and Jefferson **The Cannery**, formerly a fruit cannery, is today an attractive shopping complex. At the foot of Hyde Street **Hyde Street Pier** is home to the Maritime Museum's fleet of historic ships, several of which can be boarded and explored. Our favorite is the *Balclutha* (1886), a three-masted merchant ship typical of the hundreds that came round the Horn to San Francisco. Inspect the comfortable captain's quarters and cramped crew's quarters and exhibits of nautical gear. Just beyond the **Hyde Street cable car turnaround** lies **Ghiradelli Square**, a lovely brick building that used to house the Ghiradelli chocolate factory, now a complex of attractive stores and restaurants. The ship-shaped building in Aquatic Park (in front of Ghiradelli Square) is the land base of the **Maritime Museum**, full of displays on the history of water transportation from the 1800s to the present, including marvelous photos of old San Francisco. (415-556-3002, *www.nps.gov/safr*)

Golden Gate Bridge and **Fort Point:** San Francisco's symbol is the Golden Gate Bridge with its graceful orange arches. The visitors' viewing area on the San Francisco side offers stunning views (if the fog is not in) and access to the pedestrian walkway across the bridge (2½ miles round trip, wear warm clothing). At the base of the Golden Gate Bridge's south pier, Fort Point, built in 1861 as one of the west coast's principal points of defense, provides a fascinating insight into military life during that period. (415-556-1693, *www.nps.gov/fopo*)

Golden Gate Park: You will need to take a bus or taxi to Golden Gate Park, but don't miss it. The park encompasses over 1,000 acres, so large you really cannot hope to see it all, but many attractions are located near each other. Wander through the traditional **Japanese Tea Garden** and enjoy tea and cookies Japanese-style at the tea house (415-752-1171). The **De Young Museum** is primarily devoted to American art (415-750-3600, *www.thinker.org*) while the adjacent **Asian Art Museum** contains one of America's finest collections of Asian art. The **California Academy of Sciences** houses the Museum of Natural History, the Steinhart Aquarium, and the Morrison Planetarium. The **Museum of Natural History** offers dioramas of wildlife from African to Californian (along with an impressive collection of gems and minerals), while the neighboring **Steinhart**

Aquarium has all things fishy from a tropical swamp with alligators and turtles to a fish roundabout—an enormous donut-shaped fish tank. The **Morrison Planetarium** offers visitors daily multimedia presentations about astronomy, such as a realistic simulation of the night sky as observed from any place on Earth (415-750-7145, *www.calacademy.org*). If you are hungry, you might want to consider the **Beach Chalet**, a restaurant on the ocean side of the park near the Dutch Windmill. The menu offers good, simple fare matched with their list of brewery selections. The building once served as the changing rooms for Ocean Beach. On the first floor are beautifully restored murals of San Francisco in its early days and guests enjoy unobstructed views of the surf from tables by the second-floor expanse of window (415-386-8439).

Lombard Street: Lombard is an ordinary city street—except for one lone, brick-paved block between Hyde and Leavenworth where the street goes crazy and makes a series of hairpin turns as it twists down the hill. Pretty houses border each side of the street, and banks of hydrangeas add color. Start at the top and go down what must be the crookedest street in the world: it is lots of fun. The Hyde Street cable car makes a stop at the top of the hill and from here you can easily walk down to Fisherman's Wharf.

Mission San Francisco de Assisi: This mission at Dolores and 16th Streets is frequently referred to as the Mission Dolores. If you are interested in Californian missions, you will find a visit here worthwhile. It was on this spot that San Francisco was born when Father Francisco Palou founded his mission here in 1776. At one time this was a large complex of warehouses, workshops, granaries, a tannery, soap shop, corrals, Indian dwellings, and even an aqueduct. Today, all that is left is the chapel and next to it the garden where gravestones attest to the fragility of life. Although small, the chapel is beautiful in its simplicity with 4-foot-thick adobe walls and massive redwood timbers. (415-621-8203)

Museum of Modern Art (MOMA): A cylindrical, striped turret rising from blocks of red bricks gives a hint of what lies within this futuristic building at 151 Third Street. To help you appreciate the exhibits, an audio-cassette can be rented in the lobby to guide you through the museum's permanent collection of abstract expressionistic paintings and avant-garde photography. Even if you are not a fan of modern art, you will be awed by the building's interior: the space soars upwards from the lobby for seven stories to a broad catwalk that runs below the cylindrical glass skylight (415-357-4000, *www.sfmoma.org*). Just across the street from the MOMA lie the **Yerba Buena Gardens and Galleries**. The gardens are an oasis of tranquillity where a broad expanse of grass leads to a cascading sheet of water—a perfect place to relax and people watch. The galleries offer changing exhibits that showcase the San Francisco Bay Area's cultural diversity. On the top floor, encircled by windows and a spectacular view of the city skyline, is a new ice-skating rink. (Open daily 1 pm to 5 pm and evenings with some limitations. 750 Folsom Street between 3rd and 4th, 415-777-3726, *www.skatebowl.com.*) Just round the corner (678 Mission Street) a turn-of-the-century hardware store houses the **California Historical Society** with its bookstore and changing exhibits of photographs, paintings, and objects documenting California's growth and change. (415-357-1848, *www.calhist.org*)

Sausalito and **Tiburon:** An enjoyable excursion is to take the ferry from Pier 43½ in San Francisco to Sausalito or Tiburon, small towns just across the bay full of intriguing shops, art galleries, and wonderful restaurants. As a bonus, en route you enjoy gorgeous vistas of San Francisco and the Golden Gate Bridge. For information call the Red and White Fleet at 415-447-0597, or visit their website at *www.redandwhitefleet.com.*

Theater: For theater buffs, San Francisco offers an excellent variety of entertainment. Most theaters are located in the heart of the city within walking distance of Union Square. In addition, San Francisco has fine opera and ballet. The San Francisco Visitors Bureau, 415-391-2000, *www.sfvisitor.org*, can send you a packet with information on what is going on. You can also call the "hot line" at 415-391-2001 for a recording of all current events.

Union Square: In the center of the city sits Union Square, hallmarked by a small park around which tower deluxe hotels and fancy department stores. Do not tarry too long at the "biggies" because just beyond the square lies every specialty shop imaginable from FAO Schwartz's toy emporium to any number of "designer" boutiques. San Francisco's own exclusive and elegant Gumps at 135 Post Street certainly merits a visit. The Crocker Galleria at 50 Post houses collections from top names in international design and many fine specialty stores and restaurants.

Union Street: Union Street (between Laguna and Steiner), lined with lovely restored Victorian houses, offers a wonderful variety of quaint gift shops, elegant boutiques, beautiful antique stores, small art galleries, excellent restaurants, and a multitude of intriguing little shops hidden down tiny brick-paved lanes.

It's a three-hour drive south from San Francisco to Carmel taking the scenic Highway 280 to San Jose and Highways 17 and 1 on to Carmel. But rather than head directly to Carmel, we suggest you meander down the coast, following the contours of the spectacular coastline, enjoying a number of sights en route—a journey that will deserve a couple of days.

Leave San Francisco to the south on 19th Avenue to Highway 280 and take Highway 1 through Pacifica where the freeway ends and the road narrows to meander around the precipitous rocky promontory known as Devil's Slide. Just south of Devil's Slide is **Moss Beach**, a suburban coastal town home to Karen Brown and her inn, **Seal Cove**, named after the nearby crescent of golden sand. Seal Cove Inn and the colorful restaurant, the **Moss Beach Distillery**, 650-728-5595, known for its ghosts and beautiful ocean setting, are neighbors to the **Fitzgerald Marine Reserve** and park, where you can walk along the bluffs and investigate the tidepools at low tide (650-728-3584).

Just to the south of Moss Beach, **Princeton Harbor**, with its mass of fishing vessels and sailboats, is one of California's last true commercial fishing harbors. Sport-fishing and whale-watching boats leave early mornings from Princeton. Bookings can be made through **Huck Finn Sport Fishing** (650-726-7133). Overlooking the harbor, a popular hangout for locals is the **Half Moon Bay Brewery** (650-728-BREW), a casual eatery with good food. Look for the surfboard hanging on the wall—it was made especially for the brewery by the coastside's own surfing celebrity, Jeff Clark. If it is missing, it means the manager is in the water!

Detour off the Coastal Highway to the east at Highway 92 and take it for one block, making a right on **Half Moon Bay's** Main Street. Park just across the bridge and visit **Half Moon Bay Feed and Fuel**, an authentic country store selling saddles, rabbits, chickens, animal feed, and farm implements. Poke your head in the variety of shops, restaurants, and art galleries that line Main Street. (Another detour, traveling past Main Street farther east on Highway 92, is to the **Half Moon Bay Nursery**, nestled off the road just before it begins its climb up the mountain. An attraction in its own right with its wood-burning fireplace and classical music, the nursery also offers a bounty of reasonably priced plants.) Leaving Half Moon Bay, continue down Main Street to rejoin Highway 1 to the south of town.

Lengthy expanses of sandy beach are accessible from the many state parks along the coastline. **Pigeon Point Lighthouse** is one of the tallest lighthouses on the west coast. Tours are given on Sundays only between 10 am and 3 pm.

Thirty miles south of Half Moon Bay is the **Año Nuevo State Reserve**, home to elephant seals whose huge males with their trunk-like snouts reach a whopping 6,000 pounds. From mid-December to the end of March park docents conduct a 3-mile round-trip hike to the breeding grounds of these car-size mammals. Reservation lines open in October for the following season (800-444-7275). If you are not able to book several months in advance, call the park directly at 650-879-2025 and they may be able to advise you if last-minute tickets are available. We have, in the past, secured tickets by arriving at 8:30 am and queuing at the entrance booth for tickets for tours that day. Outside of the breeding season obtaining permits to view the seals (there are often also a great many sea lions in residence) is not a problem: tickets are issued on arrival and you follow the well-marked path to the distant beach where the seals are found. Outside of the breeding season, the best time to visit is during July and August when the juvenile males return to molt.

Ten miles south of Año Nuevo you come to the cluster of houses that makes up the town of **Davenport**. Fronting Highway 1 is the **New Davenport Cash Store**, which sells everything from handmade jewelry to local pottery and whose restaurant offers a varied and healthful menu with excellent soups and tasty vegetarian dishes (831-426-4122).

Downtown **Santa Cruz**, 11 miles south of Davenport, was badly damaged in the 1989 earthquake, but a newly revived Pacific Avenue demonstrates all the laid-back charm the town is noted for, with outdoor cafés, a variety of shops and galleries, and numerous street performers. Years ago this busy seaside town, with its bustling **boardwalk** and amusement park bordering a broad stretch of white-sand beach, was a popular day trip for workers in San Francisco. In recent years the rides and attractions have received a face-lift, making it a pleasure to visit, particularly since it is so clean and well maintained. The rides include a heart-stopping wooden roller coaster and a wonderful old-fashioned carousel.

If you enjoy riding trains, you may want to take the old-fashioned diesel that departs from the boardwalk twice a day during the summer months for the 60-minute ride to Felton. Here you board an old steam train of the **Roaring Camp Railroad**, a train that winds up into a redwood forest. The train leaves several times a day from its main station in **Felton** (except on Christmas) along narrow-gauge tracks built to carry lumber out of the forest.

Roaring Camp Railroad, Felton

The conductor tells stories of the old days as the train circles up through the trees, making a brief stop at the "cathedral," a beautiful ring of redwoods that form a natural outdoor church, before heading back to the depot. It is possible to take a picnic with you, alight at the top, and take the next train back. Call for schedules and directions: 831-335-4400.

Leave Santa Cruz heading south on Highway 1 and travel for about 20 miles to Highway 129 where you head east. Continue on the 129 for approximately 16 miles through small farms and rolling hills to **San Juan Bautista** and its most attractive **mission**. There is far more to see here than just an old church, for an area of the town has been restored to the way it was 150 years ago with the mission as its focus. Facing the square is the restored Plaza Hotel, now a museum where tickets are sold for admission to the attractions in the park. The focal point of the sightseeing is, of course, the mission, but do not end your touring there. Directly across from the mission is a most interesting house, nicely restored, and furnished as it must have looked many years ago. Adjacent to this is a blacksmith's shop and stables where there is a colorful display of old coaches. Next door to the Plaza Hotel is another home now open as a museum with period furnishings.

Follow Highway 156 west for a couple of miles until it merges with Highway 101 going south to the Monterey Peninsula. As you pass through Prunedale, begin to watch for signs indicating a sharp right-hand turn on Highway 156 west to the Monterey Peninsula. Along the way, fields of artichokes dominate the landscape as you near Castroville, the artichoke capital of the world. When you begin to smell the sea air, stay in the left lane following signs for Highway 1 south to the Monterey Peninsula. As you approach Monterey, dunes lining the sweep of the bay come into view.

The main sightseeing attractions in **Monterey** are in two areas: the old town and the marina, and the Monterey Bay Aquarium and Cannery Row. A bayside walking and biking path runs from the Marina beside Cannery Row to the Aquarium and beyond to the adjoining town of Pacific Grove. A fun way to explore Monterey is to rent a side-by-side tricycle near the aquarium and pedal to the Marina.

Kayaking lets you enjoy another perspective of Monterey—looking back at the town and gorgeous beaches from the bay. Open-deck kayaks make the sport easy even for the inexperienced and paddling out amongst the seals and otters is quite memorable. We rented from **A B Seas Kayak** and found owner, Geoff Hand, and his team to be very helpful and accommodating. All equipment, loose-fitting rain gear (although plan on getting wet), life jackets, and instruction are included in the rental price. Geoff has generously offered any of our readers a 20% discount on the $25 per person, three-hour package if they mention our guide. A B Seas Kayak is conveniently located at 32 Cannery Row, on the coastguard pier. (831-647-0147)

In **Old Town** a 3-mile walking tour links the restored buildings of early Monterey. The old adobe structures are interesting and a sharp contrast to the bustle of nearby **Fisherman's Wharf**, a quaint wooden fishing pier lined with shops and restaurants. At the end of the pier huge sea lions vie for the fish cast off the fishing boats.

Cannery Row, once the center of this area's thriving sardine industry (the fish are long gone), and brought vividly to life by John Steinbeck in his novels featuring Doc and the boys, is now filled with small stores and tucked into an old warehouse are some outlet stores. The premier attraction in Monterey is the adjacent **Monterey Bay Aquarium**. The centerpieces of the Aquarium are the huge glass tanks that showcase the underwater world of the local offshore marine habitat from the diverse tidepools to the multitude of life in the Monterey Bay: one tank is populated by huge sharks and colorful schools of fish while another contains a mature kelp forest teeming with fish. The Outer Bay exhibit, a vast tank of water representative of the outer ocean, brings a new dimension to the Aquarium and leaves the visitor with a memorable impression of just how little is known about that massive body of water. (831-648-4888)

Monterey is all hustle and bustle (especially in summer) and it is nice to continue on to the neighboring, much quieter town of **Pacific Grove**. To reach Pacific Grove, follow the road in front of the Aquarium up the hill and make a right turn onto Ocean View Boulevard, a lovely drive lined on one side with gracious Victorian homes and splendid views of the sea on the other. Besides being an affluent residential community, Pacific Grove is famous for the Monarch butterflies that return faithfully each October and cluster in the grove of trees next to Butterfly Grove Inn on Lighthouse Avenue.

Carmel lies just a few miles beyond Pacific Grove and there is no more perfect way to arrive than along the famous Seventeen-Mile Drive, which meanders around the Monterey Peninsula coastline between the two towns. The route is easy to find as the road that leads to the "drive" intersects Lighthouse Avenue and is appropriately called The Seventeen-Mile Drive.

The Seventeen-Mile Drive loops through an exclusive residential area of multi-million-dollar estates and gorgeous golf courses. Because the land is private, $7.50 per car is levied at the entrance gate, where you'll receive a map indicating points of interest along the way. The scenic drive traces the low-lying shore, passes rocky coves where kelp beds are home to sea lions, sea otters, cormorants, and gulls (remember to bring your binoculars), and meanders through woodlands where Monterey pines gnarled by the wind stand sentinel on lonely headlands. Along the drive is the famous **Pebble Beach Golf Course**, site of the National Pro-Am Golf Championship each January.

Carmel—filled with Hansel-and-Gretel-style cottages nestled under pines and surrounded by flower-filled gardens—is one of California's most appealing towns. Tourists throng the streets lined with appetizing candy shops, beckoning bakeries, a wonderful selection of restaurants, enticing boutiques, pretty gift stores, and attractive art galleries. We are especially partial to a gallery that features the work of Jann Pollard, the very talented water colorist who is responsible for our gorgeous cover paintings. **The Cottage Gallery** is located in the heart of town at the corner of 6th and Mission. The picturesque combination of fairy-tale cottages and a sparkling blue bay makes Carmel so very special. Its main street slopes gently down the hill to a glorious white-sand beach crested by windswept dunes.

Just south of town is the **Carmel Mission**, established in 1770 by Father Junipero Serra. Beautifully restored and fronted by a pretty garden, the mission was Father Serra's headquarters. It is from here that the stalwart little priest set out to expand the chain of missions. A small museum shows the simple cell in which Father Serra slept on a hard wooden bed. The church itself, with its Moorish tower, star-shaped window, and profusion of surrounding flowers, has a most romantic appearance.

Located just south of Carmel on Highway 1, **Point Lobos State Reserve** is, in our estimation, the premier place to enjoy the California coast. A small admission fee entitles you to day use of the park. Walk along the coastal trails and venture down wooden steps to secluded sandy beaches. Rocky coves are home to sea lions, harbor seals, and sea otters. Between December and May migrating gray whales surface and dive offshore. Bring your binoculars and head for Sea Lion Point and the headland on Cypress Grove Trail, the best places to see the whales. Walking trails and picnic areas are well marked and the times of guided nature walks are posted at the entrance gate. (831-624-4909)

Believe everything you ever read about the beauties of the **Big Sur Coastline**: it is truly sensational. However, hope for clear weather, because on foggy or rainy days an endless picture of stunning seascapes becomes a tortuous drive around precipitous cliff roads. (If the weather is inclement, you may wish to take the inland route to Cambria by following the picturesque Carmel Valley road east to Highway 101 where you then head south. When you come to Highway 46, turn west. The road intersects with coastal Highway 1 just south of Cambria.) As you drive south on Highway 1, you have an indication that you are approaching Big Sur when you see the road sign "Hill Curves—63 miles," which is exactly what the road does as it clings precipitously to the edge of the cliff. While the road is quite narrow, there are plenty of turnouts and opportunities for taking photos.

If you have plenty of time, you might want to consider a very scenic 10-mile detour east off Highway 1 following the **Old Coast Road** that journeys through beautiful redwood groves and country ranchland. To access the Old Coast Road, turn left just before crossing the dramatic span of Bixby Creek Bridge. You'll be on your own for most of the journey and the road will deposit you back on Highway 1, across from the entrance to the wonderful **Andrew Molera State Park**. Allow approximately one hour for the adventure, and be aware that the road is not passable after heavy rains.

If you opt to remain on scenic Highway 1, you will find its passage dramatic over the much-photographed, long concrete span of **Bixby Creek Bridge**. A few miles later the rocky volcanic outcrop topped by the Point Sur lighthouse appears. About 40 miles south of Carmel is the **Pfeiffer Big Sur State Park** with its camping facilities and many miles of hiking trails among coastal redwood groves. (831-667-2315)

If you choose only one place to stop along the Big Sur drive, make it **Nepenthe**, about 3 miles south of the entrance to Pfeiffer Big Sur State Park. Nepenthe is a casual restaurant, with a '60s-style decor, perched on a cliff high above the ocean offering unsurpassed views (on a clear day) of the coast to the south (831-667-2345). Below Nepenthe, **The Phoenix Shop** has a wonderful selection of clothes, artwork, books, and gifts (831-667-2347). Interestingly, at the heart of the complex is a cottage that Orson Welles bought for his then wife, Rita Hayworth.

Another stop along the way where you can gain a closer view of this magnificent coastline is at the **Julia Pfeiffer Burns State Park**. The parking area is to the left of the road. Leave your car and take the short walk leading under the highway and round the face of the cliff that overlooks a superb small cove with emerald-green water and a white-sand beach. From the rocky bluff a waterfall drops directly into the ocean and the restless sea beats against a craggy point. After the Ragged Point Inn, the bends become less frequent, and as the cliffs give way to the coastal plain, the driving becomes less arduous.

After the road begins to flatten out, watch for **Hearst Castle** impressively crowning the coastal hills. In 1919, William Randolph Hearst commissioned California's famous architect Julia Morgan to design a simple vacation home atop a hill on his estate overlooking the California coastline. Twenty-eight years and $10,000,000 later, he moved to Los Angeles and left his 100-room retreat, La Cuesta Encantada (the enchanted hill), which has never been completed. Hearst Castle continues to delight its millions of visitors: next to Disneyland, Hearst Castle is the most popular visitor attraction in California.

The number of visitors allowed on the hill during any one day is limited, so it is essential that you make reservations in advance. Hearst Castle is open every day except Thanksgiving, Christmas, and New Year's Day. Several different one-hour and forty-five-minute tours are available. Also from September through December, Hearst Castle offers at weekends a magical evening tour and program with a holiday theme. The castle is decorated for Christmas and the staff, dressed in appropriate and wonderful costumes, play the rolls of William Hearst and his entourage of friends as they bring Hearst Castle to life. The evening tours are tremendously popular and must be booked well in advance. If traveling with children, inquire also about the special summer children programs. Tickets for all tours are available for purchase up to eight weeks in advance. (800-444-4445, *www.hearstcastle.org*)

Plan on arriving at the visitors center at the foot of the hill at least half an hour before your scheduled departure, as the tours leave with clockwork-like precision and do not wait for stragglers. If you arrive early, you can browse through the small museum located next to the departure depot where groups assemble by number for their turn to be taken up the hill by bus. Here you also find an **Imax Theater**, a wonderful attraction in its own right. A special Imax documentary of Hearst Castle, which is only ever shown here, plays daily from 9:30 am to 5:30 pm, every hour on the half hour. Additional Imax film programs are shown daily at 11:30 am and 4:30 pm.

Of the daily tour programs, Tour 1, the overview of the castle, is the one recommended for first-time visitors. You walk through the gardens to the main house, La Casa Grande, to tour the rooms on the lower level. The sheer size and elaborate decor of the assembly room where Hearst gathered with his guests before dinner sets the opulent mood of this elegant establishment. In the adjoining refectory Hearst and his guests dined in a re-created medieval banquet hall—the bottles of Hearst's favorite ketchup on the table seem rather out of place. In the theater a short home movie of Hearst and some of his celebrity friends gives you an idea of life at the castle during the 1930s. A feeling for the opulence of the guest accommodation is given as you tour the guesthouse, Casa del Sol.

Hearst Castle

Tour 2 views suites of bedrooms, the kitchen, and the swimming pools. The indoor Roman pool has over half a million Italian mosaic tiles, vast amounts of gold leaf, and took over five years to complete. Tour 3 visits the guest wing of the castle, a guesthouse, and the pools. Tour 4, offered only in summer, does not go into the main house, but focuses on the estate's gardens.

From the Hearst-San Simeon State Historical Monument it is just an 8-mile drive south to Cambria. **Cambria** was once a whaling station and a dairy town that shipped butter and cheese to San Francisco. Now the main town lies away from the coast and encompasses two streets of art galleries, gift shops, antique stores, and restaurants.

Leave Cambria and the coast traveling east on 46 through the Santa Lucia coastal mountain range. We have always considered that Highway 46 affords one of California's most beautiful drives through gorgeous stretches of farmland and lush, gently rolling, golden hills covered with oak trees and vineyards, and it is now the best route to explore the burgeoning **Paso Robles Wine Region**. Once known for cattle ranches and grain fields and historically as a mineral springs resort area, the Paso Robles region will captivate you. The Paso Robles area has a rich history of winemaking and grape growing—the first grapes were introduced to the region by Spanish conquistadors and the Franciscan missionaries and wine was produced in 1797 at the historic Mission San Miguel Arcángel. Approximately 13 miles inland from Cambria you begin to see farmland give way to row upon row and acre after acre of vineyards.

(Note: If you have the luxury of time, detour off Highway 46 west on two separate roads to discover some of California's most beautiful scenery. Santa Rosa Creek Road offers a lovely ramble through pristine countryside to the back side of Cambria—approximately a 35-minute drive, and Old Creek Road is another charming drive—about a 20-minute trip, taking you by Whale Rock Reservoir to the beach city of Cayucos.)

Spend a few days here and you will enjoy not only drives along scenic, rural, uncrowded roads. Most of the wineries are open for tasting (most are free) and a few offer self-guided tours. Clustered just off the 46, still on the outskirts of Paso Robles, are a number of wineries: **Summerwood** is beautiful (it also offers lovely accommodation in the **Summerwood Inn** across the street) and **Castoro** is a must for tasting. Castoro Winery also hosts concerts throughout the year. Other wineries not to miss are **Dover Canyon**, **Grey Wolf**, **Midnight Cellars**, **Dark Star**, and **Fratelli Perata**. **Sycamore Farms** is also a delightful stop to pick up herbs and gifts for house and garden.

To combine wine tasting with a drive through stunningly scenic countryside, take Vineyard Drive from the 46, traveling to the north, winding through the hills that were once home to Mennonite dairy farms, grain and nut farms, and cattle ranches. Venture on to two of the most picturesque wineries, **Justin** and Carmody McKnight. Stroll through Justin's lovely gardens and sample their award-winning wines. (You can reserve one of **Just Inn**'s three elegant suites—see hotel descriptions.) From Justin Winery head over to

Carmody McKnight, an 1800s farmhouse with a pond in front, and enjoy your wine tasting while overlooking their gardens. A number of signs will tempt you off the main road down local roads to many family-run wineries. Follow Chimney Rock Road back to the heart of downtown Paso Robles.

Before continuing over to the east side of Paso Robles to visit a number of the region's larger wineries, take some time to explore historic **Paso Robles**. Begin by taking a historical walk through downtown—a guide is available at the Chamber of Commerce office on Park Street (805-238-0506). The **Carnegie Library** in the center of the town park is home to a wonderful collection of local history and a Western Art Gallery. Not far away is the **Pioneer Museum** and there is also the **Estrella Warbird Museum**, which houses a collection of WWI and WWII military fighter planes. You will be thrilled to discover the many antique shops. History is being embraced with the opening of mineral spas. **Paso Robles Hot Springs** (located 3 miles east of town off the 46 east) offers massage, facials, and therapeutic mineral baths in a serene lakeside setting.

To continue wine tasting, head out from Paso Robles on Highway 46 east to many of the area's larger wineries. **Martin-Weyrick** has a feel of Tuscany and a wonderful gift shop and tasting room. **Eberle Winery** offers picnic baskets made to order with advance notice. Enjoy your picnic on their deck, sample award-winning wines, and take time to tour the Eberle caves. **Meridian Vineyards** has lovely gardens, a great tasting room, and a gift shop. Don't leave out **Tobin James,** with its real western-flavor tasting room, great hospitality, and award-winning wines. Follow your wine map, but don't miss **Wild Horse Vineyards** in Templeton and be sure to explore country roads like Neal Springs in this "El Pomar" area. The Paso Robles Vintners have a brochure, tel: 805-239-8463, fax: 805-237-6439, or visit their website at *www.pasowine.com*.

From Paso Robles travel south on Highway 101 the short distance on to **San Luis Obispo.** If you want to visit every mission en route, when you reach San Luis Obispo take the Broad Street exit and follow signs to the **mission**, which lies at the heart of this bustling, charming college town.

About 10 miles south of San Luis Obispo, Highway 101 returns to the coast where you take the exit for Highway 1 and **Pismo Beach**, a 12-mile arc of white-sand beach backed in part by dunes. This is the home of the famous Pismo clam, which has unfortunately in recent years become rather scarce. As you travel south on Highway 1, views of the beach are blocked by apartments and motels, but do not despair: 2 miles south of town, leave the freeway by turning right into **Pismo Beach State Park**. After paying the entrance fee, pass quickly over the soft sand. Once your tires hit the well-packed, damp sand, your way feels more secure as you drive along the beach, paralleling the crashing waves. From this vantage point you can really appreciate the beautiful sweep of this white-sand bay. While it is possible to drive about 5 miles south on the beach, the auto exit ramp lies 1 mile to the south.

Leaving Pismo Beach, follow Highway 1 south passing flat, wide fields of vegetables and eucalyptus groves through Guadalupe, a rather poor agricultural town. The road becomes a divided two-lane highway as Highways 135 and 1 merge. After passing the gates of Vandenburg Air Force Base (on the approach to Lompoc), take a left turn onto Mission Purisma Road which leads to **Mission La Purisma Concepcion**, founded in 1787 and now carefully restored and maintained by the state park system. A self-guided tour offers you the opportunity to see how the Indians practiced mission crafts such as leather working, candle making, and building.The simply decorated church with its sparse furnishings, rough floors, and stenciled walls is typical of Spanish and Mexican churches of the period. One of the nicest aspects of La Purisma Concepcion Mission is its lovely setting—far in the countryside amidst rolling hills and flower-filled meadows.

Leaving the mission, follow signs for **Buelleton**, which has the redoubtable fame of being the home of split-pea soup—you come to **Andersen's Pea Soup Restaurant** just before Highway 246 crosses Highway 101. The menu has more to offer than soup, but it is still possible to sample a bowl of the food that put this little community on the map.

From Buelleton it is just a short drive into **Solvang,** a town settled originally by Danish immigrants, which has now become a rather Disneyfied version of how the perfect Danish village should look—a profusion of thatch-like roofs, painted towers, gaily colored windmills, and cobblestoned courtyards. The shops house a plethora of calorific bakeries and fudge and candy stores interspersed with lots of nifty-gifty Scandinavian-theme craft shops. Interestingly, a large portion of the town's residents truly are of Danish descent. Even if you are not a shopper, Solvang warrants a bakery stop.

Leave Solvang and rejoin Highway 246, following signs for Santa Barbara. This is another gorgeous region of horse ranches and neighboring vineyards. The towns are small, charming and country-western: **Santa Inez**, **Los Olivos**, **Ballard**—all with a main street, a few charming shops and restaurants, and the ever-present horse and feed store.

Just outside Santa Inez, Highway 246 merges with Highway 154, which takes you through the heart of this beautiful landscape and the lush green valley gives way to hills as the road climbs through the mountains up the San Marcos Pass. Rounding the crest of the pass, you see **Santa Barbara** stretched out below, hemmed between the mountains and the sea. The red-tile roofs and abundance of palm trees add an affluent look to this prosperous town.

Santa Barbara is one of California's loveliest cities. The homes and public buildings show a decidedly Spanish influence and make such a pretty picture—splashes of whitewashed walls, red-tiled roofs, and palm trees snuggled against the Santa Ynez Mountains to the east and stretching to the brilliant blue waters of the Pacific to the west.

A pleasant introduction to Santa Barbara is to follow the scenic driving tour that is outlined in the brochure published by the Chamber of Commerce. You can probably pick up a brochure at your hotel or by calling the Chamber of Commerce at 805-965-3023. You can also obtain information on the Internet at *www.sbchamber.org*. The route is well marked and gives you an overall glimpse of the city as you drive by beaches, the wharf, the old downtown area, and affluent suburbs. The brochure also outlines what is called the "Red-Tile Walking Tour" which guides you through the town's beautiful streets. It will take discipline to stay on the path as you pass the multitude of shops filled with so many tempting things to buy, but do continue on, because Santa Barbara is a beautiful city whose public buildings are lovely. The highlight of the tour is the **Santa Barbara County Courthouse**, a magnificent adobe structure with a Moorish accent.

You definitely must not leave town without visiting the splendid **Mission Santa Barbara**, which is located at the rise of the hill on the northern edge of town. This beautiful church with two bell towers faces a large park laced with rose gardens. As in many of the other missions, although the church's main purpose is for religious services, a museum is incorporated into the complex with examples of how life was lived when the Spaniards first settled in California.

When your allotted stay in Santa Barbara draws to a close, it is a little less than a 100-mile drive to the Greater Los Angeles area. The vast, often smog-filled **Los Angeles basin** is crisscrossed by a mind-boggling network of freeways, which confuses all but the resident Southern Californian. Frustrating traffic jams during the morning and afternoon rush hours are a way of life. Therefore, plot the quickest freeway route to your destination and try to travel during the middle of the day in order to avoid the worst traffic. Los Angeles does not offer a wide selection of inns, but there are many attractive, modern hotels where you can stay. The Greater Los Angeles area has an incredible wealth of places to visit and things to do—something to suit every taste. Sightseeing suggestions are described in the following *Leisurely Loop of Southern California* itinerary.

Leisurely Loop of Southern California

Disneyland

Los Angeles and San Diego are popular destinations, attracting travelers from around the world to a wealth of sightseeing treats. But in addition to visiting these justifiably famous cities, we hope to entice you to venture out into the countryside to explore lesser-known sightseeing gems: quaint Balboa Island with its handsome yachts, charming La Jolla with its idyllic beaches, picturesque Julian exuding its Gold Rush heritage, secluded Idyllwild nestled in the mountains, glamorous Palm Springs where movie stars still steal away, beautiful Arrowhead with its crystal-clear lake. Perhaps nowhere else can you discover within only a few short miles such a rich tapestry of places to visit—all so different, all so appealing. White-sand beaches, forests with towering pines, deserts rimmed with snow-peaked mountains, bountiful orchards, historical mining towns, and shimmering blue lakes all await your discovery.

Recommended Pacing: Greater Los Angeles is an enormous metropolis of cities and suburbs connected by an overwhelming maze of very busy freeways—during the commuter rush hours it can take hours to get from one side of the city to the other. Choose a hotel or motel close to the principal attraction you are visiting in Los Angeles and use it as a base for your other sightseeing. If you are just visiting Disneyland, stay in the area for two nights—the more attractions you want to include, the longer the recommended stay: if you include San Diego or La Jolla, add two nights; if you visit Palm Springs, add another and possibly include one additional night for Lake Arrowhead.

Weather Wise: The weather along the coast is warm year round and there is very little winter rain. Julian has a more temperate climate—though sometimes in the summer it has the odd very hot day and in the winter the occasional snowfall. Palm Springs can be boiling hot, but with a dry heat, during the summer, and is ideal in the winter, with warm days and cool mountain-desert nights. Lake Arrowhead is a mountain resort with warm summer weather and snow in winter.

If you are going to be staying for an extended period of time in **Los Angeles**, supplement this guide with a book totally dedicated to what to see and do. There is also a wealth of free information available from the Los Angeles Visitors Bureau—213-624-7300, *www.lacvb.com*—they will send you a very useful packet of information. We are not going to attempt to detail all of Los Angeles' sightseeing possibilities, but just briefly mention a few highlights.

Disneyland: The wonderland created by Walt Disney needs no introduction. What child from two to ninety-two has not heard of this Magic Kingdom, home to such lovable characters as Mickey Mouse, Donald Duck, Pluto, and Snow White? The park is a fantasyland of fun, divided into various theme areas. You enter into Main Street, USA and from there it is on to Tomorrowland, Fantasyland, Frontierland, and Adventureland, each with its own rides, entertainment, and restaurants. California Adventure, Disney's newest theme park, is located right next door to the main park. Disneyland is open every day of the year and is located at 1313 Harbor Boulevard in Anaheim. For information call 714-781-4565, or visit their website: *www.disney.go.com.*

The J. Paul Getty Museum: Climbing aboard the electric tram that takes you up to the Getty's mountaintop location, you soon realize that this is not your usual museum visit. Arriving at the central plaza of gleaming white travertine rock and walking up the broad staircase, you soon discover there is so much more than museum exhibits. There is the architecture to admire, exquisite gardens to stroll in, inviting tree-lined pathways to follow, places to dine, quiet corners for contemplation, reflecting pools to gaze in, and spectacular views across the city to the ocean. The exhibition galleries house collections of European paintings (Van Gogh's *Irises*, Monet's *Wheatstacks,* and David Hockney's *Pearblossom Hwy No 2* being amongst the more well known), drawings (Michelangelo's *The Holy Family with Infant St. John the Baptist*), sculpture (lots of Greek and Roman antiquities), illuminated manuscripts, decorative arts (there's a wonderful collection of Louis XIV furniture), photographs, and changing exhibits. Admission is free. You do not need a reservation for the museum BUT you do need a parking reservation ($5 fee for parking). Often parking reservations have to be made several weeks in advance. There is no convenient street parking. Buses—MTA Metro bus #561 (213-626-4455, *www.mta.net*) and Santa Monica Big Blue Bus #14 (310-451-5444, *www.bigbluebus.com*)—stop at the Getty Center. Closed Mondays and holidays, the museum is open weekends 10 am to 6 pm and weekdays 11 am to 7 pm or 9 pm. (310-440-7300, *www.getty.edu*)

Huntington Library, Art Gallery, and Botanical Gardens: The home and 207-acre estate of the late Henry Huntington are open to the public and should not be missed by any visitor to the Los Angeles area. Huntington's enormous home is now a museum featuring the work of French and English 18th-century artists. What makes the museum especially attractive is that the paintings are displayed in a homelike setting surrounded by appropriately dramatic furnishings. Nearby, in another beautiful building, is the Huntington Library—a real gem containing, among other rare books, a 15th-century copy of the Gutenberg bible, Benjamin Franklin's handwritten autobiography, and marvelous Audubon bird prints. The gardens of the estate merit a tour in themselves and include various sections such as a rose garden, a Japanese garden, a camellia garden, a cactus garden, an English garden, and a bonsai garden. Located at 1151 Oxford Road in San Marino, the estate is open Tuesday through Friday noon to 4:30 pm, and Saturday and Sunday 10:30 am to 4:30 pm. For information on special events and shows call 626-405-2281.

NBC Television Studios: Los Angeles is the television capital of the world. To get an idea of what goes on behind the screen, visit the NBC Television Studios and take their one-hour tour that gives you a look at where the stars rehearse, how costumes are designed, how stage props are made, and what goes into the special effects. The tour also visits some of the show sets. The studios are located at 3000 West Alameda Avenue in Burbank. For further information call 818-840-3537.

The Norton Simon Museum of Art: The Norton Simon Museum of Art is without doubt one of the finest private art museums in the world, set in a beautiful Moorish-style building accented by a reflecting pool and manicured gardens. Norton Simon and his actress wife, Jennifer Jones, share their incredible collection of art including paintings by such masters as Rubens, Rembrandt, Raphael, Picasso, and Matisse. The museum, open Thursday through Sunday noon to 6 pm, is located at 411 West Colorado Boulevard in Pasadena. For further information call 626-449-6840.

Pueblo de Los Angeles: With all the tinsel of modern-day Los Angeles, it is easy to forget that this city grew up around a Spanish mission. You catch a glimpse of the town's history in Pueblo de Los Angeles, a little bit of Mexico where Hispanic people sell colorful Mexican souvenirs and operate attractive restaurants. The 42-acre complex of old buildings (some dating back to the 1780s) has been restored and is now a state park. Pueblo de Los Angeles is located at 125 Paseo de la Plaza, Los Angeles. For further information call 213-628-1274.

The *Queen Mary*: If you take Highway 710 west to Long Beach, the freeway ends at the waterfront with the *Queen Mary* docked alongside: you can go aboard and wander through the biggest ocean liner ever built. A portion of the ship is a hotel, the rest a museum, re-creating the days of splendor when the *Queen Mary* was queen of the seas.

Universal Studios: Visiting Universal Studios, the biggest, busiest movie studio in the world, is like going to a vast amusement park and there is so much to see and do that you must spend a whole day here. Included in the admission price is a two-hour tram journey which takes you around the 420-acre lot, out of the real world and into make-believe: along the way you encounter the howling fury of King Kong and tremble in a terrifying 8.3 earthquake. Water World, a live sea war spectacular, Back to the Future, a time-travel ride from the age of the dinosaurs to 2015, and Backdraft's raging 10,000 degrees firestorm thrill you with their excitement, while the Animal Planet Live show and the re-creation of the zany Lucille Ball sitcoms give you the chance to laugh away all that adrenaline in your blood. The studios are just off the Hollywood Freeway at the Universal Center Drive exit in Universal City. For further information call 818-508-9600, or visit their website at *www.universalstudios.com.*

It takes only a couple of hours to whip down the freeway between Los Angeles and San Diego but, instead, follow our sightseeing suggestions and dawdle along the way to enjoy some of southern California's coastal attractions en route.

Drive south from Los Angeles on Highway 405, the San Diego Freeway, until you come to Highway 73, the Corona del Mar Freeway, which branches to the south toward the coast. Take this, then in just minutes you come to Highway 55, Newport Boulevard. Exit here and stay on the same road all the way to **Newport Beach**. Soon after crossing the bridge watch for the sign to your right for Newport Pier. (In case you get off track, the pier is at the foot of 20th Street.) Try to arrive mid-morning so that you can capture a glimpse of yesteryear when the **Dory Fleet** comes in to beach, just to the right of the pier. The dory fleet, made up of colorfully painted, open wooden fishing boats, has been putting out to sea for almost a hundred years. It is never certain exactly what time the fleet will come in (it depends upon the fishing conditions), but if you arrive mid-morning, the chances are you will see the fishermen preparing and selling their catch-of-the-day from the back of their small boats. If seeing all the fresh fish puts you in the mood for lunch, walk across the street to the **Oyster Bar & Grill**—the food is excellent and the clam chowder truly outstanding.

From Newport Beach, continue south along the long, thin peninsula: the next community you come to is **Balboa**. In the center of town there is a clearly signposted public parking area next to Balboa Pier: leave your car here and explore the area. The beach is beautiful, stretching the entire length of the peninsula, all the way from the southern tip to beyond Newport Pier. Stroll along the beach and then walk across the peninsula (about a two-block span) to the Balboa Pavilion, a colorful Victorian gingerbread creation smack in the center of the wharf. Next to the pavilion are several booths where tickets are sold for cruises into the harbor. One of the best of these excursions is on the *Pavilion Queen* that makes a 45-minute loop of the bay. Buy your ticket and, if you have time to spare until the boat leaves, wander around the nostalgic, honky-tonk boardwalk with its cotton candy, Ferris wheel, saltwater taffy shops, and penny arcade. But be back in time to board your boat because the Balboa harbor cruise should not be missed. The trip is a boat fancier's dream: over 9,000 yachts are moored in the harbor. Also of interest are the opulent homes whose lawns stretch out to the docks where their million-dollar cruisers are moored.

A block from the Balboa Pavilion is the ferry landing—you cannot miss it. After your cruise, retrieve your car and follow signs to the Balboa Ferry. You might have to wait in line a bit because the little old-fashioned ferry only takes three cars at a time. When your turn comes, it is just minutes over to **Balboa Island**, a delightful, very wealthy community. Park your car on the main street and poke about in the pretty shops, then walk a few blocks in each direction. The homes look quaint and many seem quite small and simple, but looks are deceiving—the price tags are very high.

From Balboa Island there is a bridge across the harbor to the mainland. Almost as soon as you cross the bridge, turn right, heading south on Highway 1 through the ritzy community of **Corona del Mar**. Although there is still a quaintness to the area, exclusive boutiques, expensive art galleries, palatial homes, and trendy shops hint at the fact that this is not the sleepy little town it might appear to be.

From Corona del Mar, Highway 1 parallels the sea, which washes up against a long stretch of beach bound by high bluffs. The area seems relatively undeveloped except for its beach parks. About 11 miles south of Corona del Mar the road passes through **Laguna Beach**, famous for its many art galleries, pretty boutiques, and miles of lovely sand. In summer, from mid-July through August, Laguna Beach is usually packed with tourists coming to see the Pageant of the Masters, a tableau in which town residents dress up and re-create paintings. Two dozen living paintings are staged each evening and viewed by spectators in an outdoor amphitheater.

Continue south along the Coastal Highway. Soon after passing Dana Point, take the turnoff to the east on Highway 5 to **San Juan Capistrano**. Watch for signs directing you off the highway to **Mission San Juan Capistrano** (just two blocks from the freeway). This mission, founded by Father Junipero Serra in 1776, has been carefully restored to give you a glimpse of what life was like in the early days of California. Although located in the center of town, the mission creates its own environment since it is insulated by lovely gardens and a complex of Spanish adobe buildings. Another point of special interest at San Juan Capistrano is that the swallows have chosen it as "home," arriving every March 19th (Saint Joseph's Day) and leaving October 23rd. Visit the mission and then retrace your route to Highway 5 and continue south about an hour to **San Diego.**

The San Diego Visitors Bureau—619-232-3101—will send you a packet of valuable information for touring its many attractions. A recently completed train line makes it easier and more fun than ever to get around San Diego and its environs. You can actually board the train in Old Town and journey to the Mexican border. San Diego offers a wealth of attractions and amusements—on the following pages we feature some of our favorites. (Find out more at *www.sandiego.org*.)

Balboa Park: Balboa Park is without a doubt one of the highlights of San Diego. One of the most famous attractions within the park is the **San Diego Zoo**, one of the finest in the world. For a good orientation of the zoo take either the 40-minute bus tour or the aerial tramway. Most of the more than 3,000 animals live within natural-style enclosures with very few cages. The Children's Zoo is especially fun, with a nursery for newborn animals and a petting zoo. But Balboa Park offers much more than its splendid zoo. There are fascinating museums and exhibits within the 1,400-acre park: the Museum of Man, the Aerospace Museum, the San Diego Museum of Art, the Timken Art Gallery, the Natural History Museum, the Reuben H. Fleet Space Theater and Science Center, the Hall of Champions, the Museum of Photographic Arts, the Lily Pond, and the Botanical Building. Most of the museums are housed in picturesque Spanish-style buildings. For information call 619-239-0512.

Coronado: While in San Diego take the bridge or the ferry over to Coronado, an island-like bulb of land tipping a thin isthmus that stretches south almost to the Mexican border. Here you find not only a long stretch of beautiful beach, but also the Del Coronado Hotel, a Victorian fantasy of gingerbread turrets and gables. The Del Coronado, locally referred to as "The Del," is a sightseeing attraction in its own right and makes an excellent choice for a luncheon stop or place to settle in at the beach.

The Embarcadero: The Embarcadero is the downtown port area located along Harbor Drive. From here you can take a harbor cruise or visit one of the floating museums tied up to the quay, part of the San Diego Maritime Museum, such as the *Star of India*, built in 1863, a dramatic tall-masted ship that carried passengers and cargo around the world and the *Medea*, a turn-of-the-century luxury yacht. For information, call 619-234-9153, or visit their website at *www.sdmaritime.com*.

Heritage Park: Just adjacent to **Old Town** is Heritage Park, where some of San Diego's Victorian heritage is preserved. Next to the spacious village green, a street lined with fabulous Victorian houses slopes gently uphill. The buildings were moved here from other areas of San Diego to save them from the bulldozers and now these intricate creations house small shops and offices (do not miss the doll shop with a wonderful collection of doll houses and antique toys).

La Jolla: Be sure to visit La Jolla, "The Jewel," a sophisticated town just north of San Diego. Classy shops and restaurants line the streets and on a warm sunny day there is nowhere more perfect for an informal lunch and water views than George's Ocean Terrace (858-454-4244). La Jolla is home to a branch of the University of California and within its Scripps Institution of Oceanography are an excellent aquarium and museum featuring marine life from California and Mexico. Another very interesting museum is the Museum of Contemporary Art San Diego with its spectacular ocean views, interesting exhibits, and delightful café (858-454 3541, *www.mcasandiego.org*). However, what really makes La Jolla so special is her setting—beautiful white-sand beaches sheltered in intimate little coves. You may prefer to stay here rather than in San Diego.

Mission San Diego de Alcala

Legoland: A Mecca for children between the ages of two and eight, this is the first Legoland in the United States and is modeled on the famous one in Denmark. All the attractions are built of or themed on the colorful Lego bricks. From fun rides to opportunities to see the production of the famous bricks and the chance to buy every available Lego product, this is a theme park that Lego enthusiasts will not want to miss. (760-918-5346, *www.legoland.com*)

Mexico: Mexico lies just south of San Diego. Do not judge Mexico by its border town of Tijuana, but if you would like to have a *taste* of Mexico, take one of the "shopping and sightseeing" tours that leave from downtown for the short drive to the border. You can drive across the border, but the bus tour removes the hassle from the trip. United States citizens need only carry identification such as a driver's license if they are staying in Mexico for less than 72 hours. For further information call Gray Line Tours at 619-491-0011.

Mission San Diego de Alcala: The oldest of the chain of missions that stretches up the coast is Mission San Diego de Alcala. The mission was originally closer to San Diego but was moved to its present site (10818 San Diego Mission Road) in 1774. To reach the mission, head east on Highway 8—it is signposted to the north of the highway beyond the intersection of Highway 15. For information call 619-283-7319.

Old Town: Old Town is where San Diego originated. Just southeast of the intersection of Highways 5 and 8 you see signposts for the oldest sections of San Diego. The area has been designated as a city park and several square blocks are accessible to pedestrians only. Make the Historical Museum your first stop and orient yourself by viewing a scale model of San Diego in its early days. Although small in area, Old Town is most interesting to visit as many of the buildings are open as small museums, such as the Machado-Steward Adobe, the Old School House, and the Seeley Stables (an 1860s stage depot with a good display of horse-drawn carriages). If you are in Old Town at mealtime, you can choose from many attractive restaurants. (619-291-4903, *www.oldtownsd.com*)

Seaport Village: Just a little way south of the Embarcadero is Seaport Village, a very popular tourist attraction and fun for adults and children alike. Situated right on the waterfront, it has little paths that meander through 23 acres of a village of shops and restaurants built in a colorful variety of styles from Early Spanish to Victorian. Street artists display their talents to laughing audiences. An old-time merry-go-round (an import from Coney Island) jingles its gay melody, irresistibly beckoning the child in all of us to climb aboard.

Sea World: San Diego's marine display is in Mission Bay Park. Set in a 150-acre park which includes a 1-acre children's playland, Sea World features one of California's famous personalities, Shamu, the performing killer whale who delights everyone with her wit and aquatic abilities. Penguin Encounter is a particularly fun exhibit where you watch comical penguins waddling about in their polar environment, while Shark Encounter presents one of the largest displays of sharks in the world and provides the terrifying thrill of being surrounded by these efficient killing machines as you walk through an acrylic tube. (619-226-3901, *www.seaworld.com*)

Wild Animal Park: This is a branch of the San Diego Zoo 30 miles north of the city near Escondido—truly a zoo on a grand scale. The animals roam freely in terrain designed to match their natural habitat. You feel as if you are on a safari in Africa as you watch for lions and other animals while you tour the park on the Wgasa Bushline Monorail tour. There are also several open theaters where animal shows are presented. For more information call 619-234-6541.

Leaving San Diego, Highway 8 takes you east and winds through shrub-filled canyons dotted with ever-expanding housing suburbs. About 30 minutes after the highway leaves the city, watch for the sign for Highway 79 where you turn north toward Julian. The road weaves through an Indian reservation and the scenery becomes prettier by the minute as you climb into the mountains and enter the **Cuyamaca Rancho State Park**. There are not many opportunities to sightsee en route, but if you want to break your journey, you can pause at the park headquarters and visit the Indian museum or the museum at the **Old Stonewall Mine**. Leaving the park, the road winds down into Julian.

Julian is a small town that can easily be explored in just a short time. What is especially nice is that, although it is a tourist attraction, the town is not "tacky touristy." Rather, you get the feeling you are in the last century as you wander through the streets and stop to browse at some of the antique shops, visit the small historical museum in the old brewery, and enjoy refreshment at the soda fountain in the 1880s drug store. If you want to delve deeper into mining, just a short drive (or long walk) away on the outskirts of town is the **Eagle Mine**, founded by pioneers from Georgia, many of them soldiers who came here after the Civil War. Tours are taken deep into the mine and a narration gives not only the history of the mine, but the history of Julian.

If you are in Julian in the fall, you can enjoy another of Julian's offerings—apples. Although you can sample Julian's wonderful apples throughout the year (every restaurant has its own special apple pie on the menu), the apple becomes king during the fall harvest. Beginning in October and continuing on into November, special crafts shows and events are held in the Julian Town Hall, and, of course, apples are featured at every restaurant. If you visit one of the packing plants on the edge of town you can buy not only apples, but every conceivable item that has apples as a theme.

It is only a short drive north from Julian on Highway 79 to **Santa Ysabel** where you turn right at the main intersection. At this junction you see **Dudley's Bakery**, a rather nondescript looking building that houses a great bakery: loyal customers drive all the way from San Diego just to buy one of their 21 varieties of tasty bread. As you leave Santa Ysabel you come to **Mission Santa Ysabel**, a reconstructed mission that still serves the Indians. This is one of the less interesting missions, but you may want to see the murals painted by the local Indians.

About 7 miles after leaving the mission, Highway 79 breaks off to the east and you continue north on Highway 76. In five minutes you come to Lake Henshaw. Just beyond the lake turn northeast (right) on East Grade Road which winds its way up the mountain to the **Palomar Observatory**. Just near the parking area is a museum where you learn about the observatory through photos and short films. It is a pleasant stroll up to the impressive white-domed observatory that houses the Hale telescope—the largest in the United States. A flight of steps takes you to a glass-walled area where you see the giant telescope whose lens is 200 inches in diameter, 2 feet thick, and took 11 years to polish. You cannot see the telescope in operation because it is used only at night, but it is fun to imagine scientists scanning the heavens.

After viewing the observatory, loop back down the twisting road to the main highway and when it intersects with Highway 76 turn northwest (right), driving through hills covered with groves of avocado and orange trees. In about 12 miles you come to **Pala** and the **Mission San Antonio de Pala**. Established in 1810, it is one of the few remaining active *asistencias* (missions built in outlying areas to serve the Indians). The mission is small, but the chapel is very beautiful in its rugged simplicity enhanced by thick adobe walls, rustic beamed ceiling, and Indian paintings. A bell tower stands alone to the right of the chapel, a picturesque sight. To the left are a simple museum and a souvenir shop.

From Pala it is about a ten-minute drive north on S16 to Temecula. Just before you enter town the road intersects with Highway 79 and you head east for 18 miles to Aguanga where Highway 371 takes you northeast for 21 miles to Highway 74. As you head north on 74 the mountain air becomes sweeter and the scenery increasingly prettier as you enter the forest. In about 12 miles you see signs for **Idyllwild** to the northeast. Turn here on Highway 243 and very soon you come to the small resort tucked into the mountains high above Palm Springs. Homely little restaurants, antique stores, and fascinating gift shops make up the town.

Leaving Idyllwild, continue north on Highway 342 to Banning where you turn east (right) on Highway 10. In about 12 miles you come to Highway 111 where you turn right and follow signs to Palm Springs (about a ten-minute drive). **Palm Springs** was first discovered by the Indians who came to this oasis to bathe in the hot springs, which they considered to have healing qualities. The same tribe still owns much of Palm Springs and rents their valuable real estate to homeowners and commercial enterprises. The hot springs are still in use today.

During the winter season the town is congested with traffic and the sidewalks are crammed with an assortment of people of every age, size, and shape dressed in colorful, sporty clothes. Palm Springs used to be deserted in summer when the days are very hot. However, more and more tourists are coming in June, July, and August, attracted by the lower hotel rates. Although the temperature in the summer months is frequently well above 110 degrees, it is a dry heat and not unbearable in the mornings and balmy evenings. In fact, due to the altitude, evenings often require a sweater. So if your visit is in summer, plan your sightseeing for early and late in the day and spend midday in the comfort of your air-conditioned inn.

In addition to the pleasures of basking in the sun or playing on one of the many golf courses in the area, Palm Springs offers a variety of sightseeing. The most impressive excursion is to take the **Aerial Tramway** (located just north of town off Highway 111) from the desert floor up 2½ miles into the San Jacinto Mountains. In summer you go from sizzling heat to cool mountain forests, while in winter you go from desert to snow. The weather atop the mountain is often more than 40 degrees cooler than in Palm Springs, so remember to take the appropriate clothing. At the top are observation decks with telescopes, a restaurant, and miles of hiking trails.

If you enjoy deserts, be sure not to miss the **Living Desert Outdoor Museum** (closed in summer) where 6 miles of trails wind through different types of desert that are found in the United States. Tour booklets are available at the entrance to assist you along the trails. If you are interested in the rich and famous, join a bus tour that drives by the outside of their magnificent homes. Many movie stars have second homes in Palm Springs.

Palm Springs is a convenient place to end this itinerary because it is a quick, easy drive on the freeway back to Los Angeles. But, if time permits, squeeze in one more contrasting destination, the exclusive Alpine resort of Lake Arrowhead.

Leave Palm Springs and head north on Highway 111 for about 10 miles to Highway 10 and turn west for Banning. Approximately 20 miles past Banning at Redlands, exit from the freeway on Highway 30 and drive north for a few minutes until Highway 38 travels into the hills. As the road begins to climb up from the valley the scenery becomes prettier with every curve—the dry desert brush is gradually left behind, replaced by evergreen trees. At the town of Running Springs turn west on Highway 18. This is called the "**Rim of the World Highway**," a road where sweeping vistas of the valley floor can be glimpsed through the clouds. Be aware that fog often hovers around this drive and then, instead of admiring beautiful views, you creep along in thick, gray mist.

Lake Arrowhead village is a newly built cluster of restaurants and shops along the lakefront. The lake is bordered by magnificent estates of the wealthy from southern California. The magnet of Lake Arrowhead is not any specific sightseeing, but rather the outdoors experience: although lakefront and beach access is restricted and private, you can take leisurely walks through the forest, picnic in secluded parks, explore the lake by paddle boats, or rent bicycles for a bit of fresh-air adventure. You must also take the hour-long ride on the nostalgic steamer that circles the lake.

When it is time to complete your itinerary, retrace your path back to the valley and follow Highway 10 back into Los Angeles. Unless you encounter unexpected traffic, the trip should take about two hours.

Aerial Tramway, Palm Springs

Leisurely Loop of Southern California

Yosemite, the Gold Country & Lake Tahoe

Half Dome, Yosemite

This itinerary features two of California's most spectacular natural attractions, majestic Yosemite National Park and beautiful Lake Tahoe, and links them together by one of California's best-kept secrets—the spirited, nostalgic, Gold Rush towns, which string along the Sierra foothills. These colorful towns date back to 1848 when the cry went up that gold had been found at Sutter Creek, precipitating the rush to California by men eager to make their fortunes. Overnight, boom towns sprang up around every mining camp, with a cluster of similar-style saloons, restaurants, hotels, dance halls, and homes.

Gold Rush fever quickly cooled and many of the towns were left, quietly forgotten, until tourists rediscovered their charm. Today these benignly neglected towns have been spruced up and bustle with activity: antique shops, art galleries, nifty boutiques, attractive restaurants, and appealing inns are tucked into old Victorian houses lining sleepy streets. The highway that runs through the mother lode country is numbered 49 after the gold-seeking miners who were known as the Forty-Niners.

Recommended Pacing: We recommend a minimum of two nights in Yosemite and suggest that you try to stay at accommodation in the park (see page 53). Either before or after visiting Yosemite, you have a perfect opportunity to explore California's Gold Rush Country. Rather than backtracking, plan to progress through the region, spending at least one night in the south and at least one night in the north. From the northern region of the Gold Country it is a logical continuation on to Lake Tahoe. Many people enjoy Lake Tahoe as a resort and will spend at least a week here, basking on its sandy beaches in the summer and skiing down the snow-covered peaks that ring its waters in the winter. If you are visiting Lake Tahoe as a tourist, we recommend a two-night visit.

Weather Wise: Heavy snow is the norm at Tahoe and Yosemite during the winter, while most of the Gold Rush towns are beneath the snow line and experience heavy winter rains. During summer months the days are hot in Yosemite and Tahoe, and several degrees warmer in the Gold Country.

As you read through this itinerary, please be aware that each of the areas featured could well be a destination in itself. Yosemite and Lake Tahoe are especially popular resorts and an entire vacation could easily be dedicated to either one. If that is your desire, just extract from the itinerary the portion that suits your interests. However, the Gold Country is not as well known and makes a super link between Yosemite and Tahoe—or, for that matter, a great destination in its own right.

Since Yosemite makes a most convenient first-night stop from either San Francisco or Los Angeles, driving directions are given from both so that you can tailor the trip to your own needs. Much of the first day of this itinerary is spent driving to Yosemite National

Park, about a four- to five-hour drive from San Francisco or a six- to seven-hour drive from the Greater Los Angeles area. A brief description of what to see and do during your stay in San Francisco is included in *San Francisco to Los Angeles via the Coast*, while the list of attractions of the much larger, more sprawling Los Angeles are included in *Leisurely Loop of Southern California.*

Leave San Francisco east over the Bay Bridge, in the direction of Oakland. Once across the bridge, stay in the middle lane and follow signs for Highway 580, heading east, signposted Stockton. Stay on Highway 580 for about 48 miles until you come to Livermore where Highway 580 meets Highway 205 which you take, continuing east, following signs for Manteca. Near Manteca, take Highway 120 east, directly to the northern gate of Yosemite National Park. Total driving distance is about 200 miles.

Leave Los Angeles heading north on Highway 5 until you come to the junction of Highway 99 which you take north (signposted Bakersfield). Continue on Highway 99 to the north edge of Fresno where you take Highway 41 north, directly to the southern gate of Yosemite National Park. Total driving distance is about 300 miles.

The main attractions of the over 1,000 square miles of **Yosemite National Park** lie within the narrow 7-mile-long **Yosemite Valley**, which is where you should try to stay if at all possible. A two- or three-night stay in the park is recommended. From hotels through tented cabins, all accommodations in Yosemite are controlled by the **Yosemite Concessions Services (YCS)**—for information call 209-372-0265. It is necessary year-round to make reservations well in advance by phoning 559-252-4848. Visit their homepage on the National Park Service website at *www.nps.gov/yose*.

From the stately and very expensive **Ahwahnee Hotel**, through lodges, cabins, tented camps, and regular campsites, Yosemite has accommodations to suit every pocketbook. If your taste in hotels runs to grand, stay at The Ahwahnee. **Yosemite Lodge** provides more moderately priced accommodations in both cabins and motel/hotel-type rooms. Still less expensive are the tented camps that provide canvas tents on wooden board floors (you do not need sleeping bags since beds and linens are provided). The budget choice is regular camping. But please remember—space is very limited in every category and reservations are essential.

While the attractions of staying in the valley cannot be denied, a more relaxed, serene, country atmosphere pervades the **Wawona Hotel**, located within the park, but about a 30-mile drive south of the valley on Highway 41. With its shaded verandahs overlooking broad rolling lawns, the hotel presents a welcoming picture. Bedrooms with private bathrooms are at a premium—most rooms use communal men's and women's bathrooms (sometimes situated quite a distance from your bedroom).

Yosemite Valley, an awe-inspiring monument to the forces of nature, is bounded by magnificent scraped granite formations—**Half Dome**, **El Capitan**, **Cathedral Rock**, **Clouds Rest**—beckoning rock climbers from around the world. And over the rocks, cascading to the valley far below, are numerous high waterfalls with descriptive names such as Bridalveil, Ribbon, Staircase, and Silver Strand. Below the giant walls of rock the crystal-clear River Merced wends its way through woodlands and meadows of flowers. Undeniably, this is one of the most beautiful valleys anywhere in the world.

Your first stop should be the information center to obtain pamphlets, books, and schedules. The park service offers a remarkable number of guided walks, slide shows, and educational programs—look over the possibilities and select the ones that most appeal to you.

Once you are in the valley, park your car and restrict yourself to travel aboard the free shuttle buses as you can do most of your sightseeing by combining pleasant walks with shuttle-bus rides. Alternative modes of transportation are on horseback on guided trips and by bike (bicycles can be rented in the park). Because the valley is flat, it has miles of paths for biking—a very unstrenuous, efficient way of getting around.

Be warned that during the summer months Yosemite Valley is jammed with cars and people—spring and fall are much more civilized times to visit.

Within the park, but beyond the valley floor, are many areas of great natural beauty. Situated just inside the park's southern perimeter is the **Mariposa Grove** of giant sequoias. It was here that John Muir, the great naturalist who fathered the idea of the national park system, persuaded President Theodore Roosevelt to add the 250-acre grove of trees to the Yosemite park system. A tram winds through the grove of sequoias as the driver tells the stories of these giant trees—some of the largest in the world.

To the south of the valley Highway 41 climbs for about 10 miles (stop at the viewing point just before the tunnel) to the Glacier Point turnoff. It is a 15-mile drive to the spectacular **Glacier Point**—a vista point over 3,000 feet above the valley floor. From Glacier Point everything in the valley below takes on Lilliputian proportions: the ribbon-like River Merced, the forest, meadows, and waterfalls all dwarfed by huge granite cliffs. Beyond the valley a giant panorama of undulating granite presents itself. The ideal photographic time to visit is early in the morning or evening. Rangers at Glacier Point offer evening interpretive programs.

Leave Yosemite by the northern gate on Highway 120 to **Groveland**, a handsome old town shaded by pines. The nearby town of Big Oak Flat is little more than a couple of houses strung along the road. As Highway 120 drops steeply down 5 miles of twisting road to Highway 49, the shady pine forests of the mountains give way to rolling, oak-studded foothills, the typical scenery of the Gold Country.

Heading north on Highway 49, detour into **Chinese Camp**, home to over 5,000 Chinese miners in the 1850s and now almost a ghost town sleeping under a profusion of delicate Chinese Trees of Heaven.

The main street of **Jamestown** is off Highway 49 and therefore free of thoroughfare traffic. With its wooden boardwalks, balconies, and storefronts, Jamestown has managed to retain much of the feel of the Gold Rush days. Inviting shops, particularly the emporium, merit a browse, the western-style saloons are full of local color, and the **1859 Historic National Hotel** as well as the **Jamestown Hotel** have been restored to a beauty such as the Gold Rush days never witnessed. Just above Main Street on Fifth Avenue is the **Railtown 1897 State Historic Park** where visitors can see old freight and passenger cars, steam trains, and the roundhouse. The park is open on weekends when tours of the roundhouse are conducted.

Leaving town, continue up the main street and cross Highway 49 onto a peaceful little road that takes you through the countryside to Columbia. Follow signs for Columbia or, wherever a junction is unmarked, continue straight. A 15-minute drive brings you to Parrot Ferry Road on the outskirts of the town.

In the 1850s **Columbia** was one of the largest towns in California, with many saloons, gaming halls, and stores. Today the main street is closed to car traffic and has been restored as a state park to reflect the dusty, raucous days when Columbia was the "gem of the southern mines." The renovated buildings of Main Street are like exhibits that make learning fun. Be sure to visit the Wells Fargo office, fire station, candy store, mining museum, and concession shops where costumed citizens sell goods appropriate to

City Hotel, Columbia

the period. You can enjoy a cold sarsaparilla at the saloon, munch candy rocks at the Candy Kitchen, and pan for gold at the mining shack. It is great fun to climb aboard a stagecoach for a ride through the town or take a tour to the Hidden Treasure Mine.

Both the **Fallon** and **City Hotel** have been restored (at vast expense) by the State of California to mirror the look of two of Columbia's hotels in Gold Rush days. The City Hotel on Main Street has a less ornate Victorian decor, reflecting the Columbia of the 1860s.

Parrot Ferry Road leads north from Columbia, crosses the dam and continues through hilly countryside in the direction of Murphys. If you would like to try your hand at rappelling into the largest cavern in California, you have the opportunity at **Moaning Cavern**. (You can, of course, take the saner descent down a spiral staircase into a room capable of holding the Statue of Liberty.) The rappel is exciting, and with outfitting, instruction, and a boost of confidence, you descend through a small opening into the well-lit cavern—a most exhilarating experience.

From the caves a short drive brings you to Highway 4 where you turn east (right) for about a 20-mile drive to **Calaveras Big Trees State Park**, a 6,000-acre preserve of forest including two magnificent stands of sequoia trees. A 45-minute self-guided tour takes you through the North Grove and the nearby visitors center provides information and history on these mammoth trees. If you have time and interest, you can visit the more distant South Grove of giant sequoias.

Leaving the park, retrace your route down Highway 4 and detour into **Murphys**, a sleepy Gold Rush town sheltered under locust and elm trees where several old buildings and an **Old Timers' Museum** reflect its Gold Rush heritage. Well signposted from the center of town is another cavern complex, **Mercer Caverns**, with rooms of stalactites, stalagmites, and other interesting limestone formations. You might also want to detour to a beautiful winery, **Ironstone Vineyards,** set on the hill outside Murphys. (Turn off Main Street up the road to the side of Murphy's Hotel, then at the stop sign turn right on Six Mile Road and travel 1 mile.) The grounds are absolutely gorgeous in their landscaping and at the end of an extremely informative tour it is a memorable experience to taste wine while listening to the winery's magnificent organ from the old Alhambra Theater. Complimentary tours are offered daily at 11:30 am, 1:30 pm, and 3:30 pm (no 11:30 am tour during winter months). The winery is open daily between 10 am and 5 pm (closed at Christmas and Thanksgiving) for complimentary tasting. Ironstone Winery is located at 1894 Six Mile Road, Murphys. For more information call 209-728-1251, or visit their website: *www.ironstonevineyards.com*.

At the junction of Highways 4 and 49 sits **Angels Camp**, a pleasant town with high sidewalks and wooden-fronted buildings. Today Angels Camp's fame results not from mining, but from the frog-jumping contests held every May. There is even a monument to a frog taking the place of honor on the main street along which almost all the shops sell items carrying a frog motif.

Leave Angels Camp traveling north on Highway 49 through San Andreas where nearly all evidence of Gold Rush days has been obliterated by modern shopping centers and commercial businesses. On the outskirts of the town Highway 49 makes a sharp turn to the east (right), which is signposted Jackson. A 7-mile drive brings you to **Mukulumne Hill** which in its heyday was one of the more raucous mining towns, though now it seems to be quietly fading away. Turn off Highway 49 and loop through town past the impressive (though genteelly shabby) Hotel Leger and turn left in front of the crumbling I.O.O.F building, then through the residential area and back onto the main road.

Jackson still supports roughly the same population as it had during the Gold Rush—consequently, modern shopping centers and sprawling suburbs are the order of the day. Turn right at the first stop sign in town and almost immediately left to the main street. Set above the old town in an impressive Victorian home is the **Amador County Museum**, 225 Church Street. The various rooms have rather eclectic exhibits from the Gold Rush era: for example, the kitchen is full of 19th-century cookware while a small upstairs bedroom displays Indian baskets. Set in an adjacent building is a scale working model of the North Star Stamp Mill, which crushes tiny stones.

Retrace your route to where you turned off Highway 49 and turn left on Highway 88 signposted for Lake Tahoe and Pine Grove. Just outside Pine Grove turn left (signposted for your next two destinations, Indian Grinding Rock State Park and Volcano) and follow one of the Gold Country's prettiest back roads to **Chaw'se Indian Grinding Rock State Park**. A giant slab of limestone has over 1,000 grinding mortars worn into it by Indian women grinding acorn meal. A typical Miwok village has been built nearby with a ceremonial roundhouse and various tree-bark dwellings. The adjacent cultural center, built in the style of an Indian roundhouse, has interesting displays from several local Indian tribes.

Just a short drive takes you past the turnoff for Sutter Creek and into **Volcano**, one of the smallest (population 100), prettiest Gold Country towns, which boasted the first lending library and theater group in the state. Now it is a tiny one-street town whose most impressive building is the three-storied, balconied **Saint George Hotel**. Several weathered building fronts give an impression of what the town looked like in more prosperous days. Three miles beyond the town lies **Daffodil Hill** where over 25,000 daffodils provide a colorful spring display.

Follow the narrow wooded ravine alongside Sutter Creek as it twists down to the town of the same name. **Sutter Creek** rivals Nevada City as the loveliest of the Gold Rush towns. Its main street is strung out along busy Highway 49 but somehow the noisy logging trucks, and commercial and car traffic do not detract from its beauty. False wooden store fronts support big balconies, which hang over the high sidewalks of the town. Today many of the quaint wooden buildings are home to antique, craft, and gift shops.

Amador City and **Drytown**, the first two towns you encounter after leaving Sutter Creek as you head towards Placerville on Highway 49, have an old-world charm and are worth exploring. However, following them is a string of commercial towns that offer nothing of attraction to the tourist although the intervening countryside is still most attractive. Follow Highway 49 as it weaves through the commercial sprawl of **Placerville**, crosses Highway 50, and climbs out of town.

It is an 8-mile drive along Highway 49, through apple orchards and woodlands, to Coloma where the Gold Rush began. Or you can make it a 25-mile drive by taking a right turn east just after leaving Placerville onto Highway 193, a narrow road which twists down a thickly forested canyon to Chili Bar (a popular spot for rafters to launch) and then does a spectacular weaving climb out of the valley through Kelsey and into **Georgetown**. Stop to explore Georgetown's shaded streets and then pick up Marshall Road (turn left behind the gas station), which takes you down to Highway 49 where you turn south into Coloma.

Set on the banks of the American River, the scant remains of the boom town of **Coloma** are preserved as **Marshall Gold Discovery State Historic Park**. It all began in 1848 when James Marshall discovered gold at **Sutter's Sawmill**. The remaining historic buildings are scattered over a large area, each separated by expanses of green lawn and picnic places along the banks of the river. The residential part of town is a sleepy little cluster of attractive houses set back from the river—it is hard to believe that there was once a population of over 10,000 here. The museum shows a short film on gold discovery and provides information for a self-guided tour. A duplicate of Sutter's original sawmill, looking like a big shed, sits on the bank of the river. For a change of transportation, a number of companies offer one-day rafting trips down the most famous section of the South Fork of the American River. We thoroughly enjoyed the trip that we took with **Beyond Limits Adventures**. It's a class 3 (intermediate) section of river that combines pretty scenery and whitewater as your raft plunges into Satan's Cesspool, Hospital Bar, and Ambulance Driver. Minimum age seven, season April to October. For further information call 800-234-7238, or visit their website at *www.rivertrip.com*.

Auburn lies 20 miles farther north along Highway 49, which weaves through its suburbs, crosses Highway 80, and continues as a fast, wide road for approximately 24 miles into Grass Valley. An alternative, far more attractive, and just a few miles longer route, is to take Highway 80 north to the Colfax-Grass Valley exit and follow Highway 174 through pretty woodlands and orchards into Grass Valley. (The following sightseeing suggestion, Empire Mine State Park, is signposted on your left as you near town.)

Nevada City

Grass Valley has a booming economy and sprawls far beyond its historic boundary. Its old downtown buildings housing everyday stores attest to its prosperity. Save town explorations for adjacent Nevada City and concentrate on Grass Valley's **Empire Mine State Park** at the southern end of town. This hard-rock mine produced $100,000,000-worth of gold before it closed. An exhibition depicts the mining methods used by miners who came here from the Cornish tin mines in England. Park personnel offer tours of the mine buildings, the most interesting of which is the opulent home of William Bourne, the mine's original owner.

The adjacent town of **Nevada City** is as handsome as Grass Valley is functional. The old mining stores and saloons have been cleverly converted into eateries ranging from family-style cafés to gourmet restaurants, antique stores, boutiques, bookstores, and the like. Old-fashioned gas lamps light the streets at night, providing a perfect backdrop for a horse-drawn-carriage ride. Many settlers came here from the east bringing with them the deciduous trees of their home states, so Nevada City is one of the few places in California that has the glorious fall foliage.

A great many events occur in Nevada City including the popular Victorian Christmas (Thanksgiving to Christmas—roast chestnuts and carolers), Summer Nights, and the Teddy Bear Convention (April). The town also hosts parades such as the Joe Cain Parade (Mardi Gras), markets, festivals, and tours that give you plenty of excuses to visit this delightful spot at all times of the year.

As a conclusion to your Gold Country explorations, take a 45-mile round trip to **Malakoff Diggins** where high-powered jets of water were blasted at a mountainside to extract gold. The method was very successful, but it clogged waterways for miles and left a lunar landscape where there had once been a forested mountainside. This is a very pleasant summer-evening trip, but rather than run the risk of returning down narrow country roads in the dark, make the loop as you leave Nevada City for Lake Tahoe. The route is quite well signposted, but it gives you reassurance to have in hand the map from Nevada City Chamber of Commerce. (530-265-2692, *www.ncgold.com*)

Leave Nevada City going north on Highway 49, following it through wooded countryside for 11 miles to the marker directing you right to Malakoff Diggins (signposted Tyler Foote Crossing Road). The narrow paved road leads you through the forest and, just as you are beginning to wonder quite where you are going, a signpost directs you right down a dirt road into **North Bloomfield**, a town of white-painted houses and buildings set behind picket fences under forest shade. (The town is being restored by the park service and the museum/ranger station is a useful informational stop.) The road through town leads to the diggins proper, a vast lunar landscape of awesome scars. If the weather is inclement, turn back at this point and return to Nevada City by way of the paved highway. Otherwise, continue along the well-maintained dirt road (forking left and downhill at junctions), which leads you down through some lovely scenery to a narrow wood-and-metal bridge spanning a rocky canyon of the South Yuba River where you pick up the paved road that brings you back to Highway 49 on the outskirts of Nevada City.

Leave Nevada City on Highway 20 east, a freeway which soon becomes a two-lane highway passing through forests and along a high ridge giving vistas of the Sierras. As Highway 20 ends, take Highway 80 towards Truckee, a fast freeway that climbs into the Sierra mountains through ever-more-dramatic rugged scenery.

The freeway climbs over **Donner Pass** and by **Donner Lake**, both named in honor of the group of settlers led by George Donner who in 1846 became snowbound while trying to cross the Sierra Nevada in late fall. Harsh conditions and lack of food took many lives and resulted in the survivors resorting to cannibalism.

Take Highway 89, the Tahoe City exit, and follow it alongside the rushing **Truckee River** to **River Ranch Lodge**, an inn where in summertime it is great sport to sit on the patio and watch the river tumbling by.

Follow the Truckee River to its source, **Lake Tahoe**. Tucked in a high valley, Lake Tahoe is a vast, blue, icy-cold lake ringed by pine forests and backed by high mountains. The lake has about 70 miles of shoreline, a maximum depth of 1,645 feet, and a summer temperature of about 65 degrees. When people from the San Francisco Bay Area say they are "going to the mountains," Tahoe is usually where they're heading. While certain enclaves have their share of hot dog stands, McDonald's restaurants, and glitzy gambling casinos, there are many unspoilt areas where you can enjoy the exquisite beauty of the lake and its surrounding stunning scenery. For bikers and joggers, a marvelous, seemingly endless trail traces a path along the lakefront and down the Truckee River.

Tahoe City combines rustic, folksy shops, restaurants, and everyday stores with two quite interesting tourist attractions: Fanny Bridge and the Gatekeeper's Cabin. **Fanny Bridge** is very close: just turn right at the supermarket, and there it is. You will see immediately the derivation of "Fanny" when you see the tourists leaning over the railing to watch the trout gobble up the food tossed to them. On the same side of the bridge where the fish feed, outlet gates are opened and shut to control the level of the lake—the

Emerald Bay

entire flow of water exiting from Lake Tahoe is regulated here as the water runs into the Truckee River. The other attraction of Tahoe City, the **Gatekeeper's Cabin**, sits on the bank of the Truckee. The rustic old cabin, once home to the man who controlled the river level, is now an attractive small museum operated by the local historical society.

Hugging the shoreline, Highway 89 opens up to ever-more-lovely vistas as the road travels south. Nine miles south of Tahoe City brings you to **Sugar Pine State Park** with its many miles of hiking trails, and camping and picnic sites. In summer you can tour the nicely furnished Ehrman Mansion, once the vast lakeside summer home of a wealthy San Francisco family.

You will know by the sheer beauty of your surroundings when you are at **Emerald Bay**. The road sits hundreds of feet above a sparkling, blue-green bay and miles of Lake Tahoe stretch beyond its entrance. Center stage is a small wooded island crowned by a stone tea house. A 1½-mile trail winds down to the lake—it seems a lot farther walking up—and in summer you can tour **Vikingsholm**, the 38-room lakeside mansion built in 1929 and patterned after a 9th-century Norse fortress. It is the finest example of Scandinavian architecture in America and is filled with Norwegian furniture and weavings.

Just below Emerald Bay a trail leads from the parking lot up a ¼-mile steep trail to a bridge above the cascading cataract of **Eagle Falls** which offers fantastic views of Lake Tahoe. A mile farther up the trail is **Eagle Lake**, in an isolated, picture-perfect setting.

A memorable outing from Tahoe is a day trip to Nevada's silver towns, Virginia City and Carson City. Leaving Tahoe City, follow the northernmost shore of the lake across the Nevada state line and take Highway 431 from Incline Village over Mount Rose to the stoplight at Highway 395. Cross the highway and go straight ahead up the winding Geiger Grade, Highway 341, to **Virginia City**. Built over a honeycomb of silver mines, in its heyday Virginia City had a population of over 30,000. Its wooden sidewalks, colorful saloons (you must visit the Bucket of Blood Saloon), and false-front buildings with their broad balconies make it a town straight out of a John Wayne movie. The stores sell everything from homemade candy to western boots and several have been reconstructed as museums. You can walk up to the old cemetery, take a steam-train ride, or tour a mine.

Leaving town, travel on through Gold Hill and Silver Hill to Highway 50 where you turn south for the 7-mile drive to **Carson City**, the state capital. The town itself has little of interest except for the **Nevada State Museum**, just across the street from the Nugget Casino on the main road. The highlight of the museum is the re-created silver mine in the basement. You walk along rail car lines in semi-darkness, past exhibits of miners at work and mine machinery—a lot safer than going down a working mine.

To return to Tahoe, go south on Highway 395, the main street of town, to Highway 50 west. Turn right and when you come to Lake Tahoe turn right, following the lake to Tahoe City.

Leaving Lake Tahoe, it is a fast four- to five-hour freeway drive, via Highway 80, to the San Francisco Bay area. If you are going to Los Angeles, take Highway 80 to Sacramento and Highway 5 south to Los Angeles—a fast eight- to nine-hour drive.

Yosemite, the Gold Country & Lake Tahoe

San Francisco to the Oregon Border
—and a Bit Beyond

Mendocino

If your heart leaps with joy at the sight of long stretches of deserted beaches, rugged cliffs embraced by wind-bent trees, sheep quietly grazing near crashing surf, and groves of redwoods towering above carpets of dainty ferns, then this itinerary will suit you to perfection. Nowhere else in California can you travel surrounded by so much natural splendor. Less than an hour after crossing the Golden Gate Bridge, civilization is left far behind you and your adventure into some of California's most beautiful scenery begins. The first part of this route includes many well-loved attractions: Muir Woods, the Russian River, Sonoma County wineries, the Mendocino Coast, and the Avenue of the Giant Redwoods. Then the route becomes less "touristy" as it reaches the Victorian jewel of Ferndale, the bustling town of Eureka, and the coastal hamlet of Trinidad, and concludes amongst the giant coastal redwoods of Redwood National Park.

Recommended Pacing: You can cover the distance between San Francisco and Mendocino in a day. It is approximately a four-hour drive if you are traveling inland on Highway 101 and then cutting west over at Cloverdale on Highway 128 back to the coast and Highway 1 just south of Mendocino. It is approximately a six-hour journey if you follow Highway 1 as it hugs the coast all the way north. However, if time allows, follow our routing and spend a night just north of San Francisco near Point Reyes National Seashore (more if you want to take advantage of the hiking and biking trails), and a night or two in the Healdsburg/Russian River area before arriving in Mendocino. Allow two nights for the Mendocino area and two nights for the Eureka area before continuing up the coast to Oregon.

Weather Wise: The weather along California's northern coast is unpredictable: beautiful warm summer days suddenly become overcast when the fog rolls in (July and August). The prettiest months are usually June, September, and October. Rain falls during the winter and spring, while fall enjoys beautiful crisp, clear days.

San Francisco, a city of unsurpassed beauty, is a favorite destination of tourists and it is no wonder: the city is dazzling in the sunlight, yet equally enchanting when wrapped in fog. The setting is spectacular: a cluster of hills on the tip of a peninsula. San Francisco is very walkable and if you tire, a cable car, bus, or taxi is always close at hand. Starting on page 13, we give you enough sightseeing suggestions to occupy several days.

Avoiding commuter hours and congestion, leave San Francisco on the **Golden Gate Bridge** following Highway 101 north. After you cross this famous bridge, pull into the vista point for a panoramic view of this most lovely city. For another spectacular detour, take the very first exit after the viewing area, Alexander Avenue, turn left back under the freeway, and continue as if you are heading back onto the Golden Gate Bridge but, instead, take a quick right to the **Marin Headlands**. Some of the city's most spectacular skylines are photographed from the vantage point of these windswept and rugged headlands looking back at the city through the span of the Golden Gate. The road continues through the park and eventually winds back to Highway 101. Information and maps are available at the visitors center located in the old Fort Barry Chapel. Signs in the park direct you to the center, which is open daily, 9:30 am to 4:30 pm (415-331-1540). Not to be missed is the **Marine Mammal Center**, where injured seals and other marine animals are nursed back to health by a multitude of volunteers (415-289-7325, *www.tmmc.org*).

After returning to Highway 101, continue on to the Mill Valley exit. Circle under the freeway and follow signs for Highway 1 north. As the two-lane road leaves the town behind and winds up through the trees, watch closely for a sharp right turn to **Muir Woods**. The road takes you high above open fields and down a steep ravine to the Muir Woods entrance and car park where a park volunteer gives out a map and information. Near the park entrance a cross section of a trunk of one of the stately giant coastal redwoods gives you an appreciation of the age of these great trees. Notations relate the tree's growth rings to significant historical occurrences during the tree's lifetime: 1066—the Battle of Hastings, 1215—the Magna Carta, 1492—the discovery of America, 1776—the Declaration of Independence. But this tree was only a baby—some date back over 2,000 years. Your brochure guides you on the walk beneath the redwoods or you can take a guided tour with one of the rangers. Allow about an hour for the park, longer if you take a long walk or just sit on one of the benches to soak in the beauty.

Leaving the park, continue west to the coastal road Highway 1. Turn left and then, almost immediately, right. There is a small sign marked **Muir Beach**, but it is easy to miss. Just before you come to the beach you arrive at the **Pelican Inn**, a charming re-creation of an English pub that fortunately also offers lodging. The adjacent Muir Beach is a small half-moon beach bound at each end by large rock formations.

Return to Highway 1 and head north along a challenging, winding section of this beautiful coastal road. The road descends to the small town of **Stinson Beach** where by entering the state park you can gain access to a fabulous stretch of wide white sand, bordered on one side by the sea and on the other by grassy dunes. This is a perfect spot to stretch and enjoy a walk along the beach.

Leaving Stinson Beach, the road curves inland bordering **Bolinas Lagoon,** a paradise for birds, and then leaves the water and continues north for about 10 miles to the town of Olema. At Olema you leave Highway 1 and take the road marked to Inverness, just a short drive away.

If the weather is fine, allow time to explore **Point Reyes National Seashore,** a spectacular wilderness area stretching along the sea. If you happen to be in the area on a weekend, in addition to taking advantage of the free ranger programs, call ahead on 415-663-1200 to inquire about special field trips (such as tidepool studies, bird watching, and sights and sounds of nature) that are offered for a fee. The ranger station, located in a handsome redwood building at the entrance to the park, has maps, leaflets, books, a museum, and a movie theater where a presentation gives interesting information on the park. Be sure to stop here before your explorations to obtain a map and study what you want to see and do. A short stroll away from the ranger station is the "earthquake trail"

where markers indicate changes brought about by the 1906 earthquake. Also within walking distance is the **Morgan Ranch** where Morgan horses are raised and trained for the park system. If the weather is clear, a drive out to **Point Reyes Lighthouse** is a highlight that should not be missed. As you drive for 45 minutes across windswept fields and through dairy farms to the lighthouse you realize how large the park really is. When you arrive, it is a ten-minute walk from the parking area to the viewing area. From there, steps lead down to the lighthouse. Be prepared: it is like walking down a 30-story building and once down,

Point Reyes Lighthouse

San Francisco to the Oregon Border—and a Bit Beyond

you have to come back up! In late fall and spring it is a perfect place from which to watch for migrating gray whales.

After a visit to the lighthouse, look on your map for **Drakes Bay**, one of the many beaches along this rugged strip of coast, and named for the explorer seeking lands for Queen Elizabeth I of England. He is purported to have sailed into the bay on the *Golden Hinde*, and christened it Nova Albion, meaning New England. If you are hungry, there is a café at Drakes Bay where you can have a bite to eat. Another interesting stop is at the **Johnson Oyster Company** on Sir Francis Drake Boulevard—a sign directs you to it on the left on the drive toward Point Reyes Lighthouse. Stop to see the demonstration of how oysters are cultivated in the bay for 18 months before being harvested.

If you choose to continue on to the northernmost point of the peninsula, travel Pierce Point Road which ends at the Tule Elk Range. Before 1860 thousands of tule elk roamed here but were hunted to extinction, then in 1978 two bulls and eight cows were successfully reintroduced and now the herd numbers about 250. Trails lead through this wilderness and research area to the Tomales Point Bluff or a shorter distance down to McClures Beach and Elephant Rock.

Retrace your route through the park to **Point Reyes Station** where the **Station House Café**, a delightful restaurant with delicious, imaginative food, beckons you into its dining room or tranquil, brick-paved, cottage-garden patio. Continue north on Highway 1 as the road winds through fields of pastureland and dairies and then loops back and follows for a while the northern rim of **Tomales Bay**, providing lovely vistas across the water to the wooded hills and the town of Inverness. About a 20-minute drive brings you to the village of Marshall and soon after, the road heads inland through rolling ranch land bound by picket fences, passing the towns of **Tomales** (the **Tomales Bakery**, located in the old barbershop and open Thursday through Monday, is worth visiting— rivaling anything you would sample in France) and Valley Ford before turning west to Bodega Bay and the small town of Jenner. From here it is about a 15-minute drive to **Fort Ross**. "Ross" means "Russian" and this is the site where the Russians, in the early part of the 19th century, built a fort to protect their fishing and fur interests in California. After browsing through the museum, follow the footpath through the woods and enter the courtyard bounded by the weathered wooden buildings where the settlers lived and worked. Be sure not to miss the pretty Russian Orthodox chapel in the southeast corner of the compound. When you have finished roaming through the encampment, take the dramatic walk along the bluffs above the ocean.

Leaving the fort, retrace your path to Jenner and follow Highway 116 inland along the banks of the **Russian River**. This is a tranquil stretch of road, passing through dense forests that open up conveniently to offer views of the very green water of the Russian River. (In winter after heavy rains the river can become a rushing torrent—no longer green and tranquil.) On weekends this road is very congested, but midweek and off-season this is a very pretty drive. The largest resort along the river is **Guerneville** and just a few miles beyond the town you come to the **Korbel Winery** (13250 River Road, Guerneville), a picturesque, large building banked with flowers. Three Korbel brothers came to this area from Bohemia to harvest the redwoods and ended up harvesting grapes. Korbel is famous for sparkling wines and the tour and video presentations are especially interesting. Tours of the historic champagne cellars last a little under an hour and are offered daily every hour on the hour between 10 am and 3 pm—to be safe, call to double-check the schedule. There is also a tour of the pretty rose garden nestled on the slope to the left of the winery. The winery is open daily between 9 am and 4:30 pm and offers complimentary tasting. For more information call 707-824-7000, or visit their website, *www.korbel.com.*

Sampling champagne at Korbel will whet your appetite for additional wines from Sonoma County. Leaving the winery, continue for a short distance along River Road, watching for a left-hand turn for Westside Road (if you go over the bridge, you have gone too far). Westside Road winds its way to Healdsburg, past vineyards, meadows with cows grazing, pretty apple orchards, and several wineries, including **Hop Kiln Winery** (6050 Westside Road, Healdsburg), which is open for tasting until 5 pm. The architecture at Hop Kiln is very interesting, with whimsical chimneys jutting into the sky. As the name implies, the winery was originally used for drying beer hops. For more information call Hop Kiln Winery, telephone 707-433-6491. For the **Rochioli Winery**, telephone 707-433-2305. Nearby **Healdsburg** has an attractive main square lined with quaint shops and restaurants.

Leaving Healdsburg, follow Highway 101 north for the half-hour drive to Cloverdale where you take Highway 128 heading northwest toward the coast. At first the road twists slowly up and over a rather steep pass. After the summit, the way becomes more gentle as you head down into the beautiful **Anderson Valley**, well-known for its delicious wines. Wherever the hills spread away from the road, the gentle meadows are filled with vineyards. If time permits, stop at the **Navarro Winery**, housed in an attractive contemporary building where complimentary wine tasting is offered. For further information call 707-895-3686 or visit their website at *www.navarrowine.com.* As the road leaves the sunny open fields of grapes, the sun almost disappears as you enter a majestic redwood forest, so dense that only slanting rays of light filter through the trees. Upon leaving the forest, Highway 128 soon merges with the coastal Highway 1 (about a 60-mile drive from where you left Highway 101). Here you join Highway 1 going north through Albion and Little River, and then on to Mendocino.

Mendocino is an absolute jewel: a New-England-style town built upon headlands that jut out to the ocean. It is not surprising that the town looks as if it were transported from the East Coast because its heritage goes back to adventurous fishermen who settled here from New England, and, upon arrival, built houses like those they had left behind. (In fact, the "New England" setting, seen in the popular television series *Murder She Wrote,* was filmed here.) Tucked into the many colorful wood-frame buildings you find a wealth of art galleries, gift shops, inns, and restaurants. (Mendocino Coast Chamber of Commerce, 707-961-6300, *www.mendocinocoast.com.*)

Do not let your explorations stop at the quaint town, but venture out onto the barren, windswept headlands—a visit to Mendocino would not be complete without a walk along the bluffs. In late fall or spring there is an added bonus: spouts of water off the shoreline are an indication that gray whales are present.

Mendocino makes a most convenient base for exploring the coast. However, if breathtaking views are more important to you than quaint shops and restaurants, then stay overnight instead 16 miles south of Mendocino in **Elk**, a tiny old lumber town hugging the bluffs along one of the most spectacularly beautiful stretches of the sensational Mendocino coastline. Elk has several places to stay that are described in detail in the inn section of this guide—each has its own personality, each has a magnificent ocean view. Note: If you choose to overnight in Elk instead of the town of Mendocino, when Highway 128 merges with Highway 1, go south to Elk instead of north to Mendocino.

Staying in this area, you could most successfully be entertained by doing absolutely nothing other than soaking in the natural, rugged beauty of the coast. However, there are some sightseeing possibilities. Just north of the town of Mendocino you come to **Fort Bragg**. This is a sprawling town that, when compared to the quaintness of Mendocino, has little to offer architecturally except for an extremely colorful fishing harbor. At 18220 N. Highway One you find the 47 acres of the **Mendocino Coast Botanical Gardens**. The mild, rainy winters and cool summers here provide ideal growing conditions for the collections in the gardens, which are sheltered by a native pine forest. The gardens include a fern-covered canyon, coastal bluffs, a rocky inter-tidal habitat, and wheelchair-accessible trails that connect everything together. There are lots of places to picnic including the sheltered Cliff House with its spectacular views of the ocean. Two electric carts are available for those with special needs. The gardens are open daily between 9 am and 5 pm. Admission is $6. (707-964-4352)

The most popular attraction in Fort Bragg is the **Skunk Railroad**, which runs between Fort Bragg and Willits. During the summer months you can either take the all-day trip, which makes the complete round trip to **Willits**, or choose a half-day trip leaving in the morning or the afternoon. The train follows the old logging route through the redwood

forests. Frankly, you will have already seen lovelier glens of redwood trees than those you will view on the ride, but the outing is fun, especially if you are traveling with children. The train station is in the center of town just after you pass over the rail tracks. Call ahead for reservations, 800-777-5865, or visit their website: *www.skunktrain.com.*

Leaving the Mendocino area, continue to follow the coast north and enjoy a treasury of memorable views: sometimes the bluffs drop into the sea, other times sand dunes almost hide the ocean and at one point the beach sweeps right up to the road. At Rockport Highway 1 turns inland and twists and turns its way through forests and over the coastal range on 20 miles of narrow winding road. Arriving at **Leggett** (just before the junction with Highway 101), look for a sign to your right indicating a small, privately owned redwood park where you can drive through a hole in a redwood tree.

From Leggett continue north along Highway 101 signposted for Eureka. However, rather than rushing all the way up Highway 101, follow the old highway, called the **Avenue of the Giants**, that weaves through the **Humboldt Redwoods State Park**. This is a 33-mile-long drive, but we suggest you select the most beautiful section by skipping the first part and joining the Avenue of the Giants at Myers Flat. As you exit at Myers Flat, the two-lane road passes a few stores and then glides into a spectacular glen of redwoods. A lovely section of the forest is at **Williams Grove**. Stop at the nearby park headquarters and obtain a map that directs you off the Avenue of the Giants to **Rockefeller Forest**, the oldest glen of redwoods left in the world—some date back over 2,000 years. The trees are labeled and a well-marked footpath guides you through the forest to the Big Tree, an astounding giant measuring 17 feet in diameter and soaring endlessly into the sky, and to the Flat Iron Tree (another biggie with a somewhat flattened-out trunk) located nearby in an especially serene grove of trees.

About ten minutes after rejoining Highway 101, exit to **Scotia**. Established in 1869, the entire town—homes, shops, school, hotel—is owned by the largest lumber company in the world. The picturesque little redwood homes are dominated by the **Pacific Lumber Company**. You will find the small shopping center worth visiting just for the sake of seeing the redwood building constructed from pillars made from whole tree trunks.

Drive to the museum—an all-redwood building resembling a Grecian temple with redwood-tree pillars (bark and all) instead of marble. The museum displays photos, artifacts, and machinery used in the logging camps. It is here you obtain your redwood shingle giving directions for the self-guided mill tour. Pass in hand, you follow the "yellow brick road," a well-marked trail, highlighted with yellow arrows, which guides you throughout the factory. Your first stop is at the hydraulic de-barker where you watch through windows the bark stripped from the logs by high-pressure water, which sweeps back and forth over each log like a broom. Bits of bark and sprays of water cover the windows while the entire building rumbles as the giant logs are stripped naked. The next stop is the saw mill where logs are pulled back and forth beneath a giant-sized rotary saw that slices them into large boards. Walking along the overhead ramp, you watch the entire process from the first touch of the saw until the various-sized boards are neatly wrapped and bound tightly with straps.

The Pacific Lumber Company mill is closed on weekends and holidays. Passes are given out for tours Monday through Friday, 8 am to 1:30 pm. It is best to check times in advance of your arrival by calling 707-764-2222.

Ferndale

Returning to Highway 101, about a 10-mile drive brings you to the Ferndale exit. Founded in 1852, **Ferndale** is the westernmost town (more of a village than a town) in the continental United States. Its downtown with its gaily painted Victorian buildings has changed very little since the 1890s.

Main Street is a gem, lined with delightful little galleries and stores—a favorite being the irresistible candy shop where you view, through the window, hand-dipping of delectable chocolates. Many visitors enjoy the **Repertory Theater** on Main Street where some excellent plays are produced (707-786-5483). Epitomizing the colorful character of the town are **The Gingerbread Mansion** and the historic bed and breakfast, **The Shaw House**. Stop at Ferndale's **Museum** to learn more about her past as you tour Victorian rooms and see displays of old dairy and smithying equipment. Open Tuesday through Saturday 11 am to 4 pm and Sunday 1 to 4 pm. Shaw and 3rd Street, 707-786-4466.

Centerville Beach is 5 miles west of Ferndale on Centerville Road (turn right on Ocean Avenue at the end of Ferndale). Here you have 9 miles of beaches backed by dairy farms to the north and steep cliffs to the south. Watch for harbor seals in the breakers and tundra swans, which congregate in the Eel River bottoms north of Centerville Road from mid-November to February.

Leaving Ferndale, retrace your way to Highway 101 and continue north for the 10-mile drive to **Eureka**. The area surrounding the 101 is full of fast-food chains, gas stations, and commercial establishments, but a small portion of this large town, the **Old Town**, is worth a visit (G and D between 1st and 3rd). On the northwestern edge of this restored project lies the ornate **Carson Mansion** (2nd and M), the most photographed, ornate, Victorian mansion in northern California. Just a short stroll from the Carson Mansion lie the **Carter House Inns**, a complex of three Victorian buildings offering accommodation and dining.

About 20 miles beyond Eureka exit the 101 for the coastal hamlet of **Trinidad**. Although its houses are now mostly of modern architecture, Trinidad Bay has an interesting history. It was discovered by the Portuguese in 1595, claimed by the Spaniards in 1775, flourished in the 1850s Gold Rush as a supply port for the miners, and was later kept on the map by logging. Now Trinidad is a sleepy little cluster of homes nestled on the bluffs overlooking a sheltered cove where an untouristy wharf stretches out into the bay. Next to the wharf is the **Seascape Restaurant** where you can dine on fish straight from the little fishing boats. Stroll the mile-long path along the headlands enjoying the views and in winter the crashing rollers.

Return almost to the 101 and turn left on Patrick's Point Drive as it winds through conifers often just out of view of the rocky coastline to **Patrick's Point State Park**. The $2 vehicle admission fee affords you the opportunity to stroll beside the crashing waves at Agate Beach (you may well find an agate) or enjoy the rocky vistas from the coastal trail that brings you to Wedding Rock and Patrick's Point. Also within the park is a re-created Yurok village, which recalls the days when the Yurok Indians camped in this area. (707-677-3570, *www.cal-park.ca.gov*)

From here, Highway 101 leaves the coast where the waves pound the shore and ventures inland past quiet lagoons (Big Lagoon, Stone Lagoon, and Freshwater Lagoon). At the end of Freshwater Lagoon you enter **Redwood National Park** and turn left for the **Redwood Information Center** set at the edge of the beach (1 mile south of Orick). Enjoy the exhibits, equip yourself with maps, and set off into the park, which contains some of the world's tallest trees.

Passing through **Orick**, it seems that there are more small stores advertising every imaginable item made from redwood than there are houses. So if you've always craved taking an 8-foot redwood Indian home to Aunt Tilda, this is a perfect opportunity to stop and buy one.

Turn right onto Bald Hill Road and climb steeply into the trees to **Lady Bird Johnson Grove** where you follow a 1-mile walk that loops through the stillness of a coastal redwood forest with the trees towering high above you and the forest floor carpeted with ferns.

Return to the 101 north and continue for 1½ miles, turning left on Davison Road where a large herd of elk roam the pastures that lead to **Gold Bluffs Beach** (4 miles) where traces of gold were found during the Gold Rush and on to **Fern Canyon** (8 miles from 101) where you proceed along a steep, narrow canyon walled with ferns and follow a short looping trail that crisscrosses the creek.

Returning to the 101 as it continues north, cross the Klamath River and pass through the fishing resort of **Klamath** to reach **Crescent City**, the last town in California before the Oregon border. Much of the town's waterfront was destroyed in 1964 by a tidal wave resulting from an earthquake in Alaska. While this itinerary should officially end in Crescent City (since this book is about California), we just couldn't resist taking you across the border to sample some of the awesome beauty of Oregon. If you are traveling in the summer when you are more likely to see the sun, strongly consider this extension.

A few miles after leaving Crescent City, you cross the border into Oregon—there is nothing much to mark the transition into a new state. The first town of any size you come to is **Brookings**. Don't take the time to stop now for sightseeing, just continue north on the 101.

As the highway snakes close to the coast, you glimpse views to your left of fantastic deserted beaches. You will see many signs designating roads with access to state beaches. If you have time, choose one of these roads for a quick, up-close view of the sea. However, our recommendation is to just sneak a peek at the beaches for the moment and return later in order to fully enjoy them when given the luxury of a little more time. This stretch of coast offers some of the most majestic scenery in all of Oregon (for that matter, in the entire world). Continue on to your destination, **Gold Beach**, and get settled in your hotel.

Gold Beach is a small town positioned at the mouth of the **Rogue River**. During the Gold Rush era, gold was discovered in the sandy beach. A flood in 1861 washed the last vestiges of gold into the sea, but the name "Gold Beach" remained. After the gold was depleted, Peter Hume opened a salmon cannery, which became one of the largest on the coast and dominated the economy for many years.

The "gold" today comes from tourism, and indeed there is a wealth of activities here for those who relish the joys of the out-of-doors. The steelhead and salmon fishing are superb and attract many fishing enthusiasts to the area. Also a great draw is the memorable adventure we describe further on—a jet-boat ride up the Rogue River.

We suggest two places to stay in Gold Beach, the **Tu Tu' Tun Lodge** or the **Inn at Nesika Beach**. Neither is located right in town. Tu Tu' Tun Lodge is a deluxe small fishing retreat snuggled on the banks of the Rogue River, about 7 miles inland from the coast. The Inn at Nesika Beach is a bed and breakfast overlooking the sea, about 6 miles north of town. If you want to stay at the Tu Tu' Tun Lodge, plan well in advance—the secret of this outstanding small inn has spread and space is always at a premium.

Using Gold Beach as your home base, plan to spend at least three nights here. If you are continuing up the coast to Washington, or looping back via Highway 5 to California, then "day 3" could be enjoyed as you continue onwards.

Day 1: Rogue River Jet-Boat Excursion

An absolute must is to take a trip by jet boat up the Rogue River. These excursions were originally strictly utilitarian—because the roads extended only a short distance inland, in olden days the boats were used for the delivery of mail. The round trip to the tiny hamlet of **Agness** used to take four days—by jet boat, you will arrive in just a few hours. **Rogue River Mail Boats**, the company that began the mail service in 1895, is still in operation and there are also several other companies offering jet-boat trips. The price and the excursions offered are almost identical, but because of the wider selection of departure times, we suggest **Jerry's Rogue Jet Trips**. There are three tour choices: a 64-mile round trip to Agness (six hours including a two-hour lunch or dinner break in Agness, $30 adult/$12 child); an 80-mile round trip to the lower rapids (six hours including a two-hour lunch break in Agness, $45 adult/$20 child); and a 104-mile round trip that travels far into the wilderness up a series of rapids (eight hours including lunch or dinner break, $75 adult/$35 child). By all means take the 104-mile excursion—after coming all this way, you want to experience this adventure to the fullest. The trips run from May through October, with the greatest choices of departure times from July to Labor Day. You can make reservations in advance (800-451-3645, *www.roguejets.com*).

For the 104-mile excursion, there are two departures, the first at 8:30 am and the second at 12 noon. If you are staying at the Inn at Nesika Beach, choose the noon departure (available only from July to Labor Day). This allows you ample time for a leisurely breakfast before driving to the pier.

Jerry's Rogue Jet Trips depart from a well-marked dock located on the south side of the bridge that crosses the Rogue. If you are staying at the Tu Tu' Tun Lodge, take the early departure so the boat can pick you up at the hotel's dock. You will miss the first bit of the journey, but the convenience of just climbing on board in front of your hotel is worth the loss of time on the boat. For those joining the boat in Gold Beach, Jerry's has an office by the dock where you can borrow a windbreaker for the journey. The first portion of the trip takes place in the estuary where it is often very chilly, with fog and cold winds, but there are blankets on board, which you can wrap around you to counter the elements. As you head inland, the weather warms up considerably—sometimes it can even be very hot. The best advice is to take layers of clothing.

San Francisco to the Oregon Border—and a Bit Beyond

If you have children, they will love this trip. Disneyland pales in the reality of this awesome ride. The boats first meander up the wide estuary where fishermen abound then the river narrows into a ribbon of deep green. When you reach Agness, you change to a smaller boat to more easily navigate the narrow gorges and many rapids.

Amazingly, the jet boats can navigate in about 8 inches of water, which makes this adventure up the Rogue so unforgettable. During your journey, the boat climbs 350 feet. From Agness on, you go through some narrow gorges and encounter a series of rapids, many around hairpin curves, which at first glance look impossible to navigate. However, with what seems like lightning speed, the boats successfully climb the shallow rocky rapids and when the going gets quiet, the guides spin the boats in a circle, splashing water on the laughing children on board.

The turnaround point for the trip is at **Paradise Lodge** where guests get off to enjoy a simple, hearty meal. There is no access except by boat, so this is a rustic retreat. If you so desire, you can arrange in advance when you book the excursion to spend the night here and return on the boat the next day. The guestrooms are small and plainly furnished, but appropriate for a lodge so far from civilization.

Your journey downstream is just as much fun. Along the way you will spot a profusion of birds, probably river otter, perhaps some deer, and, if you are lucky, even a bear.

Day 2: Exploring the Beaches South of Gold Beach

Because your time was too short to enjoy the rugged coastal area en route to Gold Beach, you should allow a day to retrace your steps and explore this astounding area at your leisure. Although the entire coast of Oregon is beautiful, most agree that this particular area between the California border and Gold Beach is especially outstanding—there seems to be a special splendor to these beaches because they are so untouched and so serene. Frequently you can have miles of beach to call your own. This particular section of the coast, sometimes called the Banana Belt, is supposed to have the warmest weather and the most sun, but don't take the tourist board too seriously—the days are usually chilly, often foggy, and there are over 90 inches of rain a year, so dress appropriately.

But in sun or fog, there is almost a mystical aura to walking these deserted, driftwood-strewn beaches with gigantic rocks thrusting from the sea just off shore.

Practically the entire Oregon coast seems to be a necklace of state parks but it is impossible to visit all the beaches. First make a stop at **Cape Sebastian**, just 6 miles south of Gold Beach. This park includes 1,104 acres of woodlands and open areas, with the highlight being a headland 700 feet above the sea offering a splendid vista of the coast both north and south. About 15 miles south of Gold Beach is the **Samuel H. Boardman State Park**, a glorious 10-mile stretch of coastline that includes the Arch Rock Point, Natural Bridges Cove, House Rock, and Rainbow Rock.

San Francisco to the Oregon Border—and a Bit Beyond

The beaches are definitely the highlight here, but for those who love flowers, visit the area just south of Brookings where more than 75% of all the Easter lilies in the United States are grown. The season is from late June to early September. You can visit **Flora Pacifica,** 15447 Ocean Drive in Harbor to enjoy their garden and browse through their gift shop. They are open from 10 am to 5 pm, Tuesday through Sunday (541-469-9741).

Day 3: Gold Beach North to Bandon

Day 3 could conveniently be made as a round-trip excursion from Gold Beach. The other option is to include the following sightseeing as you move on to your next destination. Whichever option you choose, be sure to save time to enjoy the coast north of Gold Beach. As you drive up Highway 101, you soon come to **Port Orford**, the first place settled in Oregon and one of the most westerly towns in the continental USA. About 4 miles north of Port Orford, take the road signposted to **Cape Blanco State Park**. The road weaves 5 miles west to the coast where the remarkably photogenic **Cape Blanco Lighthouse** comes into view, perched above the sea. Dating back to 1870, this 300,000-candle-power beacon (which can be seen 21 miles out to sea) is Oregon's oldest still-functioning lighthouse. In the same park, in a small meadow above the winding Sixes River, is the **Hughes House**, a beautifully restored, wooden Victorian built by Jane and Patrick Hughes, pioneer dairy farmers who settled in this remote area in 1898. Both the lighthouse and Hughes House are open for tours from April to November, Thursday through Monday, 10 am to 4 pm.

Your next target is **Bandon**, a small town founded by Irish immigrants in the middle of the 19th century. Before swifter means of transportation, Bandon was a stop for the coastal steamers on the popular San Francisco to Seattle run. You must visit the **Bandon Beach State Park**, a glorious stretch of beach highlighted by soaring rock formations with such whimsical names as Elephant Rock and Garden of the Gods. There is an amazingly well-laid-out path on the headlands with signs along the way describing various sights and telling you about the wildlife. During high season, docents are frequently there to further enlighten you about the wonders of nature at your fingertips.

As an added attraction, the beaches are especially popular since the ardent beachcomber can sometimes find semi-precious stones such as agates and jasper. In addition, Bandon has a tiny "Old Town," which, although not exceptionally quaint, is fun to visit. If driftwood interests you, stop at the **Bandon Driftwood Museum**, located in an old general store on 1st and Baltimore streets (541-347-3719).

Cranberries were introduced to Bandon in the late 1800s by settlers from Cape Cod. Today you see great cranberry bogs, both north and south of town. Dairy farming was also popular in pioneer days, and cheese is still an important commodity. Stop at the **Bandon Cheese Company** (on the left side of the highway as you leave town) to see how cheddar cheese is produced (541-347-2456).

This itinerary ends in Bandon. From here, you might be returning to your hub, Gold Beach. However, if you are continuing north on the 101 to Washington, do not miss the incredible **Oregon Dunes National Recreation Area**, which stretches for 40 miles from Reedsport to Florence. This is the most gigantic area of sand dunes in the world—the average height is 250 feet and sometimes the dunes extend 2½ miles inland. If you visit the sand dunes, stop first at the Oregon Dunes Recreation Area headquarters in Reedsport to see a movie on how the sand dunes are formed.

A highly recommended option for continuing this itinerary is to make a loop back to San Francisco, stopping en route in the charming town of **Ashland**. To do this, from Bandon take the 42 west to Highway 5 and head south to Ashland. In Ashland there is a rich selection of bed and breakfasts where you can settle for a few days to enjoy the excellent **Shakespeare Festival** (in addition to Shakespearean plays in the lovely outdoor Elizabethan theater, there are other more modern productions being performed simultaneously). The Shakespeare Festival runs from mid-June to early October. To reserve seats in advance, call 541-482-4331. From Ashland, it is about a six-hour drive back to San Francisco.

Wandering through the Wine Country

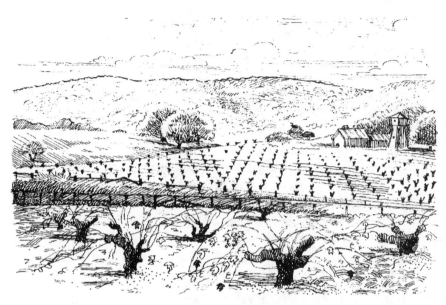

The Napa Valley

The Napa and Sonoma Valleys, just north of San Francisco, have earned a well-merited reputation for the excellence of their wines. Happily for the tourist, many of the wineries are open to the public for tours and tasting. But it is not only visiting the wineries that makes this area so special—these valleys are also memorable for their beauty. A visit to the wine country makes a pleasant excursion any time of year. In summer the days are long and warm, perfect for bike rides, picnics, music festivals, concerts, and art shows. As summer days give way to the cooler afternoons and crisp evenings of fall, the lush foliage on the thousands of acres of grapevines turns to red, gold, and yellow—a colorful reminder that it is time for harvest. You can sense the energy of the crush as vintners work against the clock and weather to pick grapes at their prime. In winter, cool days are often washed by rain, but this is also an excellent time to visit since this is "off season" and the winery tours will be almost private as you travel from one winery to the next. Spring is glorious: mustard blossoms paint the valleys yellow, contrasting dramatically with the dark bark of the vines laced with the delicate green of new leaves.

Recommended Pacing: The Napa and Sonoma wine regions can possibly be squeezed into a day's journey from San Francisco with time to visit one or two wineries. It requires only about an hour to drive from San Francisco to the southern boundaries of either valley. Running north and south, Napa Valley spans a territory of approximately 35 miles while the Sonoma Valley stretches about 17 miles. However, since the primary attractions in either valley are its vineyards, and wine tasting is offered at almost every one, it is most restful to investigate a few in the space of an afternoon, sample their wines, and then incorporate a nap or a laze by a pool into the day's schedule. Since the prospect of returning to San Francisco and battling traffic at rush hour is not a welcome notion, we recommend that you plan to leisurely spend a minimum of one to two nights in the Napa Valley and one to two nights in the Sonoma Valley. With the distance between the valleys being only about 10 to 12 miles, you can also use either valley as a base from which to explore both wine regions.

Weather Wise: The Napa and Sonoma Valleys have very similar climates. Summer days can be scorching hot and roads are often clogged with visitors. Autumn gives way to mild, sunny days, cooler afternoons, and crisp evenings. From autumn to spring you can expect some rain although many days will be sunny. In winter, temperatures are mild yet several degrees cooler than in the nearby San Francisco Bay Area.

Note: We have tried to be as accurate as possible when giving information about touring wineries, but things change, so be certain to give each winery a call in advance to see whether or not they are open and whether you need an appointment for a tour or tasting.

This itinerary, which wends up the Napa Valley and down the Sonoma Valley, is an introduction and a sampling of what the wine country has to offer. This itinerary is not intended to be strictly adhered to in its exact routing. Rather, it is meant as an overall plan from which you can pick and choose what sounds most interesting to you. Use it as a framework to plan your own holiday, taking various segments as they fit in with your time frame. The featured wineries have been chosen for a variety of reasons such as their historical interest, the excellence of their wines, the appeal of their tour, and their special ambiance. Some wineries offer wine tasting free of charge, others charge a fee.

From San Francisco, travel east on Highway 80 across the San Francisco-Oakland Bay Bridge. After crossing the bridge, stay in the left-hand lane and follow signs for Highway 80 in the direction of Sacramento. Approximately 5 miles after crossing the Carquinez Bridge, watch for the Marine World Parkway (Highway 37) turnoff. Take this parkway for 2 miles and turn north on Highway 29, which travels in the direction of Napa. The road widens and the scenery improves dramatically as the road nears the base of the Napa Valley. There are two parallel roads that stretch the length of the valley—Highway 29 and the Silverado Trail. Highway 29 is the busier road and the address for many of the valley's larger wineries and all the towns. The Silverado Trail, the more scenic, less commercial route, hugs the eastern hills, and twists and winds amongst smaller vineyards, often offering a welcome escape from the summer crowds and traffic. This itinerary suggests a route north through the Napa Valley, crisscrossing back and forth between Highway 29 and the Silverado Trail, and then travels west to follow a route south through the Sonoma Wine Valley.

For our first suggested winery stop, the Jarvis Winery, continue on Highway 29. When the road divides, take the east (right) fork, Highway 121, which goes to Napa and on to Lake Berryessa. To reach the Jarvis Winery, stay on Highway 121, continuing to follow signs to Lake Berryessa. When Highway 121 makes a turn to the east and leaves the valley floor, it begins to climb into the wooded hills and assumes the name Monticello Road. After the turnoff, continue toward Lake Berryessa for about 4 miles. Watch for a gate on the left marking the Jarvis entrance at 2970 Monticello Road, Napa. The gates will automatically open after you give your name and say you have a reservation for the tour.

A tour of the **Jarvis Winery** necessitates a reservation well in advance. If you are watching your pennies, you can bypass this tour ($15 per person) and proceed on to the next stop. However, the structure of the Jarvis Winery is different from that of any other winery you will see in the Napa Valley. It also produces excellent wines (Cabernet Franc, Cabernet Sauvignon, Chardonnay, and Merlot) and offers a fun tour. All you see as you approach are two massive doors built into the hillside—it looks like an entrance into a bunker. But inside, another world opens up as you find yourself in a giant cave. Tour groups are limited to a very small number, which makes the tour very personal. You follow a path that forms a loop around the cave, passing by an underground stream and a waterfall, and visiting the Crystal Chamber, a grand reception hall. The tour ends in an intimate room where guests sample fine wines at a small table surrounded by gilded chairs with blue velvet upholstery. Tours are offered daily at 10 am and 1:30 pm. Based on demand, extra tours are sometimes added. For information and reservations call 707-255-5280 or 800-255-5280, or visit their website at *www.jarviswines.com*.

Leaving the Jarvis Winery, retrace your route back down the hill until Highway 121 (Monticello Road) intersects the Silverado Trail. Turn right (north) on the Silverado Trail until you come to Oak Knoll Avenue. Turn west on Oak Knoll, a beautiful drive bounded by walnut trees and vineyards, and watch for a small signpost on your right marking the entrance of **Trefethen Vineyards** at 1160 Oak Knoll Avenue, Napa. Surrounded by its own grapevines, Trefethen Vineyards is housed in the oldest wooden winery in the Napa Valley. Pumpkin in color with a brown roof, this handsome complex celebrated its one hundredth birthday not long ago and there was much reason to celebrate, as the Trefethen family fortunately rescued and lovingly restored the property. This wonderful old winery was designed by the same architect responsible for the Niebaum-Coppola and Beaulieu wineries. Trefethen Vineyards is a delightful small winery, family-owned and -operated, which has proved that size is in no way a factor in excellence. The Trefethens have converted a bulk winery to the production of fine estate-grown Chardonnay, Riesling, and Cabernet Sauvignon. Trefethen wines are featured in some of the finest restaurants. Old farming implements border the parking area and a brick walk encircles a handsome oak in front of the winery where you can sample the wines. The winery is open to the public from 10 am to 4:30 pm, and offers daily tours, but you must make an appointment. For more information call 707-255-7700, or visit their website at *www.trefethen.com.*

After a visit to the Trefethen Vineyards, continue west on Oak Knoll Avenue and in a few minutes you come to Highway 29 where you turn right and continue north up the valley. When you come to the small town of **Yountville**, take the first exit, keep to your right, then turn left at the first street, which is Washington. You will see on your left **Vintage 1870**, a wonderful complex of 40 shops and restaurants housed in a quaint old brick winery. Even non-shoppers will enjoy a stroll through this lovely building: the old brick, heavy beams, and tiled and cobbled floors are dramatic against a meticulously groomed backdrop of green lawn and flowers. A variety of specialty shops makes any purchase possible: toys, antiques, handmade sweaters, books, kitchenware, jewelry, or art. An assortment of restaurants will appease most appetites whether you desire a gourmet salad, pastries, or simply a refreshing ice cream cone. You can also arrange for an early-morning balloon ride—the office for **Adventures Aloft** is located in Vintage 1870, next to the Pacific Blues Café. Departures are at sunrise, the best possible time as the winds are gentle and the air is cool. The flights are expensive, but memorable. For more information call 707-255-8688 or 800-944-4408.

Drive south from Yountville on California Drive, crossing under Highway 29 in the direction of the Veterans' Home. Just after passing under the freeway, turn right onto the property of **Domaine Chandon** at One California Drive, Yountville. When the proprietors of Moët & Chandon first came to the valley with the intention of making sparkling wine following the principles and rigid process of true French champagne, *methode champenoise*, they contracted to use Trefethen Vineyards. Successful in their venture, their sparkling wine was well received and they moved to the present location and established their own winery, Domaine Chandon. Roses front the vineyards, a French tradition, copied both for its practicality as well as for its aesthetic value. The roses add a grace and beauty to the planted fields, but they are also susceptible to the same root diseases and insect problems. If the roses are blemished, vintners know to investigate the vines closely.

Although the winery is relatively new, mature oak trees shade a lovely lawn and a series of terraced ponds with fountains. A wooden footbridge spans the creek-fed ponds to the stone winery tucked back into the hillside. Complimentary tours are offered daily on the hour between 11 am and 5 pm and are hosted by courteous guides who are well informed about the aspects of *methode champenoise*. Visitors see first the traditional storage of the wine in polished stainless-steel tanks and then continue on to observe the additional steps involved in making champagne. In the cellar, bottles of sparkling wine are aged and riddled (turned). In the bottling room you see the process of freezing then disgorging the sediment, corking, cleaning, and labeling the bottles. A visit here shows French and Californian vintners sharing expertise and working side by side. After the tour visitors are invited back to the salon where Domaine Chandon's sparkling wines may be purchased by the glass—at $8 to $12 per glass. From the salon you can view Domaine Chandon's elegant restaurant through a glass partition. The visitors center is closed on Mondays and Tuesdays from January through April. For further information call 707-944-2280. Reservations can be made online at *www.dchandon.com*.

From Domaine Chandon, return to Highway 29, heading north a few miles to the roadside town of **Oakville**. A few buildings comprise this town, the principal one being the original **Oakville Grocery**. If you plan to picnic, stop here for supplies and gourmet treats to accompany your wine-tasting purchases.

Just to the north of Oakville, on the right of Highway 29 you soon come to **Opus One** (the address is 7900 Saint Helena Highway, Highway 29, Oakville). This winery is a masterpiece and the showplace of Robert Mondavi and the Rothschild family. The purpose of their joint venture was to combine the talents of the best French winemakers with the know-how of California's Mondavi family to produce some of the world's finest wines. The gleaming white, circular structure looks a bit like a luxurious, futuristic, coliseum—it is totally different in ambiance from the typical Napa Valley winery. It certainly makes a statement, which is just want the owners wanted to do. As you enter the impressive building, it is immediately obvious that no expense was spared: everything is of the finest quality. Visitors are treated as honored guests and wait in an elegant lounge before the free tour begins (you must sign up two to four weeks in advance). The optional tasting of their current vintage is $25, and the tasting room is open daily from 10:30 am to 3:30 pm. For more information call 707-944-9442, or visit their website at *www.opusonewinery.com*.

Your next stop, the **Robert Mondavi Winery** (the same Robert Mondavi who is a partner in Opus One, which you have just visited), is just a little bit farther north, on the left side of the highway (7801 Saint Helena Highway, Highway 29, Oakville). This modern winery with an original Bufano statue of Saint Francis at its entrance was styled after the Franciscan missions, with an open-arched entry framing an idyllic view of vineyards. Seven different tours varying in length and cost are offered. The hour-and-a-half vineyard and winery tour, offered daily at various times throughout the day, is extremely informative and provides a good general introduction to the essentials of winemaking ($10 per person). By special arrangement, you can also make reservations for the three- to four-hour advanced winegrowing tour ($25 per person), offered Sundays and Wednesdays at 10 am, touring the fields and studying the grapes as well as the winery. After each tour guests are invited into the tasting room to sample the wines. The lovely lawn at the back is the site of summer concerts and art shows. Reservations are recommended. For further information call 707-259-9463 or 888-766-6328, or visit their website at *www.robertmondaviwinery.com*.

After visiting the Robert Mondavi Winery, your next stop is another real winner, the **Niebaum-Coppola Winery**. Continue north on Highway 29 for a few miles beyond the Robert Mondavi winery. Just past Niebaum Lane on the left, you will see the entrance to the winery (1991 Saint Helena Highway, Highway 29, Rutherford). In the late 1870s a Finnish sea captain, Gustave Niebaum, retired from shipping to invest his fortune in the Napa Valley, envisioning a winery that would produce magnificent wines, even surpassing the finest French wines. After his death, Niebaum's property was divided, but in 1995 the Coppola family (owners of the Niebaum-Coppola Winery since 1975) purchased the adjacent Inglenook château and its vineyards, thus uniting once again the original historic estate. Francis Ford Coppola (world-renowned movie director) and his wife, Eleanor, have great respect for wine and the enormous potential of the land. They carry on the Niebaum tradition by growing, producing, and bottling all on the estate—a rare occurrence in today's viticultural world. Niebaum-Coppola is a handsome winery

Wandering through the Wine Country

and enjoys a superb setting nestled against the western foothills of the Napa Valley. Since the winery dates back to the 19th century, it is able to offer what the valley's new wineries cannot—character achieved with age and time. At a cost of $20, you can enjoy a historic estate tour through the original stone aging cellar containing some magnificent large German oak casks. The tour includes the tasting of four wines.

The magnificent château has been restored to its original splendor, and a museum to commemorate Gustave Niebaum and to explore the creative workings of film and the work of Francis Ford Coppola has been opened. Tours are offered Monday through Friday and Sunday at 10:30 am and 2:30 pm, Saturday at 12:30 pm, on a first-come, first-served basis. The tasting rooms are open to the public daily from 10 am to 5 pm. There is a $7.50 charge for the tasting of four wines. For information call 707-963-9099 or visit their website at *www.niebaum-coppola.com*.

Across Highway 29 from Niebaum-Coppola on the corner of Rutherford Road in a complex of buildings is **Beaulieu Vineyards** (1960 Saint Helena Highway, Rutherford). Referred to as BV, Beaulieu is known for some excellent wines. Tours and wine tasting are complimentary. Wine tasting is offered daily from 10 am to 5 pm in the Main Visitors Center, and you can also request the Private Reserve Room to sample four to six reserve wines at a flat rate of $12.50 (open from 10:30 am to 4:30 pm daily). For information call 707-967-5200 or log on to *www.beaulieuvineyards.com*.

Rutherford Road affords a scenic drive shaded by an archway of oak trees. Travel the short distance to its end, past the Louis Honig Winery, and then turn north on Conn Creek Road, which then intersects with the Silverado Trail. Turn north on the Silverado Trail, but drive slowly as you want to take the first right turn onto Rutherford Hill Road, which winds up past the Auberge du Soleil, to the Rutherford Hill Winery.

Although relatively new, the **Rutherford Hill Winery** (200 Rutherford Hill Road, Rutherford) is housed in a stunning building of weathered redwood in the shape of a chalet-barn, draped with Virginia creeper and wisteria and bounded by grass and flowers.

The winery crowns a plateau and enjoys a spectacular valley view. Paths lead down the hillside to picnic tables set under olive trees where the views will tempt you to wile away an afternoon. Rutherford Hill is the dream of a number of independent vintners who together purchased what was once the Souverain Winery (now located in the Sonoma Valley) in order to process and control the production of their limited quantities of grapes into wine. By now, Rutherford Hill Winery is widely considered the leading producer of Merlot in the Napa Valley. The owners also constructed what was at the time the largest expanse of underground caves in the valley—these maintain a constant natural temperature of 58 degrees, minimizing evaporation far more successfully than when temperatures are controlled by air conditioning. The complimentary half-hour tour, offered daily at 11:30 am, 1:30, and 3:30 pm, includes a visit to these caves. Guides at Rutherford Hill are friendly and quite proud of (as well as knowledgeable about) the winery and visitors are encouraged to ask questions. Although all winemaking procedures are basically the same, Rutherford Hill is a small winery and the guide's explanation of the step-by-step process seems easier to understand than the same explanation at a much grander winery. The tasting room is open daily from 10 am to 5 pm. Wine tasting is $5 per glass, reserve tasting is $10 per glass. Advance reservations are not needed. For more information call 707-963-1871 or visit their website at *www.rutherfordhill.com.*

From Rutherford Hill travel north on the Silverado Trail, cross over to Highway 29 on Zinfandel Road, and then jog north on Highway 29 (approaching the town of Saint Helena) to visit the **V. Sattui Winery**, at 1111 White Lane Street, Saint Helena. Sattui winemaking history dates back to 1885 when Vittorio Sattui founded the winery in the North Beach district of San Francisco. Great-grandson Daryl Sattui revived the family tradition in 1973 by moving the winery to Saint Helena. Currently 15 vintage-dated wines are produced, all of which are sold exclusively at the winery or by mail order. V. Sattui wines are not available in any stores, wine shops, or restaurants. With a lovely garden setting, this is an attractive winery where you can also purchase picnic supplies—

Wandering through the Wine Country

such as over 200 different kinds of cheeses, homemade salads, patés, breads, and desserts. The winery has a wonderful picnic spot, with tables set on the lawn beneath shady trees. Tours are self-guided and tasting is complimentary. The winery, deli, and picnic grounds are open daily from 9 am to 6 pm in summer, 9 am to 5 pm in winter. For further information call 707-963-7774, or visit their website at *www.vsattui.com*.

It is just a couple of miles to **Saint Helena**. Highway 29 becomes this lovely town's Main Street, lined with elegant stores, boutiques, and restaurants. Detour east two blocks off Main Street via Adams Street to Saint Helena's **Library and Museum**. The library has a very interesting section on wine and one wing of the museum is dedicated to Robert Louis Stevenson, the great Scotsman who settled with his new bride in an old miner's shack northeast of Calistoga. It was here that he wrote *Silverado Squatters*, a book romantically promoting the beauty of the Napa Valley. Stevenson buffs can also visit the **Robert Louis Stevenson Park** on Highway 29 between Calistoga and Middletown and also make an appointment to tour Schramsburg Vineyards, the winery Stevenson featured in his chronicles of the wine country.

As Highway 29 leaves the commercial district of Saint Helena and enters a very exclusive residential district on its northern borders, watch carefully for the gated entry to **Beringer Vineyards** (2000 Main Street, Highway 29, Saint Helena), set on a knoll, surrounded by beautifully landscaped grounds of mature trees, lawns, and gardens. What was once the home of the founding Beringer family now houses a wine and gift shop. Reflecting its heritage and standing as a tribute to one of the valley's founding wineries, the dramatic stone and half-timbered building with a slate roof was one of two family homes built as a replica of the German home that Frederick and his brother Jacob left behind when they emigrated. A 45-minute guided tour is offered daily every half hour, Monday through Friday between 10 am and 5 pm (from November to March the last tour is at 4 pm), Saturday and Sunday starting at 9:30 am (availability is on a first-come, first-served basis). Tours are $5 per person and tickets may be purchased starting at 9:30 am for any tour time that same day. Tours emphasize the historical aspect of the winery and include a memorable visit through the tunnels and caverns where the wine is aged in barrels. There is a fee of $2 if you want to sample the reserve wines, otherwise tasting is complimentary. For information you can call 707-963-4812 or visit their website at *www.beringer.com.*

Also in Saint Helena, just north of Beringer Vineyards, at 2555 Main Street (which is also named Highway 29), is the **Culinary Institute of America**, a fascinating place to dine. The prestigious institute, which opened in the fall of 1995, is housed in what has long been a landmark of the Napa Valley—the Christian Brothers Winery. On the second floor of the right wing of the massive old winery is the **Greystone Restaurant**, a super place to eat lunch or dinner (reservations are recommended and can be made up to one month in advance). The culinary team is made up entirely of Culinary Institute graduates or advanced students who display their skills at an open-to-view kitchen, set center stage in the room. Greystone's own organic gardens inspire the menu, which mingles Mediterranean flavors and textures with the culinary aesthetics of Northern California. The food is delicious and the price is an excellent value. Lunch is served from 11:30 am to 2:45 pm, a light "tasting" menu from 3 to 5:30 pm, and dinner from 5:30 to 10 pm daily. For reservations call 707-967-1010. In the left wing of the Culinary Institute is a museum where you can see many antique tools used for winemaking and an extensive display of antique corkscrews. You can visit their website at *www.ciachef.edu.*

From the Culinary Institute of America head north on Highway 29 to the south of Calistoga where you will find **Schramsberg Vineyards**, tucked in the western foothills of the Napa Valley just off Highway 29 (1400 Schramsberg Road, Calistoga). Schramsberg Vineyards offers tours by appointment. Over 2 miles of tunnels are devoted to the production of sparkling wine in this historic winery. Wine tasting is offered at a charge of $7.50–$20.00 for three current releases, but only in conjunction with the tour. To make an appointment, call 707-942-4558. For further information visit their website at *www.schramsberg.com.*

Beyond the Schramsberg Vineyards, a large sign on Highway 29 instructs you to turn just a few miles farther north on Highway 29 at Dunaweal Lane to visit **Sterling Vineyards** (1111 Dunaweal Lane, Calistoga). Reminiscent of the architectural style of the Greek island of Mykonos, Sterling Vineyards enjoys a crowning position on a hill idyllically set in the middle of the valley. From the winery you can savor panoramic views looking down through tall pines to a checkerboard of vineyards. Access to Sterling is possible only by small gondolas. For a fee of $6 (the fee for children under 18 is $3, which includes juice at the top) you can ride the aerial tramway from the parking lot to the winery and back (first tram 10:30 am, last 4:30 pm). Arrows and detailed signs direct you on an informative, but impersonal, self-guided tour through the maze of rooms that comprise the winery. For general information, call 800-726-6136 or visit their website at *www.sterlingvineyards.com*. Monday through Friday, group tours can be arranged by appointment—call 707-942-3359. At the end of the tour, a flight of steps leads up to a tasting room with limited views of the valley. The wines are lovely, and another inviting feature about Sterling is the wonderful melodic sound of bells that ring out every quarter-hour. These bells once hung in London's Saint Dunstan's-in-the-East Church. Wine tasting is complimentary.

Across the street at 1060 Dunaweal Lane you will find **Clos Pegase**, a joy for those who appreciate wine and art. When owner Jan Isaac Shrem, a Paris-based businessman and art collector, turned 50, he decided to move to Napa Valley and take up viticulture. Shrem enlisted the help of the San Francisco Museum of Modern Art to help him find an architect to design his winery. That person turned out to be Michael Graves, who designed the structure with influences that range from ancient Rome to art deco. The result is a beautiful building that the *Washington Post* called "America's first monument to wine as art." Here you will have the pleasure of touring the winemaking facilities and viewing the abundance of 20th-century art and artifacts. Clos Pegase is open daily from 10:30 am to 5 pm with guided tours at 11 am and 2 pm. Tours are complimentary and reservations are not required, although afternoon weekend tours tend to be crowded.

Wine tasting of three current-release premium wines starts at $2.50. For information call 707-942-4981, or visit their website at *www.clospegase.com*.

The delightful town of **Calistoga** is just a few miles north at the intersection of Highway 29 and Highway 128. Bounded by rugged foothills and vineyards, Calistoga is an attractive town servicing local residents and tourists alike. Its main street, Lincoln Avenue, is lined on both sides by attractive shops and numerous restaurants. This charming town has been famous ever since Spanish explorers arrived in 1823 and observed Indians taking mud baths in steamy marshes. Sam Brannan, who purchased a square mile of land at the foot of Mount Saint Helena, gave the town its name: he wanted the place to be the "Saratoga of California"

and so called it Calistoga. He bought the land in the early 1860s and by 1866 was ready to open his resort of a few cottages and palm trees. The oldest surviving railroad depot in California, now serving as a quaint and historic shopping mall, received its first trainload of passengers when they came to Calistoga for the much-publicized opening of Sam Brannan's resort. For more than a hundred years, Calistoga has attracted visitors from all over the world, primarily for its hot springs and spas. People came in search of its glorious, healing waters long before the region became a popular destination for its wineries.

There are many spa facilities to choose from. At the eastern end of town look for the **Calistoga Spa and Hot Springs**, 1006 Washington Street. Their facilities, which include separate women's and men's bath houses, four outdoor mineral-water pools, and exercise and aerobics rooms, are newly renovated, expansive, and modern and the attendants are professional and very nice. Offered are volcanic ash mud baths, mineral and steam baths, blanket wraps, and massage. The entire package, "the works," takes almost two hours and their rates are very competitive. For more information call 707-942-6269 or visit their website at *www.calistogaspa.com.*

If you are feeling adventurous, you can take a balloon flight with **Calistoga Ballooning**, which is affiliated with **Bonaventura** out of Saint Helena. A sunrise launch is arranged for a flight over the premier area of the valley and a selection of its wineries. Depending on winds, departure points vary but are normally from the upper valley. Each balloon is committed to just one journey per day and the number of passengers is limited to maximize individual enjoyment. Various options include a full breakfast at Meadowood, a picnic, or a Continental breakfast. For further information call 800-359-6272 (800-FLY-NAPA) or 707-944-2822, or log on to *www.calistogaballooning.com.*

If you have never seen a geyser, travel a few miles farther north from Calistoga on Highway 128 in the direction of Lakeport to Tubbs Lane. Turn right onto Tubbs Lane and in half a mile you see the entrance to the **Old Faithful Geyser** on the left. Old Faithful, one of only three such regularly erupting geysers in the world, erupts at varying intervals of every 15 to 50 minutes with a spume of about 4,000 gallons of water reaching more than 60 feet into the air. This is certainly an interesting phenomenon, although the staging is a bit honky-tonk. Old Faithful Geyser can be viewed from 9 am to 6 pm during the summer (9 am to 5 pm in winter). For more information call 707-942-6463, or log on to *www.oldfaithfulgeyser.com.*

Leaving Calistoga, take the Petrified Forest Road west in the direction of Santa Rosa, forsaking the Napa Valley for the neighboring Sonoma Wine Valley. The road climbs and winds a scenic 10 miles through forest and past meadows where cattle graze next to neighboring vineyards and orchards of apples and almonds. You may wish to stop at the rather commercial **California Petrified Forest**, a grove of redwoods that was petrified by ash from the volcanic eruption of Mount Saint Helena over 6,000,000 years ago. It is this same ash that is responsible for the fertile wine-valley soil.

On the residential outskirts of Santa Rosa the Petrified Forest Road merges with Highway 12 and then turns south (left) toward Sonoma. This highway travels down the center of Sonoma Valley, often referred to as the "Valley of the Moon" after Jack London's famous novel of the same name. London fell in love with Sonoma Valley's magnificent landscape—a wondrous mix of high hills, oak-covered knolls, open pastures, forests of oaks, madrones, fir, and redwood trees, grassy fields, and streams. The author chose the valley as his home—"a quiet place in the country to write, loaf in and get out of nature that something which we all need, only most of us don't know it."

Your first destination in this lovely valley, **Château St. Jean**, lies about 7 miles south of Santa Rosa on the left, at 8555 Sonoma Highway, Highway 12, Kenwood. An extremely pretty road winds up through the vineyards to the strikingly beautiful winery and main house surrounded by lush lawns. With the exception of its mock tower, Château St. Jean is Mediterranean-French in its architecture, its red-tile roofs and arched entries stunning against a backdrop of green hills. The estate is dedicated exclusively to the production of premium wines, but as a visitor you will feel that the winery's chief concern is making visitors feel welcome by outlining a very comprehensive self-guided tour of the winemaking process. After the tour you cross the courtyard to the original "château" for tasting. The winery is open daily from 9 am to 6 pm (to 5 pm in winter). Wine tasting in the main tasting room is $5, $10 to taste three premium wines in the reserve room. Questions you have will be answered graciously. For additional information call 707-833-4134, or visit their website at *www.chateaustjean.com*.

Your next stop, **Kenwood Vineyards**, is just beyond Château St. Jean, but completely different in character. Kenwood (9592 Sonoma Highway, Highway 12, Kenwood) occupies an attractive complex of old wooden barns where wine is produced, stored, and tasted. Kenwood Vineyards is open daily between 10 am and 4:30 pm. Mini tours of this small winery are offered daily between 11:30 am and 2:30 pm on request, based on the availability of the winemaker. There is no fee for tasting or tours. For more information call 707-833-5891, or visit their website at *www.kenwoodvineyards.com*.

The next winery you come to (just beyond Kenwood Winery on the same side of the road) is the **Kunde Winery** at 10155 Sonoma Highway, Highway 12, Kenwood. The founder, Louis Kunde, settled in the Sonoma Valley in 1904. The present-day winery, which re-creates an 1883 barn that previously stood on the same site, houses a reception area with wine tasting and a small shop where you can find attractive, wine-oriented gift items. Complimentary wine tasting is available daily between 10:30 am and 4 pm. Complimentary tours of the barrel-aging caves, which feature half a mile of interconnecting tunnels, are available approximately every half hour on Fridays, Saturdays, and Sundays. For tour hours and further information call 707-833-5501, or visit their website at *www.kunde.com*.

As you travel south on Highway 12, take a turnoff to the right marked to Glen Ellen. Travel this main road through Glen Ellen, following signs for Jack London State Park. Before you reach the park, stop to visit the Benziger Winery, which will be on the right.

The **Benziger Winery**, located in Glen Ellen at 1883 London Ranch Road, is family-run in the truest sense of the word—signs warn to watch for children at play. From babies to Goober, the family dog and "official reception committee," everyone at Benziger is warm and friendly. The Benziger family were wine importers in New York before moving to the Sonoma Valley to produce their own wines.

If it's close to lunchtime, take advantage of picnic tables set under redwood trees. The tasting room is quite a hike from the parking lot, so if someone in your party has difficulty with a hilly driveway, continue on to the handicapped area, or circle round to drop them off in the front. The tour here is truly a treat: guests climb onto a trolley, pulled by a cheerful bright red tractor, for a tour of the vineyards, which lasts approximately 45 minutes. The day we took the tour, Goober climbed aboard and sat on the bench next to the other guests, happily wagging his tail as the tram moved through the fields. Stops are made en route where a guide explains the production of wines. Reservations are not taken, and space on the trolley is limited, so arrive early. Weather permitting, the tours are at 11:30 am, 12:30 pm, and every half hour from 1 to 3:30 pm.

After the tour, visit the gift shop and stay to taste some of the excellent wines. Both the tour and tasting are complimentary. For further information call 707-935-3000, or visit their website at *www.benziger.com*.

Trolley at Benziger Winery

Continue on to **Jack London State Park** where Jack London is buried. This is a lovely wooded park, established as a tribute to the famous author who has had such an impact on the Sonoma Valley. This strikingly handsome man lived a life of rugged adventure and wrote passionately about life's struggles and how to survive them with integrity. In the 16 years prior to his death at age 40, he wrote 50 novels, which were immensely popular and are today considered classics. Two of his more renowned novels are *Call of the Wild* and *Sea Wolf.* This park offers a fitting tribute to Jack London, a courageous, dynamic man, full of life and concern for others. Open all year, admission is $3 per vehicle. (707-938-5216, or *www.parks.sonoma.net/jlpark.html*)

In the park you can visit the ruins of Wolf House (London's dream house, which mysteriously burned to the ground the night of its completion), Beauty Cottage (the cottage where London wrote much of his later work), and the House of Happy Walls (the home that Charmian London built after her husband's death). The House of Happy Walls is now an interesting museum that depicts London's life through numerous photographs, writings, and furnishings that belonged to the author. From the museum, paths lead to the other homes and the grave site. From the park return to Arnold Drive and travel south (past the Sonoma State Home) to Madrone where you turn left, crossing over to Highway 12, which takes you into Sonoma. Note: If you're hungry, just a short detour north of Madrone on Highway 12 is the wonderful **Garden Court Café and Bakery**, great for breakfast, lunch, or gourmet picnics-to-go. Open daily from 7 am to 2 pm (707-935-1565).

Sonoma is a gem of a town. By simply exploring the boundaries of its main square you will glimpse some of California's most important periods in history. (A small admission price is charged to tour Sonoma's historic buildings.) On the square's northern edge sits the **Sonoma Barracks**, a two-story adobe building that was the Mexican provincial headquarters for the Northern Frontier under the command of General Vallejo. The adjacent wood-frame **Toscano Hotel** has been restored and on weekends guides lead interesting tours through the rooms. The nearby **Mission San Francisco Solano de Sonoma**, the last Franciscan mission built in California, was restored in the early 1900s.

If you visit during the week, you may see elementary-school children, dressed as missionaries with their simple cloaks and rope ties, experiencing history "hands on" as they work with crafts and tools from the days of the missionaries. In one hall of the mission is an unusually beautiful collection of watercolor paintings of many of California's missions. The long, low adobe building across the way, the Blue Wig Inn, originally built to house soldiers assigned to the mission, enjoyed a more colorful existence as a saloon and gambling room during the Gold Rush days.

In addition to the historic sites on Sonoma's plaza, there are numerous shops and boutiques to investigate, including some wonderful specialty food stores where you can purchase picnic supplies. The **Sonoma Cheese Factory** on Spain Street is interesting to visit. The front of the shop has a deli and at the back, behind a glass partition, you can observe the making of cheese. (Open daily from 8:30 am to 5 pm, tel: 707-996-1000.) On First Street East you can purchase delicious bread at the **Sonoma French Bread Shop** and enjoy a tasty ice cream at the ice cream parlor.

Mission San Francisco Solano de Sonoma

Leaving the Square, go east on Napa Street for 2 miles to Old Winery Road where you turn left to the **Buena Vista Winery**, the region's oldest winery, located at 18000 Old Winery Road, Sonoma. Nestled in a wooded glen, the old stone, ivy-covered buildings are very picturesque with arched caverns and stone walls. Picnic tables are set under the trees (it is hard to find a spot in the summer). Complimentary wine tasting is offered from 10:30 am to 5 pm daily in the old press house, and a self-guided tour directs you to the cellar building. At 2 pm daily a tour guide gives a presentation of the historical founding of the winery. Call 800-926-1266, or visit *www.buenavistawinery.com*.

General Vallejo, the military commander and director of colonization of the Northern Frontier (until the Bear Flag Revolution established California as a free and independent republic), lived nearby with his wife and their 12 children. Vallejo's Home, "**Lachryma Montis**" (translated to mean mountain tear, an adaptation of the Indian name given to a free-flowing spring that surrounds the property), is well signposted on the outskirts of town on Spain Street. In its day this lovely Victorian-style house was considered one of the most elegant and lavishly decorated homes in the area, and is still attractively furnished.

After you leave the Sonoma Valley, when Highway 12 dead-ends at Highway 116, turn right onto Highway 116 (signposted Petaluma) and at the intersection of Highway 121 turn left in the direction of San Francisco. A short drive brings you to the **Gloria Ferrer Champagne Caves**. The Ferrer family, who brought their expertise on Spanish sparkling wines to the Sonoma Valley in 1982, hails from Catalonia, Spain and, consequently, the winery with its stucco walls and tiled roof resembles a small Catalonian village.

A wide road sweeps up to the winery through the vineyards. The very informative free tours last half an hour and are available daily at various times between 11 am and 4 pm. They start from the tasting room, a spacious room whose windows look out over the vineyards and valley. Most of the narrative is given in a room decorated with winemaking instruments used a half a century ago in the Ferrers' winery in Spain. The riddling of the bottles to capture the sediment is explained, and then you go to the observation room to see the process of freezing then disgorging the sediment, corking, cleaning, and labeling the bottles of sparkling wine. The tour then descends into a maze of interconnected wine-storage tunnels. It is awesome to stand next to towering heights of stacked bottles. The tour concludes back in the tasting room next to their beautiful Vista Terrace overlooking the Mayacamas Mountains, which separate the Napa and Sonoma Valleys. Wine tasting is $3.50 to $6 per glass. For further information call 707-996-7256, or visit their website at *www.gloriaferrer.com*.

One more winery awaits you before you return to San Francisco. Just a short drive from the Gloria Ferrer Winery on Highway 121 you come to the **Viansa Winery and Italian Marketplace** at 25200 Arnold Drive (Highway 121). Founded in 1990 by Vicki and Sam Sebastiani, Sam being a third-generation Sonoma Valley winemaker, this lovely hilltop winery produces Italian varietals, all of which are sold exclusively at the winery or by mail order. The grounds are especially inviting and offer a wonderful picnic area with tables set overlooking the vineyards and 90 acres of restored natural wetland. In the marketplace visitors can purchase gifts, wine, and delicious food items prepared daily in the Viansa kitchen, or sample one of the many pantry foods set out for tasting. Private group tours (20 or more) are offered of the underground aging cellar. Wetland tours are offered on specified Saturday mornings from March to October and include a guided walk, informal talk, and video presentation. The winery is open daily for complimentary tasting and self-guided tours from 10 am to 5 pm. For more information call 707-935-4700, or visit their website at *www.viansa.com*.

From the Viansa Winery it is about an hour's drive back to San Francisco by continuing along Highway 121 to Highway 37 and onto Highway 101, which takes you over the Golden Gate Bridge into the city.

Places to Stay

The location of the Albion River Inn is splendid—right on the bluff overlooking the handsome bay formed by the mouth of the River Albion as it flows into the ocean. The architecture creates the ambiance of a New England village: softly hued clusters of cottages perch on the cliffs surrounded by a meadow where long grass waves in the wind. Gardens filled with brightly colored flowers line the walkways along the bluff and the quiet is broken only by the deep-throated call of the foghorn. Each of the bedrooms offers a sweeping view of the inlet where the fishing boats bob about in the ever-changing tides. All of the rooms are spacious, romantic, and very private and all have fireplaces and binoculars for whale watching. Other extras include complimentary wine, newspapers, and coffee makers. The decor is most attractive and although not antique, reflects the hand of a professional decorator. The acclaimed Albion River Inn Restaurant with its award-winning wine list is adjacent to the inn with picture windows overlooking the sea—it is a good idea to request dinner reservations in advance. A hearty breakfast is served including fresh fruits, juices, homemade breads, and other specialties of the house. *Directions*: From San Francisco drive north on Highway 101 to Cloverdale, west on Highway 128 to Highway 1, and north 3 miles to Albion. The Albion River Inn is on the northwest side of the Albion bridge.

ALBION RIVER INN
Owners: Flurry Healy & Peter Wells
Manager: Karen Malone Deitz
3790 N. Highway 1
P.O. Box 100, Albion, CA 95410
Tel: (707) 937-1919 or (800) 479-7944
Fax: (707) 937-2604, Email: ari@mcn.org
20 rooms, Double: $200–$310
Open all year
Credit cards: all major
Restaurant, Children welcome
Wheelchair friendly
www.karenbrown.com/california/albionriverinn.html

Amador City with its quaint old west-style houses was a bustle of activity during the Gold Rush days. Now it's a peaceful place (except for the logging trucks that rumble through town periodically), with its old wooden stores full of craft and antique shops and the Imperial Hotel, looking as though it belongs in a cowboy movie. There is immediate charm as soon as you walk into this renovated western hotel where you wouldn't be surprised to see prospectors leaning at the bar. Beyond the bar lies a spacious, high-ceilinged dining room, its red-brick walls hung with fanciful Victorian art. Dining is casual and the menu is short: usually three appetizers, seven entrees, five or six desserts. Upstairs, the six bedrooms are a delight—nothing fancy or frilly, but each thoughtfully appointed and accompanied by a small, sparkling bathroom with tub or shower and heated towel bar. Room 6, decorated warmly in tans and navy, is a real winner with an elaborate art-deco bed. The whimsical hand-painted headboard in room 5 is echoed in the paintings of clothes on the closet in room 3. Rooms 1 and 2 share the large balcony at the front of the hotel. There are two sets of adjoining rooms. Guests help themselves to early-morning coffee and tea before going in for breakfast. *Directions:* Amador City straddles Highway 49, 6 miles north of Jackson. The Imperial Hotel is on your right at the bend in the main street.

IMPERIAL HOTEL
Owners: Bruce Sherrill & Dale Martin
14202 Highway 49
P.O. Box 195
Amador City, CA 95601
Tel: (209) 267-9172 or (800) 242-5594
Fax: (209) 267-9249
6 rooms, Double: $85–$115
Open all year
Credit cards: all major
Restaurant closed Monday
Children welcome

It was wonderful to find that the grand Bayview Hotel, built in 1878, has been attractively refurbished and once again offers comfortable and reasonable accommodation in the seaside village of Aptos. A lovely wood-banistered stairway winds up to the second and third floors and the 12 guestrooms. The rooms are all attractive in their individual decor and vary in size, which is reflected in the price: from the Amelia at $149 (named for the daughter of the man who built the hotel whose presence is still said to haunt the building), which is a cozy, second-floor room with a pretty white iron bed, to one of the most expensive at $249, the Colonial, tucked under the eaves of the third floor, a handsome room with a fireplace and Roman tub for two. All the guestrooms have private baths, direct-dial phones and television sets. This hotel has changed hands a few times since it was restored and reopened and we "discovered" it. Although we have visited, we have not had an opportunity to meet the current owners and would welcome readers' feedback. This is lovely old hotel set on the main street that travels through the heart of the beach town of Aptos. *Directions:* Located 10 miles south of Santa Cruz. Take the State Park Drive exit off Highway 1 and go east away from the ocean. Turn right on Soquel Drive and drive about ¾ mile into the village. The Bayview Hotel is on the left.

BAYVIEW HOTEL
Owners: Sandy & Roland Held
8041 Soquel Drive
Aptos, CA 95003
Tel: (831) 668-8654 or (800) 422-9843
Fax: (831) 688-5128
Email: lodging@bayviewhotel.com
12 rooms, Double: $149–$249
Open all year
Credit cards: all major
No restaurant
Children welcome
www.karenbrown.com/california/bayviewhotel.html

Aptos, two hours south of San Francisco, is best known as a beach resort. Most tourists never realize that tucked into the coastal hills are beautiful redwood glens and that adjacent to a forest of redwoods, creeks, and trails is Mangels House, a large and elegant redwood home built in the 1880s, painted white and wrapped in a two-tiered verandah. Once the holiday home of the wealthy Mangels family, whose fortune was in sugar beets, Mangels House belongs now to Jacqueline Fisher. You enter into a large living room dominated by a tall stone fireplace surrounded by two comfortable floral-patterned sofas and an easy chair. To the left is a formal dining room where a full breakfast is served each morning. The six delightful bedrooms at the top of a lovely staircase vary considerably in size and each is individual in decor and pretty and fresh in its furnishings. One of the nicest aspects of Mangels House is that it is nestled in a woodland of 10,000 acres of creeks and hiking trails, yet is only a five-minute drive to the beach. *Directions:* From Santa Cruz, drive 6 miles south on Highway 1, taking the State Park Drive exit and crossing over the freeway (away from the bay). Turn right at the traffic light onto Soquel Drive and go 1/3 mile, under the railroad bridge. Take the first left at Aptos Creek Road (just before the Aptos Station Shopping Center), through the entrance to the state park. Mangels House is ½ mile farther on the right.

MANGELS HOUSE
Owner: Jacqueline Fisher
570 Aptos Creek Road, Aptos, CA 95003
Mailing address:
P.O. Box 302, Aptos, CA 95001
Tel: (831) 688-7982, Fax:none
Email: mangels@cruzio.com
6 rooms, Double: $145–$190
Closed 4 days at Christmas
Credit cards: MC, VS
No restaurant
Children over 11 welcome
www.karenbrown.com/california/mangelshouse.html

We don't often include resorts in our book, but the stunning location of the Seascape Resort prompted us to make an exception. This sprawling complex of seven buildings rests on the bluffs overlooking the Monterey Bay—you can't get much closer without being on the beach. On a stretch of residential street, the resort is quiet and low key. The beach is a short walk down a private paved path (or take the golf-cart shuttle if you prefer) and there are three pools with outdoor Jacuzzis. Guests can choose from studios, one-bedroom suites, or two-bedroom villas. Each suite is handsomely furnished in light colors and offers a private balcony with ocean view, fireplace, full kitchen, and television. Families are easily accommodated in the larger villas (averaging 1200 square feet). Children are quite welcome here: in fact, there is a "kids' club" during the summer months and most holidays featuring planned activities for children between five and ten years old. Sanderlings Restaurant, set on two levels of the main building and offering spectacular vistas, is named after the scurrying shorebirds on the beach. The resort makes a good home base for visiting the Monterey Bay Aquarium, taking children to the Santa Cruz Beach Boardwalk, and golfing on nearby courses. *Directions*: About 9 miles south of Santa Cruz, take the Larkin Valley Road exit off Highway 1 and go west on San Andreas Road. Turn right on Seascape Boulevard.

SEASCAPE RESORT–MONTEREY BAY
General Manager: Jim Maggio
One Seascape Resort Drive
Aptos, CA 95003
Tel: (800) 929-7727, Fax: (831) 685-0615
Email: tani@seascaperesort.com
285 suites & villas
Double: $250–$550
Breakfast: $12–$15 per person
Open all year, Credit cards: all major
Restaurant, Children welcome
Wheelchair friendly
www.karenbrown.com/california/seascaperesort.html

You'll find a little bit of Europe in the Central Coast region outside the town of Atascadero in the form of Oak Hill Manor, an English Tudor-style home sitting on top of a small hill with picturesque views of the Santa Lucia Mountains. This welcoming inn reflects the owners' love of Europe, with rooms named for European cities or themes such as the St. Andrews or Alpine Suites. You can even enjoy a game of pool, cards, or darts in the common Pub Room. The luxurious guestrooms, all appropriately termed suites, are decorated with rich colors and fabrics and many have large Jacuzzi tubs and fireplaces for utter relaxation and comfort. Three of the suites are in the Manor House and the remaining five in the Carriage House, a separate building which affords guests a little more privacy. Settle on the patio of the Parisienne Suite with a glass of wine and views of the mountains or splurge and reserve the Alpine Suite if you would like to be quite undisturbed, as it is the only accommodation on the second floor of the Carriage House. With the Edna Valley to the south and Paso Robles to the north, Atascadero is perfectly located for wine-tasting get-aways. Hearst Castle is a 45-minute drive away. The beach towns of Cambria, Morro Bay, and Cayucos are even closer *Directions*: Halfway between San Francisco and Los Angeles. Take Highway 101 to the Santa Barbara Road exit, turn east and drive ½ mile, turning right on Hampton Court.

OAK HILL MANOR **New**
Owners: Risë & Maurice Macaré
12345 Hampton Court
Atascadero, CA 93422
Tel: (805) 462-9317, Fax: (805) 462-0331
Email macare@oakhillmanorbandb.com
8 rooms, Double: $145–$325
Open all year
Credit cards: all major
No restaurant, Children over 10 welcome
Wheelchair friendly
www.karenbrown.com/california/oakhillmanor

The lovely Ballard Inn is located in the Santa Ynez Valley, a lush region of rolling hills planted with vineyards or sectioned off with white picket fences. Set just off the road, the Ballard was built as an inn but carries the appearance of a gracious sprawling residence. White picket fences enclose its narrow front garden and a wide porch winds round it. The dining room, serving bountiful breakfasts (with two or three hot selections) and gourmet dinners (Wednesday through Sunday evenings), is located just off the entry to the right. To the left, another cozy room invites you to linger over a buffet of afternoon hors d'oeuvres, or venture on into the sitting room where large deep sofas steal you away for lazy conversations in front of an open fireplace. Guestrooms are located upstairs or in a neighboring wing just off the graveled driveway. Rooms are comfortable and attractively decorated, each with a small, functional private bathroom. Although, at first, rooms overlooking the front garden seem preferable to those overlooking the parking area, rooms at the back are quieter since locals do head off to work and early-morning traffic breaks the silence of the country morning. A final note: If you like horses, ask about the neighboring miniature horse farm. We visited in spring when every mother was matched with a tiny foal—adorable. *Directions:* From Highway 101, take the Solvang exit, following Route 246E through Solvang to Alamo Pintado. Turn left, drive 3 miles to Baseline Avenue, then turn right. The inn is on the right side.

THE BALLARD INN
Owners: Steve Hyslop & Larry Stone
2436 Baseline Avenue
Ballard, CA 93463
Tel: (805) 688-7770 or (800) 638-2466
Fax: (805) 688-9560
Email: innkeeper@ballardinn.com
15 rooms, Double: $195–$275
Closed Christmas Day, Credit cards: all major
Restaurant, Children over 12 welcome, Wheelchair friendly
www.karenbrown.com/california/theballardinn.html

Deetjen's Big Sur Inn, a cluster of rustic, weathered redwood houses, trimmed in white and topped by green roofs, was built in the early 1930s by Helmuth Deetjen, who crafted the cabins in the style of his native Norway. If you are looking for the amenities of a modern hotel, Deetjen's is definitely not your cup of tea. However, those who appreciate old-fashioned charm and the splendor of nature will be enthralled by this very special property—it exemplifies the lifestyle of those who first came to the magnificent Big Sur area to enjoy a gentle life, uncluttered by possessions. The guestrooms are nestled in amongst the redwoods in buildings with individual names and characters. Old hand-hewn doors (without locks or keys) open to a medley of varying room configurations, all warmed by fireplaces, wood-burning stoves, or electric heaters. The accommodations are charming in their simplicity and tastefully decorated with antique accents and pretty fabrics. The doorway of Château Fiasco, like a tree house with vaulted ceilings and a private deck, is framed by a tree limb and accessed by climbing a rambling stairway. Downstairs in the same building the Franklin Room is cozy with dark-paneled walls and a fire-stove. In some of the rooms you are lulled to sleep by the sound of the rushing stream below. There are four exceptionally romantic dining rooms with a cozy fireplace, low-beamed ceilings, soft lighting, country antiques, painted furniture, and tables dressed with linens. *Directions*: Located on the east side of Highway 1, about 3 miles south of Big Sur.

DEETJEN'S BIG SUR INN
Innkeeper: Laura Moran
Highway 1
Big Sur, CA 93920
Tel: (831) 667-2377, Fax: (831) 667-0466
20 rooms, 15 with private bathrooms
Double: $75–$195
Open all year, Credit cards: MC, VS
Restaurant
Children over 12 welcome
www.karenbrown.com/california/deetjensbigsurinn.html

Ventana, surrounded by 240 acres of meadows and forests, is nestled in Big Sur, a gorgeous stretch of coast where the hills plunge down to meet the crashing sea. In contrast to the coastline, there is nothing rugged about Ventana. It pretends to be somewhat rustic, but in reality, behind the weathered wooden façade of the cottages lies a most sophisticated, deluxe resort where guests are pampered and provided with every luxury. The Ventana has grown in stages, so each cluster of natural-wood buildings has its own patina of age. The exteriors are not outstanding but, inside, each guestroom is spacious and decorator-perfect. The decor varies (depending upon which section you are in) but each guestroom has the same country ambiance with natural-wood paneling, luxurious fabrics, and leather chairs. Most rooms have a large terrace with a latticed wood screen—some have private hot tubs. All have a pretty view either of the hills and forest or to the sea on the far horizon. There are three lounges: one where wine and cheese are served in the afternoon and two where breakfast (a scrumptious buffet of home-baked pastries and fruit) is set out each morning. Guests can either take a tray to their room, or eat on one of the tables in the lounge or outside on the terrace. There are two 75-foot swimming pools with adjacent hot tubs (some areas are designated as clothing-optional), and a gourmet restaurant. In 1999 a new spa and four more deluxe suites were added. *Directions:* Thirty miles south of Carmel on the east side of Highway 1, just south of the Big Sur State Park.

VENTANA INN & SPA
General Manager: Sal Abaunza
Highway 1
Big Sur, CA 93920
Tel: (800) 628-6500 or (800) 628-6500
Fax: (831) 667-2419
62 rooms, Double: $340–$975
Open all year
Credit cards: all major
Restaurant
Inappropriate for children
Wheelchair friendly

The Château de Vie is an intimate bed and breakfast, sweetly tucked away behind a white lattice fence in lush gardens of beautiful roses, exotic flowers, and mature fruit trees. Built in 1981, it was designed to resemble a small French country château. The decor is elegant, and the use of dark, rich wall colors adds an air of masculinity. The comfortable living room is done in soothing tones of olive and taupe, with linen window-coverings and French doors leading to a deck with umbrella-covered tables and a small refrigerator—a handy place to cool a bottle of wine purchased while exploring the nearby vineyards. After enjoying the coffee or tea that arrives outside their door in the morning, guests mosey down to the handsome dining room with forest-green walls and a large window seat, or to the back deck, for a gourmet breakfast of fresh-baked scones, breads, and muffins, sausage, and vegetable quiche. All of the guestrooms overlook the pretty garden and are appealingly decorated in bold colors and textures. Each has a queen-sized bed and a private bathroom (although one is down the hall). Your exceptionally gracious hosts, Felipe and Peter, are constantly upgrading their small inn. The latest enhancement is a large Jacuzzi tucked behind a white picket fence, with a romantic view over the adjacent vineyards. *Directions*: From Calistoga take Highway 128 north. When you reach Tubbs Lane, go ¼ mile farther—turn right along a small lane and the Château de Vie is the first house on your right.

CHÂTEAU DE VIE
Owners: Felipe Barragan & Peter Weatherman
3250 Highway 128
Calistoga, CA 94515
Tel: (707) 942-6446, Fax: (707) 942-6456
Email: chateaudv@aol.com
4 rooms, 3 en suite
Double: $189–$249
Open all year, Credit cards: all major
No restaurant
Children welcome
www.karenbrown.com/california/chateaudevie.html

The delightful Christopher's Inn is superbly located just a few steps from the quaint town of Calistoga with its boutiques and cute restaurants. This intimate, family-run property displays the remarkable talents of Christopher Layton, a San Francisco architect and landscape designer, who took eight nondescript, small homes and magically transformed them into an exceptionally charming inn. The guestrooms in the original inn, which range from pocket-sized to commodious, are all decorated in a cozy English-country style with Laura Ashley linens and window and wall coverings. In addition, there are two cottages (each with two bedrooms). These are ideal for families and groups since each bedroom has a queen-sized bed and there is also a trundle bed in the sitting room. There are nine splendid suites facing the garden, which are extremely spacious and have a French-country flair. Each suite has either a porch or private garden patio, and several offer the romance of a fireplace and Jacuzzi tub. In the morning a basket is delivered to your room with a bounty of delicious treats: fresh coffee, juice, croissants or Danish pastries, fresh fruit with yogurt, or warm baked cobbler. Details such as the lovingly tended gardens, bouquets of fresh flowers, and beautiful antiques make this an appealing place to stay. Every time we visit, Adele and Christopher have added more enhancements to make this small inn even more enchanting. *Directions*: Coming north on Highway 29, the inn is 500 yards past the John Deer tractor sales barn, on the right side of the road, before the blinking light at the intersection of Foothill Boulevard and Lincoln.

CHRISTOPHER'S INN
Owners: Adele & Christopher Layton
1010 Foothill Boulevard
Calistoga, CA 94515
Tel: (707) 942-5755, Fax: (707) 942-6895
Email:christophersinn@verio.com
22 rooms, Double: $165–$425
Open all year, Credit cards: all major
No restaurant, Children welcome
Wheelchair friendly
www.karenbrown.com/california/christophersinn.html

In the 1970s Monica Bootcheck, Tom Stimpert, and Bob Beck shared a three-apartment houseboat in Sausalito. Their friendship endured and 20 years later, along with their spouses, they pooled their talents of architecture, contracting, interior design, and marketing and built the Cottage Grove Inn. The inn is a complex of 16 individual cottages tucked into a beautiful grove of century-old Siberian Elm trees. Although of new construction, the property reflects the nostalgic charm of yesteryear. From the outside, each of the sweet, doll-house-like cottages has a similar appearance—a clapboard exterior painted a warm dove gray, accented by deep-coral-colored shutters and crisp white trim. A romantic porch stretches across the front of each cottage with two white wicker rockers just begging you to relax with a good book. Each cottage has its own personality, achieved through decorative accessories, beautiful wall colors, fine fabrics, lovely linens, and high-quality furnishings. Another bonus: each has a wood-burning fireplace and an enormous bathroom featuring a wonderful, deep Jacuzzi tub big enough for two (and cozy bathrobes). *Directions:* From Highway 29, turn east on Lincoln. Just before the road curves left as it leaves town, you will see the inn on your left.

COTTAGE GROVE INN
Owner: Valerie Beck
1711 Lincoln Avenue
Calistoga, CA 94515
Tel: (707) 942-8400 or (800) 799-2284
Fax: (707) 942-2653
Email: cottage@sonic.net
16 cottages, Double: $235–$295
Open all year, Credit cards: all major
No restaurant
Children over 12 welcome
Wheelchair friendly
www.karenbrown.com/california/cottagegrove.html

Located at the northernmost end of the Napa Valley, Meadowlark Country Inn is buffered from noise by a long drive and graced by a white covered bridge and 20 acres of grounds embracing ponds, woodland walks, and a pasture grazed by magnificent sport horses. The two-story country inn, originally built in 1886, is decorated with English antiques and comfortable contemporary furniture. Inside, light-wood floors contrast beautifully with country-pine antiques and handsome fabrics. The atmosphere of sophisticated elegance and the hospitality reflect Kurt Stevens's European background—he sets guests at ease and wants them to enjoy his inn as if it were their home in the country. The spacious living room and library with fireplace has French doors opening to a large verandah. There is also a country-French dining room where guests gather for breakfast. There are four guestrooms in the inn and in the wing next door are three lovely bedrooms decorated in earth tones with four-poster beds, French doors, and private patios. All rooms enjoy a queen bed, private bath, air conditioning, TV with VCR, and telephone. Surrounded by a flagstone deck is a large, clothing-optional swimming pool. Adjacent to the private sunbathing deck is the newly built pool house, which features a hot tub and sauna. Meadowlark's guest register reflects numerous repeat visitors. *Directions*: Traveling north on Highway 101 past Santa Rosa, take the River Road/Guerneville exit and turn right onto Mark West Springs Road (follow it for about 20 minutes to the end). Turn left onto Petrified Forest Road and turn right onto the white covered bridge.

MEADOWLARK COUNTRY INN
Owner: Kurt Stevens
601 Petrified Forest Road
Calistoga, CA 94515
Tel: (800) 942-5651, Fax: (707) 942-5023
Email: none
7 rooms, Double: $165–$265
Open all year, Credit cards: all major
No restaurant, Inappropriate for children
www.karenbrown.com/california/meadowlark.html

Although located on the Silverado Trail, one of the two main arteries through the Napa Valley, Scarlett's Country Inn, tucked in a pocket canyon, is hidden from the road. The inn consists of two buildings: the original turn-of-the century farmhouse and behind it, a newer ranch house with dining room, kitchen, and one guestroom. Ask to stay in the original farmhouse, which is charming, with just two suites, each with its private entrance. The Gamay Suite has a bathroom on the first floor and upstairs a small parlor plus a bedroom tucked under the eaves. The Camellia Suite on the first floor is a real prize, with a living room with sofa bed, wood-burning fireplace, and a wet bar, plus a separate bedroom. Each room has a microwave and mini refrigerator. In the rear garden is a beautiful swimming pool, set tranquilly amongst the trees. In addition there is an aviary with colorful finches and two plump hens (Blondie and Blackie). Although small, Scarlett's Country Inn offers many niceties: fresh flowers daily in each of the rooms, turn-down service at night, and complimentary wine upon check-in. *Directions:* From Napa go north on Highway 29 to 5 miles past St. Helena, make a right on Bale Lane, then go left on the Silverado Trail. Drive half a mile and turn right at 3918 (street address).

SCARLETT'S COUNTRY INN
Owner: Scarlett Dwyer
Innkeepers: Derek Dwyer & Andrea Day
3918 Silverado Trail North
Calistoga, CA 94515
Tel & fax: (707) 942-6669
Email: scarletts@aol.com
3 rooms, Double: $135–$205
Open all year
Credit cards: none
No restaurant, Children welcome
www.karenbrown.com/california/scarlettscountryinn.html

As an alternative to the bed and breakfasts near Cambria's shops and galleries, the Blue Whale Inn offers guests more privacy and the opportunity to stroll for miles along Moonstone Beach. The front room and parlor enjoy views across the road to the beach and expansive ocean through six large picture windows. It is here that guests are served a delicious breakfast and wine, cheese, and cookies are set out in the afternoon. Stretching out behind the main building are the newly constructed guestrooms, each opening at an angle onto a border of front garden that buffers the rooms from the parallel parking. Country in their decor, the rooms are attractive with light-pine furnishings, chintz and floral fabrics, and canopy beds. Each of the spacious ocean-view mini suites has a television, telephone, refrigerator, and a tiled modern bathroom. Motels and hotels line the beach frontage and without a doubt the Blue Whale Inn is the best of the bunch. Karen and Jay, the resident innkeepers, are definitely part of the reason this inn is so popular. They truly enjoy their role and extend a warm welcome to both new and their many returning guests. *Directions:* Turn west off Highway 1 north at the exit sign for Moonstone Beach. Follow Moonstone Beach Drive past the hotels that line this coastal frontage to the Blue Whale Inn.

BLUE WHALE INN
Owners: Jan Crowther & Kate McGill
Innkeepers: Jay & Karen Peavler
6736 Moonstone Beach Drive
Cambria, CA 93428
Tel: (805) 927-4647
Fax: (805) 927-3852
6 rooms, Double: $190–$250
Open all year
Credit cards: MC, VS
No restaurant
Inappropriate for children

The J. Patrick House benefits from the enthusiasm and care of its owners, John and Ann. They first came to know the J. Patrick House as appreciative guests and decided to leave Huntington Beach and their former careers when the property became available. Happily settled in as innkeepers, John describes their changes as decorating with a "touch of elegance." Built as an authentic log cabin, the J. Patrick House, lovingly named for the original owner's father, is a contemporary inn where great care has successfully established an old-world ambiance. The comfortable living room is inviting with its country-cozy decor and open log fire surrounded by comfy sofa and chairs. In the evenings guests gather for appetizers offered with a selection of three wines. A full breakfast is served in a cheerful room overlooking a small but lovely garden. One bedroom is upstairs in the main house while the remainder are in the "carriage house" across the back garden. Named for counties in Ireland, each room has a wood-burning fireplace or stove, window seat, and antiques. Each room has its own personality and all have a private bath and shower except one, which has only a shower. The back bedrooms enjoy a little sitting room. One very important tradition that John and Ann have maintained is the evening offering of "killer" chocolate chip cookies and milk. *Directions*: Exit off Highway 1 east on Burton Drive and travel half a mile. The house is on the right.

J. PATRICK HOUSE
Owners: John Arnott & Ann O'Connor
2990 Burton Drive
Cambria, CA 93428
Tel: (805) 927-3812 or (800) 341-5258
Fax: (805) 927-6759
Email: innkeeper@jpatrickhouse.com
8 rooms, Double: $135–$200
Open all year
Credit cards: MC, VS
Children welcome
www.karenbrown.com/california/jpatrick.html

This pretty little Victorian, freshly painted in a warm butter-cream and dressed with green trim, sits at the heart of the original downtown area of Cambria. A gate in the picket fence opens to a brick walkway leading through the garden to the small porch and entry of this lovely inn. Inside, the decor is refreshing, clean, light, and attractive, with whitewashed walls and the warm patina of natural pine floors. Named for the couple who inhabited the home for much of its century-plus history, the inn has photos and memorabilia of their lives proudly displayed throughout its rooms. The house has five simple and extremely tasteful guestrooms, all intimate in size, with modern, functional bathrooms. Downstairs at the back of the inn overlooking a wooded garden, the Garden Room, formerly the kitchen, enjoys its own private entrance and porch. At the front of the inn, the Parlor Room, once used as a school classroom, is now a pretty bedroom with a bay window and bird's-eye-maple furnishings. Upstairs, the Village Room, the Gothic Room, and Louise's Room are all attractive and enjoy the character added by the pitches and angles of the roofline. *Directions:* From Highway 1 turn east on Burton Drive to Cambria Village.

THE SQUIBB HOUSE
Owner: Bruce Black
Innkeeper: Lynn Walters
4063 Burton Drive
Cambria, CA 93428
Tel: (805) 927-9600
Fax: (805) 927-9606
5 rooms, Double: $95–$155
Open all year
Credit cards: all major
No restaurant, Children over 12 welcome

The Inn at Depot Hill, just two blocks up the hill from the beach and picturesque village of Capitola-by-the-Sea, dates back to 1901 when it was built as a Southern Pacific railroad station. The property does not sit on a large lot, so the grounds are minimal. Inside, the inn's imaginative decor reflects the theme of first-class train travel at the turn of the century: the bedrooms are handsomely decorated and named after different parts of the world—as if a guest were taking a railway journey and stopping at different destinations. The rooms feature many caring touches such as cutwork lace sheets and pillowcases, and sumptuous feather beds. There is a wealth of other amenities: writing desks, tasteful cupboarded televisions and VCRs, fireplaces, bathrobes, hairdryers, luxurious marble bathrooms, some Jacuzzi tubs on private outdoor patios, and even mini televisions in all of the bathrooms. An elegant full breakfast is served each morning either in the dining room, the romantic walled garden, or your room. Complimentary early-evening wine and hors d'oeuvres and late-evening desserts and port are served from the dining-room buffet. *Directions:* South on Highway 1 from Santa Cruz. Take the Park Avenue exit, turn right and go 1 mile. Turn left onto Monterey, then immediately left into the inn's driveway.

THE INN AT DEPOT HILL
Manager: Tom Cole
250 Monterey Avenue
Capitola, CA 95010
Tel: (800) 572-2632, Fax: (831) 462-3697
Email: lodging@innatdepothill.com
12 rooms, Double: $220–$325
Open all year
Credit cards: all major
No restaurant
Children welcome
Wheelchair friendly
www.karenbrown.com/california/innatdepothill.html

The Mission Ranch, which in days long past was a working farm, was bought and renovated with great sensitivity to its heritage by Clint Eastwood. The inn is located on 22 acres, just a pleasant walk from the center of Carmel, yet a world away in tranquillity (in fact, sheep still graze in the meadow that stretches out to the sea in front of the hotel). The ranch offers a wide range of accommodations in terms of setting, views, and price. The least expensive guestrooms are found in the old barn, while more deluxe rooms are located in small meadow-front cottages. The latter have fireplaces and private porches with old-fashioned rocking chairs that beckon you to watch the sun set over the sea. There are also six bedrooms in the charming old farmhouse, which has an ornate Victorian-style living room with heavy oak furniture and grand piano. Whichever room you choose, you cannot help being captivated by the peaceful beauty of the property and its well-maintained gardens. For exercise, there are six tennis courts and a workout room, plus, of course, a lovely beach within a 15-minute walk. A Continental buffet breakfast including fruits, cereals, juices, and pastries is served in the clubhouse next to the tennis courts. The Restaurant at Mission Ranch, open for dinner, has an attractive terrace where guests can dine outside on warm evenings. *Directions:* From Highway 1, turn west onto Rio Road, then left at the Mission (Lausuen Road), and wind round the Mission to the ranch.

MISSION RANCH
General Manager: Theresa Jung
26270 Dolores
Carmel, CA 93923
Tel: (831) 624-6436, Fax: (831) 626-4163
31 rooms, Double: $95–$275
Open all year
Credit cards: all major
Restaurant
Children welcome
Wheelchair friendly

Monte Verde Inn has a super location in the heart of Carmel—just steps from Ocean Avenue with its intriguing boutiques and restaurants and just three short blocks from the beach. But location is not all this intimate inn has to offer. It is cute as it can be from the outside: a white two-story, stucco house with an upstairs balcony extending across the front to create a cozy entrance. Flowers, vines, and a tall pine tree complete the picture. A wide driveway on the left leads to the ample guest parking, a real bonus in Carmel where parking is difficult. Whereas many of the places to stay in Carmel began as private homes, the Monte Verde has been an inn since it first opened in 1900. Of course it has been constantly upgraded through the years, but although all the rooms now have a private bath and all the proper modern amenities, the charm of the past still lingers. There is a sweet reception room where you will be warmly greeted. A Continental breakfast is set out downstairs or guests can take a tray up to their room. A staircase leads upstairs to where some of the guestrooms are located, all of which are very attractively decorated with a simple, country flair. One of my favorites, number 4, is an especially spacious room with a queen bed, a fireplace, and a deck overlooking the street. Besides the rooms above the reception, there are also rooms that extend behind the hotel. All are attractive and each has its own attribute. Some have fireplaces, some have a sitting room, some have an ocean view, and one even has a kitchen. *Directions*: Take the Ocean Avenue exit from Highway 1. Continue on Ocean Avenue then turn left on Monte Verde.

MONTE VERDE INN
Owners: Willa & Ernest Aylaian
Ocean Avenue & Monte Verde
P.O. Box 394
Carmel, CA 93921
Tel: (831) 624-6046 or (800) 328-7707
Fax: (831) 624-6904
14 rooms, Double: $99–$155
Open all year
Credit cards: all major
No restaurant, Children welcome

The Normandy Inn, one of the first hotels in Carmel, exudes the charm and storybook quality that make this town so famous. As you walk down the main street toward the ocean, you cannot help stopping and smiling at this whimsical inn, which stretches for the better part of two blocks in the heart of town. Over the years it has grown to include not only the two-story building where the reception parlor, breakfast room, and many of the bedrooms are located, but also several cozy cottages and three houses—each house has three bedrooms, two bathrooms, and a kitchen. It is especially pleasing to see that, although the buildings vary architecturally, there is a pleasing continuity of style that blends them harmoniously. If you want to splurge, ask for one of the cottages. These are especially adorable, with a Hansel and Gretel look. The gardens too are absolutely stunning. Carmel is famous for its flowers—shops and hotels all vie to outdo their neighbors with the finest floral displays, but the Normandy Inn wins the prize. Like the exterior, the guestrooms have a similarity of feel. Each exudes a country-French ambiance and is attractively decorated in a color scheme of blue and white. This is an extremely well-run, friendly small hotel where guests are warmly greeted, a Continental breakfast is included, sherry is offered in the afternoon, and free parking is available. As an added bonus, the Normandy Inn has one of the few swimming pools in town. *Directions*: Leave Highway 1 at Ocean Avenue. Continue on Ocean Avenue and the Normandy Inn is on your left, just past Monte Verde.

NORMANDY INN
Innkeeper: Sandra Backinger
Ocean Avenue & Monte Verde
P.O. Box 1706, Carmel, CA 93921
Tel: (831) 624-3825 or (800) 343-3825
Fax: (831) 624-4614
48 rooms, Double: $99–$500
Open all year
Credit cards: all major
No restaurant, Children welcome

With the ocean three blocks away, Sea View Inn is within easy walking distance of the much-photographed Carmel beach and it is possible to catch the tiniest glimpse of the ocean through the trees from the third floor of the inn. This large Victorian house looks as though it were once a large home, when in fact it has always been an inn. Deep-red-colored board-and-batten wainscoting accented by a plate rail displaying antiques and interesting bric-a-brac sets the welcoming mood for the living room and adjacent parlor where Continental breakfast, afternoon tea and coffee, and evening wine and sherry are served. Both rooms are warmed by cozy fireplaces, with games, books, and magazines scattered about, which add a comfortable, lived-in feel. The largest bedrooms are found on the second floor. Room 6 has a new, elegant decor with an Oriental rug, Ralph Lauren prints, and white shutters at the window. The adjacent room 7 has stark white walls and window blinds and a dramatic Oriental-style four-poster bed draped with blue-and-white Chinese-motif fabric. The four tiny bedrooms tucked under the steeply slanting attic ceilings on the third floor provide the very snuggest of accommodation. Each is lavishly decorated in a Provence floral print gathered into canopies and covering huge bed pillows. *Directions:* Take the Ocean Avenue exit from Highway 1 to Camino Real where you turn left—Sea View Inn is just after 11th Street on the left-hand side.

SEA VIEW INN
Owners: Diane & Marshall Hydorn
Innkeeper: Margo Thomas
Camino Real between 11th & 12th Streets
P.O. Box 4138, Carmel, CA 93921
Tel: (831) 624-8778, Fax: (831) 625-5901
Email: seaviewinn@mymailstation.com
8 rooms, 6 with private bathrooms
Double: $95–$165
Open all year
Credit cards: all major
No restaurant, Children over 12 welcome
www.karenbrown.com/california/seaviewinn.html

Carmel's quaint gingerbread architecture, profusion of colorful flowers, and tall, shady trees are all happily combined at the Vagabond's House Inn. Set around a flagstone courtyard shaded by a giant oak tree and surrounded by fuchsias, azaleas, camellias, and rhododendrons, the inn is made up of a group of attached storybook English cottages, brick and half-timbered, topped by a thick shake roof, making this one of Carmel's most appealing-looking inns. Most of the guestrooms open directly onto the courtyard with its fountain and profusion of flowers including colorful fuchsias cascading from hanging boxes set in the oak tree. Many of the bedrooms have been refurbished and are very inviting, with pretty coordinating fabrics on the comforters, cushions, and window coverings. Every bedroom has at least two antique clocks and many have their own fireplace (be sure to request a room with a wood-burning as opposed to gas fireplace) and cozy sitting nook. In the morning you phone reception to let them know when you would like a breakfast tray brought to your room. When you check in, be sure not to miss the antique toy collection in the lounge. *Directions:* Take the Ocean Avenue West exit from Highway 1, turn right on Dolores Street, and go three blocks to 4th Street. The Vagabond's House Inn is on the corner of 4th Street and Dolores.

VAGABOND'S HOUSE INN
Owner: Dennis LeVett
Innkeeper: Dawn Dull
Dolores & 4th Street
P.O. Box 2747, Carmel, CA 93921
Tel: (831) 624-7738 or (800) 262-1262
Fax: (831) 626-1243
Email: innkeeper@vagabondshouseinn.com
11 rooms, Double: $125–$250
Open all year
Credit cards: all major
No restaurant, Children over 10 welcome
www.karenbrown.com/california/vagabonds.html

We tend not to recommend hotels (as opposed to inns), and yet every once in a while we happen on one, be it large or small, where the service is exceptional and welcoming and we find we want to share it with our readers. The Tickle Pink Inn is a lovely, romantic retreat and the fact that it is family-owned and -operated is evident in the quality and caring of the service. Set high on the hillside above the well-known Highlands Inn, the Tickle Pink is a two-story motel-like building, which hugs the hillside and looks out through the greenery of cypress trees to the distant rugged ocean. Rooms are attractively decorated with light-pine furnishings in warm colors of beiges, creams, and pinks. Most guestrooms have their own private deck and handsome stone fireplace; all enjoy a TV with VCR (movies are available for rent), lush terrycloth robes, and coffee service. Included in the room rate is a lovely evening buffet of wine and an assortment of cheeses and fruit, and a Continental breakfast served either in your room or on the patio off the lounge. Ocean views vary depending on the location within the inn, but the staff is extremely helpful in describing the differences in accommodation and patient in assisting you with a selection over the phone. *Directions:* The Tickle Pink is located 4 miles south of Rio Road in Carmel just off Highway 1. Highland Drive is marked by a sign for both the Highlands Inn and the Tickle Pink Inn.

TICKLE PINK INN
General Manager: Mark Watson
155 Highland Drive
Carmel Highlands, CA 93923
Tel: (831) 624-1244 or (800) 635-4774
Fax: (831) 626-9516
Email: info@ticklepinkinn.com
34 rooms, Double: $249–$379
Open all year
Credit cards: all major
No restaurant
Children over 12 welcome
www.karenbrown.com/california/ticklepink.html

Threading into the hills east of Carmel is the beautiful Carmel Valley where, unlike Carmel, which tends to be foggy, almost every day is blessed with sunshine. Here, tucked into its own 330-acre oasis, is Stonepine, built by the Crockers, an early-California dynasty of great wealth. Anticipation of the very special treat waiting builds as impressive, wrought-iron gates open magically, allowing you to enter. The road crosses a small bridge then winds through the trees, ending in the courtyard of a beautiful home, Italian in feel, with a muted-pink façade accented with red-tile roof, shuttered windows, and fancy grille-work. Inside, a quiet elegance emanates from every niche and corner. No expense is spared in the splendid furnishings, which give no hint that this is a commercial operation. You definitely feel like a guest in a private mansion as you roam from library to sitting room to dining room, each decorated to perfection. The dining room, handsomely lined in mellow antique paneling, is set exquisitely for dinner each night with fine crystal and china. Upstairs are eight beautiful guestrooms. There are four additional bedrooms in the paddock house and two more in the Briar Rose Cottage. A luxurious addition to the property is Hermés House, a French-styled two-bedroom cottage just outside the walled gates, perched on a bluff overlooking the racetrack. Although there are a swimming pool and a tennis court, Stonepine was built as a ranch, and horses are the main attraction—there is a superb equestrian center. Stonepine is very expensive and exclusive. *Directions:* Signposted on the right after leaving Carmel Valley Village going east on G16.

STONEPINE
Owner: Gordon Hentschel
150 E. Carmel Valley Road
Carmel Valley, CA 93924
Tel: (831) 659-2245, Fax: (831) 659-5160
16 rooms, 3 cottages, Double: $375–$1,250
Open all year
Credit cards: all major
Restaurant
Children welcome in cottages

Staying at the Inn on Mt. Ada is like stepping into a fairy tale—suddenly you are "king of the mountain." This is not too far from reality, since the inn is the beautiful Wrigley family mansion (chewing gum, you know), their vacation "cottage" built high on the hill overlooking Avalon harbor. If you arrive by ferry at Catalina Island, you cannot miss the house: the mansion appears like a white wedding cake to your left above the harbor. The inn is expensive, but money seems almost immaterial, because, once through the door, you have bought a dream. You are truly like a pampered guest in a millionaire's home, with hardly a hint of commercialism (until you pay the bill) to put a damper on the illusion. The lounges and dining room have been redecorated with soft, pretty colors and traditional furniture and fabrics appropriate to the era when the house was built. Upstairs are six individually decorated bedrooms, the grandest having a fireplace, sitting area, and a terrace with breathtaking views of the harbor. Rates include all the extras such as complimentary use of your own golf cart, a full scrumptious breakfast, and lunch. Coffee, tea, soft drinks, fruit juice, and freshly baked cookies are always available in the den and sun porch. *Directions*: By boat from Long Beach, San Pedro, and Newport Beach. By helicopter from Long Beach and San Pedro.

INN ON MT. ADA
Owners: Susan Griffin & Marlene McAdam
P .O. Box 2560
398 Wrigley Road
Avalon, Catalina, CA 90704
Tel: (310) 510-2030
Fax: (310) 510-2237
6 rooms, Double: $330–$620*
*Includes breakfast & lunch
Closed Christmas Eve & Christmas Day
Credit cards: MC, VS
No restaurant, Children over 14 welcome

The Coloma Country Inn, a handsome early-American farmhouse, was built in 1852, four years after gold was discovered at Sutter's Mill, just down the street. Today Coloma is a sleepy little village where the scant remains of the heady Gold Rush days are separated by wide green lawns sloping up from the American River, giving it the air of being a well-kept park. The Coloma Country Inn sits in the middle of the park, its wraparound porch inviting guests to relax and sip a glass of wine while soaking in the beauty of the surrounding tranquil countryside. Inside, the decor is very appealing, American-country style, with handmade quilts, fresh flowers, and other country accents. Your room might feature a balcony or brick patio with a rose garden. An 1898 carriage house offers a suite with its own flowering courtyard, sitting room and kitchenette—perfect if you are traveling with children. Behind the inn is a cheerful pond with a colorful collection of wild ducks begging to be fed from the dock. The surrounding Gold Country holds many great attractions to visitors to these parts. In addition to exploring the historic sites, or hiking or biking on the many mountain and river trails, outdoor activity abounds. One of the most popular whitewater rafting destinations in the country, the South Fork of the American River offers Class III rapids for exciting but safe family fun. For those with loftier goals, a hot-air-balloon ride down the river canyon is breathtaking. (Your innkeepers can assist you in arranging these adventures.) *Directions:* Take Highway 50 from Sacramento to Placerville and exit on Highway 49, going north for 8 miles to Coloma.

COLOMA COUNTRY INN
Owners: Candie & Kerry Bliss
345 High Street, P.O. Box 502
Coloma, CA 95613
Tel: (530) 622-6919, Fax: (530) 626-4959
Email: info@colomacountryinn.com
6 rooms, Double: $105–$225
Open all year, Credit cards: none
No restaurant
Children welcome
www.karenbrown.com/california/colomacountryinn.html

Columbia is a state-preserved town whose shops and stores have been re-created to show life in the heyday of the California Gold Rush. On Main Street is the exquisitely restored City Hotel. Prior to 1874 the building was a gold assay office, the state company headquarters, an opera house, and a newspaper office. Now it is owned by the State of California and partially staffed by students from Columbia College's hotel management program (consequently the staff, dressed in their period costumes, are exceedingly young and wonderfully friendly). The excellent restaurant and the conviviality of the adjacent What Cheer bar provide an especially pleasant way to spend an evening. The high-ceilinged bedrooms have Victorian or early-American furniture. The very nicest rooms open directly onto the parlor, rooms 1 and 2 having the added attraction of balconies overlooking Main Street. All the bedrooms have private en-suite toilets and washbasins. It is not a problem to have showers down the hallway when slippers, robes, and little wicker baskets to carry soap, shampoo, and towels are provided. A bountiful Continental breakfast is served on the buffet in the dining room. *Directions:* From Highway 99 take Highway 108 east to Sonora, then Highway 49 north for the 4-mile drive to Columbia.

CITY HOTEL
General Manager: Tom Bender
Main Street
Columbia State Historic Park, CA 95310
Tel: (209) 532-1479 or (800) 532-1479
Fax: (209) 532-7027
Email: info@cityhotel.com
10 rooms with half baths, showers down the hall
Double: $105–$125
Open all year
Credit cards: all major
Restaurant closed Monday
Children welcome
www.karenbrown.com/california/cityhotel.html

The Fallon Hotel is owned and operated in the same way as the nearby City Hotel in this gem of a Gold-Rush town. The hotel opened in 1986 after receiving a $4,000,000 refurbishment from the State of California. The bedrooms are perfect reflections of the opulent 1880s, with patterned ceilings, colorful, ornate wallpaper, and grand antique furniture. Front rooms have shaded balconies. All have en-suite pull-chain toilets and ornate washbasins. Like the nearby City Hotel, showers are down the hall and slippers, bathrobes, and baskets of toiletries are handily provided. One downstairs room has wider doors for wheelchair access. A simple buffet-style Continental breakfast is served in the adjoining ice-cream parlor. In the Fallon Hotel building is the Fallon Theater, offering a year-round schedule of contemporary dramas, musicals, and melodramas. When making reservations at either the City or Fallon hotels, ask about their excellent-value-for-money theater and dinner packages. *Directions:* From Highway 99 take Highway 108 east to Sonora, then Highway 49 north to Columbia.

FALLON HOTEL
General Manager: Tom Bender
Washington Street
Columbia State Historic Park, CA 95310
Tel: (209) 532-1470 or (800) 532-1479
Fax: (209) 532-7027
Email: info@cityhotel.com
14 rooms with half baths, showers down the hall
Double: $60–$125
Closed Monday to Wednesday in winter
Credit cards: all major
Restaurant closed Monday
Children welcome
Wheelchair friendly
www.karenbrown.com/california/fallonhotel.html

Barbara Gage's lovely old two-story home with its weathered brick exterior, a restored former stage stop, sits just a garden's distance from the Middle Fork of the Feather River. You enter into the coolness of the house into the front room with a lovely old trestle table banked by two wonderful old benches set before a large open fireplace. Stools are drawn up to a counter in front of the open country kitchen. The two guestrooms on the first floor are off the large porch of the home, set with wicker furniture, and both have private bathrooms. The Parlor Room is for the romantic—a warm paneled library room with a fireplace and double Victorian brass bed, while the larger Trading Post Room has a seating area and one single and one queen bed. Cross the bridge and follow a forested footpath to the charming white two-bedroom cottage with its inviting porch, dear little kitchen, lovely small central sitting area with wood-burning pot-bellied stove, and small back bedroom with private bath. In the larger Creekside Cabin you will find the dramatic bedroom cantilevered directly over Jackson Creek. The sunny kitchen, dining room, and living room with cozy sleeping alcove all add to the cozy ambiance. The inn is set on 250 acres and Barbara proudly claims her 1-mile frontage on the Feather River (a perfect location for country weddings, large or small), long known as an excellent trout fishery. *Directions*: From Cromberg on Highway 89/70 take the Old Cromberg Road and follow it as it winds past the old cemetery to the bottom of the hill and Twenty Mile House.

TWENTY MILE HOUSE
Owner: Barbara Gage
Old Cromberg Road
P.O. Box 30001
Cromberg, CA 96103
Tel: (530) 836-0375, Fax: (530) 836-2128
2 rooms, 2 cottages, Double: $125–$160
Open all year, Credit cards: none
No restaurant
Children welcome
Wheelchair friendly

The Blue Lantern Inn, perched on a bluff offering unparalleled views of the fascinating harbor of Dana Point and the blue Pacific, is an outstanding inn on southern California's Riviera. The new construction is designed in a Cape Code style—a most appealing building whose many gables, towers, and jutting rooflines create a whimsical look. The façade is painted a soft gray made even prettier by its crisp white trim. Inside, the color scheme reflects the sea with the use of hues of periwinkle blue, soft lavender, and sea-foam green. Each of the 29 guestrooms is individually decorated—some with light-pine, some with wicker, others with dark-mahogany furniture. The traditional-style furnishings are mostly reproductions and are of excellent quality. Each room has a gas log fireplace and spacious bathroom with Jacuzzi tub. Many of the rooms capture magnificent views of the sea. Breakfast is served each morning in the lounge, a cheerful room where sunlight streams through the wall of windows. Off the reception area is the library where tea is served in the afternoon. Other amenities include a conference room and a well-equipped exercise room. The Blue Lantern is more of a sophisticated small hotel than a cozy bed and breakfast, but the management is superb and the warmth of welcome cannot be surpassed. *Directions:* From the Pacific Coast Highway 1, turn west on Street of the Blue Lantern and go one block.

BLUE LANTERN INN
Innkeeper: Patricia Olsen
34343 Street of the Blue Lantern
Dana Point, CA 92629
Tel: (949) 661-1304 or (800) 950-1236
Fax: (949) 496-1483
Email: none
29 rooms, Double: $155–$500
Open all year, Credit cards: all major
No restaurant
Children welcome
Wheelchair friendly
www.karenbrown.com/california/bluelanterninn.html

Deep within Lassen National Park lies Drakesbad Guest Ranch, set in an idyllic high mountain valley. A broad sweep of grassy meadow cut by a tumbling river gives way to towering pines rising to rocky peaks. There's no electricity at Drakesbad—the warm glow of a kerosene lamp lights your cozy paneled bedroom. Furnishings are simple: polished pine-log chairs and beds topped by quilts, simple country curtains, and a pine dresser and bedside table. Our favorite rooms are in the little cabins that nestle at the very edge of the meadow with their smart modern bathrooms and sliding doors opening to a tiny deck where you can sit and watch the deer grazing at twilight. Other cabins nestle in the pines. Rooms upstairs in the main lodge have half baths. Evenings are for books, games, and conviviality by the fireplace in the lodge, conversation around the campfire, or stargazing from the soothing warmth of the swimming pool, which is fed by the natural warmth of a hot spring. Days are for walks, horseback riding, and swimming. A bell is rung to announce meals, which are served in the rustic pine dining room whose tables are topped with flowery mats and napkins. It's a family place full of people who came as children returning year after year with children and grandchildren. Some even remember when guests slept in tents on the meadow. *Directions:* Take Highway 36 to Chester. Turn left at the fire station and go 17 miles. The last 4 miles are dirt road.

DRAKESBAD GUEST RANCH
Innkeepers: Billie & Ed Fiebiger
End of Warner Valley Road
Chester, CA 96020
Winter tel: (530) 529-1512 ext 120
Summer tel: ask AT&T operator for Drakesbad toll station
  #2 via 530 area code
Fax: (530) 529-4511
19 rooms, Double: $232–$262 (includes all meals)
Open June to October
Credit cards: MC, VS
Restaurant
Children welcome, Wheelchair friendly

The Elk Cove Inn is one of the town's cutest Victorian houses, with perky gables and a million-dollar view of cove and towering rock weathered by the crashing sea. Its owner, Elaine Bryant, a charming hostess, takes great pride in extending a warm welcome and lavishing southern hospitality and attention on her guests. In the main house, the gathering room is set with breakfast tables in front of two walls of windows looking out to the spectacular coastline—a memorable spot for a morning repast. Another intimate nook to settle is the cozy oceanfront bar where you can enjoy beer, wine, and cocktails. All bedrooms have fresh flowers from the garden and a welcome gift basket with wine, fruit, and fresh homemade cookies. Some of the rooms are in the main house where the three upstairs share an intimate sitting area with television, VCR, microwave, and refrigerator. There are also four bedrooms in two separate cottages enjoying full ocean views through large picture windows. The most deluxe accommodations are four suites built on a bluff overlooking the sea, each with a large living room with a spectacular view, a spacious bedroom, a private deck, and a large bath equipped with Jacuzzi. The latest enhancement is a hot tub with a view. *Directions*: Elk is 15 miles south of Mendocino, 6½ miles south of the junction of Highway 128 on Highway 1. The inn is on the south edge of Elk as the road winds down the hill.

ELK COVE INN
Owner: Elaine Bryant
6300 South Highway 1
P.O. Box 367, Elk, CA 95432
Tel: (707) 877-3321 or (800) 275-2967
Fax: (707) 877-1808
Email: elkcove@mcn.org
14 rooms, Double: $148–$328
Open all year, Credit cards: all major
No restaurant, Children over 12 welcome
Wheelchair friendly
www.karenbrown.com/california/elkcoveinn.html

The Griffin House, a pretty little clapboard house painted gray with white trim and with a white picket fence, dates back to the late 1800s when it served as the local doctor's office and pharmacy. Later, five cottages were added behind the office to house some of the lumbermen coming to the growing town of Elk. The pub offers evening meals and good cheer (hours vary). The garden cottages are pleasant, but truly outstanding are the doll-house-like cottages on the edge of the bluff. In fact, these three separate little houses offer the most sensational views anywhere on the California coast. Each of these cottages, named after one of the early settlers of Elk, has a wood-burning stove, a sitting area, a wall of windows overlooking the coast, and a private redwood deck with chairs and table. These tiny cottages are very simple in decor, with nothing contrived or quaintly cute, just providing old-fashioned, basic comfort but with a vista so breathtaking that you will be back again and again. Patty Sarb, the new owner, relocated from a country town in the Shenandoah Valley of Virginia to this dear little coastside hamlet. Returning guests will be pleased to see her improvements: the cottages are all freshly painted inside and out and embraced by beautiful new landscaping, and the pub has been remodeled and is open seven days a week—lighter fare is offered midweek and steak and salmon at weekends. *Directions:* Off the west side of Highway 1, at the center of Elk.

GRIFFIN HOUSE
Owner: Patty Sarb
Innkeepers: Terry Smith & Lisa Nelson
5910 South Highway 1
P.O. Box 190
Elk, CA 95432
Tel: (707) 877-3422, Fax: (707) 877-1853
Email: griffinn@mcn.org
4 rooms, 3 cottages, Double: $100–$250
Open all year, Credit cards: all major
Pub, Children over 3 welcome in cottages
Wheelchair friendly
www.karenbrown.com/california/griffinhouse.html

The Harbor House has a fantastic location on one of the most spectacular bluffs along the Mendocino coast. There is even a little path, with benches along the way, winding down the cliff to a secluded private beach. The home was built in 1916 as a guesthouse for the Goodyear Redwood Lumber Company, so it is no wonder that everything inside and outside is built of redwood. The inn is appealing, with the ambiance of a beautiful, elegant country lodge. You enter into a redwood-paneled living room dominated by a large fireplace, also made of redwood. An Oriental carpet, comfortable sofas, beamed ceiling, soft lighting, and a grand piano add to the inviting warmth. Doors lead from the lounge to the verandah-like dining room, stretching the length of the building, with picture windows looking out to the sea. A broad wooden staircase leads upstairs to six spacious, sophisticated, beautifully furnished bedrooms that make you feel as if you are a guest in a private home. Four cottages flanking the main house, set among the trees, are simple, intimate, and tastefully appointed. Most of the accommodations have sea views, and all but one have fireplaces. All rooms feature down comforters, feather beds, robes, hairdryers, and CD players. Included in the room rate is an award-winning four-course dinner featuring the flavors of Tuscany and Provence. For the quality of accommodations and the excellent dining, this is a great value. *Directions:* Take Highway 101 north from San Francisco to Highway 128 west. At Highway 1 turn left and drive south for 5 miles.

THE HARBOR HOUSE INN
Owners: Elle & Sam Haynes
5600 South Highway 1
P.O. Box 369, Elk, CA 95432
Tel: (707) 877-3203 or (800) 720-7474
Fax: (707) 877-3452
Email: harborhs@mcn.org
10 rooms, Double: $225–$450*
*Includes breakfast & dinner
Open all year, Credit cards: all major, Restaurant
Children over 16 welcome, Wheelchair friendly
www.karenbrown.com/california/harborhouseinn.html

The Sandpiper House Inn is superbly positioned on a bluff overlooking the most beautiful section of the Mendocino coast. The front of the gray-shingled house, enclosed with a white picket fence, is most inviting, but it is not until you come inside and look out the windows to the ocean that you realize what a prize you have discovered. Behind the house, a beautifully tended green lawn embraced by an English garden stretches out to the edge of the bluff below which the waves crash against awesome rock formations. Benches are strategically placed to capture the glory. A path leads down the steep incline with a halfway resting point before continuing on down to the private beach. Because of the setting the house would be a winner if it were just a shell within, but, happily, the interior does justice to the setting. The decor is unpretentiously lovely, with an elegant, homelike ambiance and excellent taste. Four of the bedrooms capture the sensational view and as I saw each one it became my favorite. Choose Evergreen for complete privacy, a luxurious bathroom with a tub for two, and fireplace; Headlands for its recently added fireplace, two-person soaking tub, garden patio, and view-capturing sitting area; Clifton for its bay window with chairs placed to savor the view; and Weston for its fireplace and breathtaking panoramic view of rocky headland and vast expanse of sea through windows at the foot of the bed. The owners are as warm and gracious as their home. *Directions:* Take Highway 101 north to Cloverdale. At the north Cloverdale exit, take Highway 1. The Sandpiper House Inn is located on Highway 1 at the Navarro River. NOTE: We have learned just as this book goes to press that this inn is currently for sale and may sell as a private home and not as an inn.

SANDPIPER HOUSE INN
Owners: Claire & Richard Melrose
5520 South Highway 1
P.O. Box 149, Elk, CA 95432
Tel: (707) 877-3587 or (800) 894-9016, Fax: none
5 rooms, Double: $150–$250
Open all year, Credit cards: all major
No restaurant, Children over 12 welcome

Carter House Inns are a group of four buildings: the majestic Carter House, the adorable Bell Cottage and the Carter Cottage next door, and the adjacent Hotel Carter. The inns are the dream of Mark Carter who grew up in Eureka and, after restoring several Victorian homes, chose to build his own (the Carter House), using the original plans for a Victorian house designed by the architect who built the Carson Mansion, a Victorian showplace in Eureka. All of their bedrooms are generously appointed with antique furniture, original artwork, and cozy flannel robes to make guests really feel "at home." While the Carter House offers the most delightful antique-filled rooms, if you are in the mood for something more sensuous, opt for a suite. The suites at the Hotel Carter offer large whirlpool tubs (in the bedroom) with marina views, fireplaces, king beds, large showers with two heads, entertainment centers, and well-stocked refrigerators (not complimentary). The Hotel Carter's lobby and dining room are the center for socializing— guests enjoy hors d'oeuvres and wine in the early evening, a nightcap of homemade cookies and tea before bed, outstanding dinners, and bountiful breakfasts. The inn's Restaurant 301 is among 81 dining establishments worldwide to hold a *Wine Spectator* Grand Award, its cellars yielding one of the most extensive wine lists in North America. The ebullient Mark Carter sets the friendly, welcoming tone for this delightful inn. *Directions:* Take Highway 101 north to Eureka. The highway turns into 5th Street. From 5th Street, turn left on L Street and go two blocks.

CARTER HOUSE INNS
Owners: Christi & Mark Carter
301 L Street, Eureka, CA 95501
Tel: (707) 444-8062 or (800) 404-1390
Fax: (707) 444-8067
Email: reserve@carterhouse.com
31 rooms, Double: $125–$495
Open all year
Credit cards: all major, Restaurant
Children welcome, Wheelchair friendly
www.karenbrown.com/california/carterhousevictorians.html

Brothers Cornelius and John Daly came from Ireland to Eureka and in 1895 founded a successful chain of northern California clothing shops. When their business flourished, the brothers returned to Ireland in search of wives, married sisters Annie and Eileen, and returned to Eureka to build them impressive homes next door to each another. Now Annie and Con's home is a delightful bed and breakfast run with warm enthusiasm by Sue and Gene Clinesmith who fell in love with the house while visiting their son at Humboldt State University. Sue and Gene have lavished time and attention on their lovely home and the result is that it is an extremely comfortable place for guests to stay. Enjoy wine and cheese in the parlor, watch a movie in the den, or relax in the wicker parlor or on the back patio overlooking the newly landscaped garden. Upstairs, I particularly enjoyed the Garden View and Victorian Rose suites with their spacious bedrooms, sitting rooms (in what were once sleeping porches), and modern bathrooms. A short walk takes you through Eureka's more commercial district to its handsome historic old town (between D and G and 1st and 3rd streets) where attractive shops and restaurants occupy restored buildings. *Directions*: From San Francisco take Highway 101 275 miles north to Eureka. The highway turns into 5th Street. From 5th Street turn right into H Street—The Cornelius Daly Inn is on your left.

THE CORNELIUS DALY INN
Owners: Sue & Gene Clinesmith
1125 H Street, Eureka, CA 95501
Tel: (707) 445-3638 or (800) 321-9656
Fax: (707) 444-3636
Email: innkeeper@dalyinn.com
5 rooms, 3 with private bathrooms
Double: $85–$150
Open all year
Credit cards: all major
No restaurant, Children welcome
www.karenbrown.com/california/thedalyinn.html

Ferndale is a jewel—a wonderfully preserved Victorian town 5 miles from the northern California coast. Happily, the town's most beautiful Victorian, a fantasy of ornate turrets and gables, is an inn: The Gingerbread Mansion. Walking through the parlors and breakfast room is like taking a step back into Victorian times. While the bedrooms continue the Victorian theme, I feel certain that the prude Victorians would be quite aghast at several of Ken Torbert's more sensuous rooms. If money is no object, request the Empire Suite, an open-plan bedroom and bathroom combination where you can soak in a claw-foot tub in front of one of the fireplaces (there are two), relish the complexity of operating a shower with eight heads, and sleep in a king-size bed where towering Ionic columns (pillars) soar to the rafters. Alternatively, request your room according to whether you want a tub in the room (Lilac), his-and-her tubs in the room (Gingerbread), fireplaces (five rooms), or a sleeping loft for a child (Hideaway). I particularly enjoyed the Garden Room with its fireplace, old-style bathroom, and French windows opening onto a private balcony overlooking the clipped hedges and colorful flowerbeds of the garden. Guests often combine their stay with a play performed by the Ferndale Repertory Company. *Directions:* Ferndale is approximately 250 miles north of San Francisco. From Highway 101 traveling north, take the Fernbridge/Ferndale exit, following signs to Ferndale. When you reach Main Street, turn left at Six Rivers and go one block.

THE GINGERBREAD MANSION
Owner: Ken Torbert
400 Berding Street
Ferndale, CA 95536
Tel: (707) 786-4000 or (800) 952-4136
Fax: (707) 786-4381
Email: innkeeper@gingerbread-mansion.com
11 rooms, Double: $150–$385
Open all year
Credit cards: all major
No restaurant, Children over 12 welcome
www.karenbrown.com/california/thegingerbreadmansion.html

You would think you were in England instead of northern California when you first see the large Tudor-style Benbow Inn. The English theme continues as you step inside the lounge with its large antique fireplace flanked by comfortable sofas, antique chests, paintings, needlepoint, cherry-wood wainscoting, two grandfather clocks, potted green plants, and a splendid Oriental carpet. At tea time complimentary English tea and scones are served. The dining room, too, is very English: a beautiful, sunny room with beamed ceiling and dark-oak Windsor chairs. Both the reception hall and the dining room open out to a pretty courtyard overlooking the river. The traditionally decorated bedrooms vary in size—all the way up from small bedrooms located both in the main hotel and in an annex, which also opens onto the courtyard. The one disadvantage of the Benbow Inn is its proximity to the freeway, but loyal guests do not seem to mind. A wonderful feature here is the very special Christmas celebration with wondrous decorations, music, and dining (the whole month of December). The Benbow Inn is also justifiably proud to share the news of their award of excellence by the *Wine Spectator*. *Directions:* Drive north on Highway 101. Just south of Garberville, take the Benbow exit—the hotel is on the west side of the freeway.

BENBOW INN
Owners: Teresa & John Porter
445 Lake Benbow Drive
Garberville, CA 95442
Tel: (707) 923-2124 or (800) 355-3301
Fax: (707) 923-2122
Email: benbow@benbowinn.com
55 rooms, Double: $99–$325
Breakfast: $9 per person
Open April 1 to January 2
Credit cards: all major
Restaurant
Children welcome
www.karenbrown.com/california/benbowinn.html

It is hard not to notice Beltane Ranch, a pale-yellow board-and-batten house encircled on both stories by broad verandahs, set on the hillside off the Valley of the Moon Road. Rosemary, the owner, will probably be in the cozy country kitchen when you arrive, but if away from home, she will write you a welcoming note on the chalkboard hung by the back door. The house has no internal staircase, so each room has a private entrance off the verandah—which was probably a very handy thing when this was the weekend retreat of a San Francisco madam. Incidentally, this also explains the southern architecture of the house as "madam" hailed from Louisiana. The bedrooms, decorated in family antiques, have a very comfortable ambiance. Chairs and hammocks are placed on the verandah outside each room and offer a wonderful spot to settle and enjoy peaceful countryside views beyond Rosemary's well-tended garden. A small yellow cottage behind the main house has a private entrance and French doors leading to a patio. The decor is tasteful and simple. Beltane has been in the family for 70 years and produces a well-known Chardonnay as well as its own label of olive oil. For the energetic, there are walking trails and a tennis court. Beltane Ranch remains a personal favorite. *Directions:* From Sonoma take Highway 12 towards Santa Rosa: Beltane Ranch is on your right shortly after passing the turnoff to Glen Ellen.

BELTANE RANCH
Owner: Rosemary Wood
Innkeeper: Anne Soulier
11775 Highway 12 (Sonoma Highway)
P.O. Box 395
Glen Ellen, CA 95442
Tel: (707) 996-6501,
6 rooms, Double: $140–$220
Open all year
Credit cards: none
No restaurant
Children over 8 welcome
www.karenbrown.com/california/beltaneranch.html

On the main road that weaves through the quaint town of Glen Ellen, the Gaige House is an elegant inn whose owners, Greg and Ken, are making their own statement as to decor with contemporary, Indonesian, and Japanese details. Since acquiring the inn a few years ago, they have made major upgrades and added six guestrooms. They take great pride in their home, and it shows from the bountiful gourmet breakfasts to the hand-ironed quality linens. There is a sense of perfection, and everything is fresh and handsome, airy and light. Each of the bedrooms has its own personality, but all exude a similar ambiance with a predominant use of Calvin Klein fabrics. The Gaige Suite is a spacious, sunny room with large windows on three sides and a wraparound deck overlooking the garden. Dominating the room is a four-poster bed with a lace-canopy trim and a bathroom (with Jacuzzi tub) as large as bedrooms in some hotels. Three brand-new suites are housed in a building next to the pool. Though all are sophisticated, the Creekside Suite is outstanding with its interesting contemporary design and a private deck overlooking the creek. An added bonus—a large pool and spa are set in the lawn in the rear garden. *Directions:* Driving north on Highway 12 from Sonoma, turn left on Arnold Drive, which is signposted to Glen Ellen. The inn is on the right, just before you arrive in town.

GAIGE HOUSE INN
Owners: Ken Burnet & Greg Nemrow
Innkeeper: Susan Burnet
13540 Arnold Drive
Glen Ellen, CA 95442
Tel: (707) 935-0237 or (800) 935-0237
Fax: (707) 935-6411
Email: gaige@sprynet.com
17 rooms, Double: $150–$600
Open all year
Credit cards: all major
No restaurant
Children over 12 welcome, Wheelchair friendly
www.karenbrown.com/california/gaigehouseinn.html

The Inn at Nesika Beach, painted a soft blue-gray, was built along the appealing lines of a handsome, large New England home. There is a wraparound porch, many gables, and a steeply pitched roof accented by chimneys. The setting also could be Cape Cod, but instead of overlooking the Atlantic, the Inn at Nesika Beach is perched on a romantic wind-blown bluff overlooking the blue Pacific. The setting is superb. Below it (and accessible by a nearby footpath) is a deserted sweep of beach that stretches for miles, while just offshore giant rock formations catch the impact of crashing waves. Whereas many bed and breakfasts started out first as a family home, the Inn at Nesika Beach was purpose-built to take guests, so all the rooms have a private bathroom and are especially commodious. If you stay here, be sure to splurge—request one of the two guestrooms facing the back, overlooking the sea. Except for the decor, these two especially large bedrooms are carbon copies of each other, with gas fireplaces, oversized feather beds, and spacious bathrooms with Jacuzzi tubs big enough for two. But what makes these rooms truly memorable is that each has a large balcony overlooking the ocean. *Directions*: Driving north on Highway 101, go over the Rogue River bridge and continue for 5½ miles, then turn left at the blinking yellow light. Go for almost a mile and the inn is on your left.

INN AT NESIKA BEACH
Owners: Ann & Larry Minnich
33026 Nesika Road
Gold Beach, OR 97444
Tel & fax: (541) 247-6434
4 rooms, Double: $125–$160
Open all year
Credit cards: none
No restaurant
Children over 12 welcome

Tu Tu' Tun (pronounced "too–toot'–tun") is a delightful small fishing lodge hugging the banks of the Rogue River, 7 miles from the coast. Although it is appealing at first glance, when you go inside you realize how truly special Tu Tu' Tun Lodge is and why its rooms are booked solid all season (often months ahead). The heart of the inn includes a spacious lounge with a massive stone fireplace and a wall of windows facing the river, an intimate bar, cozy library, and a nationally acclaimed gourmet dining room. A separate two-story wing, joined by a walkway to the lounge-dining area, houses the guestrooms. All have tall windows overlooking the river, and decks or patios with dramatic views. Many of the bedrooms have fireplaces and some even have outdoor soaking tubs. Throughout the lodge, the furnishings are of fine quality and the tasteful decor exudes a rustic yet sophisticated simplicity. Stretching across the entire side of the lodge, facing the intensely green water of the Rogue, is a large deck—a favorite place for guests to relax with a good book during the day or to gather around the "camp fire" in the evening. Terraced below the deck is a swimming pool, and below that the lawn sweeps down to the banks of the river where there is a small boat pier from which guests leave each morning for fishing excursions or jet-boat trips up the Rogue. *Directions*: From Gold Beach, drive north over the bridge and immediately turn right on the North Rogue. Continue for about 6 miles, following signs for the inn.

TU TU' TUN LODGE
Owners: Laurie & Dirk Van Zante
96550 North Bank Rogue, Gold Beach, OR 97444
Tel: (541) 247-6664 or (800) 864-6357
Fax: (541) 247-0672
Email: tututun@harborside.com
20 rooms, Double: $85–$325
Breakfast: $6 per person
Open all year
Credit cards: MC, VS, Restaurant
Children welcome, Wheelchair friendly
www.karenbrown.com/california/tututunlodge.html

Groveland is a quaint Gold Rush town just half an hour from the west entrance to Yosemite. Highway 120 becomes Groveland's one main street as it transects the charming town. It is a great place to break the drive and stop for either breakfast or lunch at the corner PJ's Café and for those who choose to overnight and just take a day trip into the park, the Groveland Hotel offers very comfortable and attractive accommodation. Fronting Main Street, the Groveland Hotel is actually two buildings dating from 1849 and 1914 joined by a wraparound verandah. One building dates from the Gold Rush and the other was built as a boarding house to accommodate the executives from San Francisco here to oversee the building of the massive Hetch Hetchy water project. No two rooms are alike and yet each is pleasing in its decor, decorated with a blend of antiques and attractive fabrics. Although opening onto the street, some of the main floor and front upstairs rooms enjoy lovely bay windows and there are two rooms, one with a queen, the other twin beds, which each have only one window and therefore no views, but they are a great value for their price. An extensive Continental breakfast and evening glass of wine are included in the room rate, and the Victorian Room restaurant also offers dinner complemented by an award-winning wine list. *Directions:* Groveland is two hours from Sacramento along the historic stretch of Highway 120.

THE GROVELAND HOTEL
Owner: Peggy Mosley
18767 Main Street
P.O. Box 481
Groveland, CA 95321
Tel: (209) 962-4000 or (800) 273-3314
Fax: (209) 962-6674
Email: peggy@groveland.com
17 rooms, Double: $135–$210
Open all year, Credit cards: all major
Restaurant, Children welcome in some rooms
Wheelchair friendly
www.karenbrown.com/california/groveland.html

With a backdrop of towering redwood and pine trees, the weathered, wood-sided cottages of the North Coast Country Inn step up the hillside just off the east side of Highway 1. Although it does not have ocean views, the inn's wooded setting is lovely and the accommodation is some of the best in the area. Maureen and Bill Shupe use the original old farmhouse, once part of a local sheep ranch, as their private residence and patterned the neighboring cottages after its rustic and appealing design. Each spacious guestroom cottage is attractive in its individual, country decor, enjoys its own private entrance off a porch or surrounding deck, and is equipped with a dining area (four guestrooms have kitchenettes), a wood-burning fireplace, and a private bathroom. Although it was hard to select a favorite, I loved the space of the Aquitaine Room with its handsome four-poster bed, beamed ceiling, and large windows. A maze of brick walkways weaves through an immaculately-cared-for garden of green lawn and fruit trees, while a wooded path winds up the hillside to a secluded hot tub set into a two-level redwood deck, magical at night under the beauty of dramatic stars whose intensity is not diminished by city lights. The price includes a wonderful full breakfast served in the new breakfast room. *Directions:* Located at Highway 1 and Fish Rock Road, 4 miles north of Gualala and ¼ mile north of Anchor Bay.

NORTH COAST COUNTRY INN
Owners: Maureen & Bill Shupe
34591 South Highway 1
Gualala, CA 95445
Tel: (707) 884-4537 or (800) 959-4537
Fax: (707) 884-1833
Email: ncci@mcn.org
6 rooms, Double: $175–$195
Open all year
Credit cards: all major
No restaurant
Children welcome
www.karenbrown.com/california/northcoastinn.html

Beach House, situated on the coast 3½ miles from the town of Half Moon Bay, offers stunning views of the ocean and the boats of Princeton Harbor. Welcoming guests since 1997, the Beach House has 54 lofts, each with a patio or balcony, most boasting spectacular vistas of the entire 7-mile stretch of crescent-shaped coastline aptly named Half Moon Bay. Although the hotel fronts a highway, double-paned windows on the street-facing rooms block the noise, and inside, the highway is quickly forgotten. Each loft is a tastefully decorated two-tiered suite (separate living room and bedroom areas) with a king-size bed and sleeper sofa. Designed with the guest's comfort in mind, every loft enjoys a wood-burning fireplace, wet bar, refrigerator, CD/stereo system, robes, and bathroom with double sinks and deep tub. If you are traveling with children, ask about their "family accommodation"—two neighboring lofts that share a common main door. Those on a budget might opt for a non-view room. For extra space and comfort, the 625-square-foot Half Moon Suite has two decks, vaulted ceilings, and a sitting area in the bedroom. Guests enjoy a Continental breakfast buffet of croissants, muffins, scones, and fruit either on the outdoor patio or in their rooms. With its breathtaking views of the ocean combined with the comforts of a quality hotel, Beach House is sure to please. *Directions*: From San Francisco take Highway 1 south (about 25 miles). Beach House is on the right just after Pillar Point Harbor.

BEACH HOUSE
Manager: Dana Dahl
4100 North Cabrillo Highway
P.O. Box 129
Half Moon Bay, CA 94019-0129
Tel: (650) 712-0220 or (800) 315-9366
Fax: (650) 712-0693, Email: view@beach-house.com
54 rooms, Double: $209–$425
Open all year
Credit cards: all major, No restaurant
Children welcome, Wheelchair friendly
www.karenbrown.com/california/beachhouse.html

For those who love to be lulled to sleep by the rhythmic sound of crashing waves, the Cypress Inn will be just your cup of tea. It is positioned directly across the road from the 5-mile-long sandy stretch of Miramar Beach. The Cypress Inn is a contemporary building with a weathered-wood façade with turquoise trim. Giving credence to the inn's name, a windswept cypress tree towers by the entrance. Inside, a native-folk-art theme prevails. As you enter, there is a snug sitting area to your left with wicker chairs and sofa grouped around a fireplace. Bedrooms in the main building tend to be on the cozy size and are delightfully decorated in inviting, bright colors. Atop the inn the large top-floor suite offers million-dollar ocean views and a rooftop patio. Each of the rooms has a television, gas-log fireplace, built-in bed with reading lamps, wicker chairs, writing desk, and glass doors opening onto private balconies—each overlooking the ocean. The adjacent Beach House offers four more-quietly-decorated king-bedded rooms, three of which have filtered ocean views. Plans are underway to build six additional oceanfront rooms with king-sized beds and Jacuzzi tubs. *Directions:* Take Highway 1 south from San Francisco. Turn right on Medio Avenue (1½ miles beyond the stop light at Pillar Point Harbor). Cypress Inn is at the end of the street.

CYPRESS INN ON MIRAMAR BEACH
Innkeeper: Kelly Robinson
407 Mirada Road
Miramar Beach
Half Moon Bay, CA 94019
Tel: (650) 726-6076, Fax: (650) 712-0380
Email: lodging@cypressinn.com
12 rooms, Double: $215–$365
Open all year
Credit cards: all major
No restaurant
Inappropriate for children
Wheelchair friendly
www.karenbrown.com/california/cypressinn.html

Half Moon Bay is a delightful little beachside town just 45 minutes south of San Francisco, packed with interesting shops, galleries, and restaurants. One of the most attractive of several lovely Victorians along Main Street is the 1890s Old Thyme Inn, bordered by a white picket fence and named for the herb found in the inn's fragrant cottage garden. The seven bedrooms also take their names from the garden: Mint is decorated in shades of restful green, its queen four-poster decked with crisp white linens before a fireplace. For the most spacious of quarters, opt for the Garden Room, which has a queen four-poster bed, a Jacuzzi tub for two tucked into a corner of the room, and its own private garden entrance. Rick and Kathy really focus on a full breakfast—on the day of my visit it was pears with plum sauce, blueberry almond coffee cake, and scrambled egg tortillas served at the large round table in the parlor/dining area. The parlor is the center of activity at the inn though on sunny evenings guest often enjoy sherry and hors d'oeuvres on the patio. The beach is six blocks away and it's an easy stroll to places to eat that range from an excellent pizza parlor to Pasta Moon, one of our favorite restaurants. San Francisco and the many nearby beaches (one of them, Año Nuevo, is the breeding ground of giant elephant seals) are huge attractions *Directions:* Take Highway 1 south from San Francisco to Half Moon Bay (30 miles). Turn left at the first stop light onto Main Street. Drive through town and watch for the Old Thyme Inn on the left.

OLD THYME INN   **New**
Owners: Kathy & Rick Ellis
779 Main Street
Half Moon Bay, CA 94019
Tel: (650) 726-1616 or (800) 720-4277
Fax: (650) 726-6394
Email: innkeeper@oldthymeinn.com
7 rooms, Double: $130–$290
Open all year, Credit cards: all major
No restaurant
Children over 11 welcome
www.karenbrown.com/california/oldthyme.html

The Belle de Jour Inn, a complex of farm cottages built in 1873, has a wonderful rural, hillside setting. It is approached by a long drive shaded by pines. The impeccably maintained complex has five cottages with guestrooms plus a single-story farmhouse, which is the home of Brenda and Tom. They run their small inn with a professional eye to detail and genuine warmth of welcome that keep guests coming back year after year. Once the grain and tack room, the Caretaker's Suite has French doors opening onto a trellised deck and a pine four-poster, king-size canopy bed topped with Battenberg lace. The Terrace Room is charming, with a fireplace and a whirlpool tub for two, overlooking terrace and valley. The Morning Hill Room is cozy with a fireplace and a shuttered window seat. The Atelier, with sitting room, is large and lovely. The Carriage House accommodates a magnificent deluxe, second-floor country suite with vaulted ceilings, plank-wood floors, antique pine furniture, fireplace, and a whirlpool tub for two in its own stained-glass alcove—very romantic. All rooms have gas fireplaces, refrigerators, CD players, robes, and hairdryers. A full country breakfast is served in the owners' breakfast room. For a memorable wine-tasting experience, Tom will take you in his 1925 vintage auto along the backroads of the wine country. *Directions:* Traveling north on Highway 101, exit at Dry Creek Road then go east to Healdsburg Avenue. Turn left at the lights and go north for 1 mile. The entrance is directly across from the Simi Winery.

BELLE DE JOUR INN
Owners: Brenda & Tom Hearn
16276 Healdsburg Avenue
Healdsburg, CA 95448
Tel: (707) 431-9777, Fax: (707) 431-7412
Email: none
5 rooms, Double: $185–$300
Open all year, Credit cards: all major
No restaurant
Inappropriate for children
www.karenbrown.com/california/belledejourinn.html

Haydon Street Inn is set in a very quiet neighborhood of Healdsburg four blocks from the main plaza of this especially nice town. Like the town, the inn is most attractive: a soft-blue Victorian with a crisp, white trim, fronted by a white picket fence heavily laden with pink roses. Cody, the Bertapelles' dog, greets guests at the door. The main house has a lovely country living room, sitting room, and dining area for guests' use. The six bedrooms, one downstairs and five upstairs, are decorated with homey, comfortable furnishings. The Turret Room, a smaller room, has a fireplace and lovely claw-foot soaking tub. The Rose Room on the first floor has a queen and single bed, plus a Jacuzzi tub, and comfortably accommodates three people. At the rear of the lovely garden is a Victorian-style cottage with two large guestrooms occupying the upper floor. Each cottage room has a private entrance and beautiful pine floors. As an added touch of luxury, the bathrooms in the cottage have double whirlpool bathtubs. A new suite, The Victorian Cottage, enjoys a living room, dining room, separate bedroom, kitchen, fireplace, outdoor hot tub, and private garden. The Bertapelles prepare a full country breakfast and serve it on Luneville French or Spode china in the dining room. After a day of wine-tasting, guests can enjoy a leisurely afternoon under the umbrellas on the lawn of this charming bed and breakfast. *Directions*: Traveling north on Highway 101, take the Central Healdsburg exit. Turn right on Matheson to Fitch then right on Fitch to Haydon and left on Haydon.

HAYDON STREET INN
Owners: Pat & Dick Bertapelle
321 Haydon Street, Healdsburg, CA 94558
Tel: (707) 433-5228 or (800) 528-3703
Fax: (707) 433-6637
Email: innkeeper@haydon.com
9 rooms, Double: $110–$250
Open all year, Credit cards: MC, VS
No restaurant
Children welcome
www.karenbrown.com/california/haydonstreet.html

The Honor Mansion, a soft-beige Victorian with white trim and a maroon door, sits behind a white picket fence on a lovely residential street. In one corner of the immaculate yard you'll notice a bench under a gazebo covered with tiny white flowers. The first floor houses the gathering areas—a parlor and dining room, tastefully decorated with rich colors and traditional furnishings. From the deck just off the parlor guests can enjoy the gentle sound of water falling into the Koi pond. The guestrooms are found on the second floor and are well appointed with everything from lush robes to bath salts to garment steamers to lap desks, while the feather beds, down comforters, and fine linens will make you want to just melt into bed. Guests have the use of two small refrigerators, which are stocked with soda and bottled water. A back staircase leads to a lap pool and lounge chairs. For more privacy there is a spacious cottage next to the house, which has a private entrance and all the comforts you could desire. The luxurious, two-story Tower Suite also has a private entrance and enjoys a private deck and an outdoor, canopied Jacuzzi tub. Homemade refreshments are set out in the afternoon, followed by wine and an elaborate spread of hors d' oeuvres in the evening. An ample gourmet breakfast is served at two sittings in the dining room. If you prefer to stay at a bed and breakfast but don't want to sacrifice any of the amenities of a hotel, The Honor Mansion might be just your cup of tea. *Directions:* Traveling north on Highway 101, exit at Dry Creek Road and turn right. At the first stoplight, Grove Street, turn right. The Honor Mansion is on your right.

THE HONOR MANSION
Owners: Cathi & Steve Fowler
General Manager: Tracy Harris
14891 Grove Street, Healdsburg, CA 95448
Tel: (800) 554-4667, Fax: (707) 431-7173
Email: innkeeper@honormansion.com
9 rooms, Double: $150–$350
Open all year, Credit cards: MC, VS
No restaurant, Children over 16 welcome
Wheelchair friendly
www.karenbrown.com/california/honormansion.html

Healdsburg's main square is a green park bordered by shops and restaurants. If you want to stay in this charming town, the Inn on the Plaza overlooking the main square is a great choice. Entrance to the inn is through double doors into a freshly painted, high-ceilinged reception area that doubles as an art gallery and gift shop. A dramatic, long flight of stairs winds up to a central lounge where a jigsaw puzzle is left for each successive guest to work on a bit. Off the lounge are ten bedrooms decorated in a very Victorian style, a few of which overlook the old plaza through bay windows or open onto balconies in the rear of the building. All rooms enjoy air conditioning, a TV with VCR, and telephone, most have fireplaces, and some have whirlpool tubs for two. An enclosed solarium has lace-covered tables and chairs and lots of greenery. The carriage house behind the main building is quite large and has a full kitchen, fireplace, and deck off the bedroom. There are two breakfast servings: cereal, toast, jam, and hot beverages are available for early risers and later, around 9 am, a hot egg dish plus fresh fruit platter, hot muffins, and juice are served. Complimentary wine, fresh buttered popcorn, and party trays are set out at 5:30 pm. The Inn on the Plaza is a very friendly, welcoming hotel and Genny or her competent staff is always there to greet you. *Directions*: From San Francisco, take Highway 101 north to the Central Healdsburg exit. Drive down Healdsburg Avenue north and make a right on Matheson Street.

INN ON THE PLAZA
Owners: Genny Jenkins & LeRoy Steck
110 Matheson Street
Healdsburg, CA 95448
Tel: (707) 433-6991 or (800) 431-8663
Fax: (707) 433-9513
Email: innpressions@earthlink.net
11 rooms, Double: $215–$285
Open all year, Credit cards: MC, VS
No restaurant
Children welcome in some rooms
www.karenbrown.com/california/innontheplaza.html

Madrona Manor, although just a few minutes from the heart of Healdsburg, is secluded in 8 acres of glorious grounds. A lane leads from a gated entrance up to the fantasy gingerbread mansion perched atop a gentle knoll. The building, which is on the National Register of Historic Places, was built in 1881 by John Alexander Paxton, a tycoon of the day who acquired his great wealth through lumber, mining, and banking. The main building (which when it was built was the talk of the town with 17 rooms, 7 fireplaces, and *even* 3½ baths) houses the reception area, several lounges, and a spacious dining room opening onto a large covered terrace. Antiques abound, emphasizing the Victorian mood of the home. A flight of stairs leads up to the four most romantic guestrooms, which are decorated with handsome Victorian furniture original to the house. Other guestrooms are found in the Carriage House, the Meadow Wood Complex (which was the original kitchen), and the Garden Cottage (with its own private garden and sheltered deck). The Schoolhouse Suites are located in the original schoolhouse for the ranch—two suites each with sitting room, Jacuzzi, private deck, and garden. Lush lawns, perfectly manicured gardens, towering trees, and secluded nooks provide a haven of beauty and tranquillity. A swimming pool offers a refreshing interlude after a day of visiting the nearby Sonoma vineyards. *Directions:* Driving north on Highway 101, take the Central Healdsburg exit, turn left at the second traffic light and go under the freeway. You will be on Westside Road and will see the hotel entrance straight ahead as the road bends to the left.

MADRONA MANOR
Owners: Trudi & Bill Konrad
1001 Westside Road
Healdsburg, CA 95448
Tel: (707) 433-4231 or (800) 258-4003
Fax: (707) 433-0703
Email: madronaman@aol.com
22 rooms, Double: $185–$445
Open all year, Credit cards: MC, VS
Restaurant, Children over 12 welcome
www.karenbrown.com/california/madronamanor.html

The Beach House at Hermosa Beach occupies a spectacular location on the beach just steps from the heart of this lively southern California town. Even if you have no desire to join in all the fun on the sand or roller-blade, bike, run, walk, or stroll the path that separates the beach from the inn, you will relish the people watching that this location affords. The rooms are referred to as "lofts" and all have a patio or balcony. Each loft is a tastefully decorated two-tiered suite (separate living room and bedroom areas) with a king-size bed and sleeper sofa. Designed with the guest's comfort in mind, every loft enjoys a wood-burning fireplace, wet bar, refrigerator, CD/stereo system, robes, and bathroom with deep tub. If you are traveling with children, ask about their family accommodation—two neighboring lofts that have an interconnecting door. Those on a budget might opt for a non-view room. The Continental breakfast buffet of croissants, muffins, scones, and fruit is served either in the beachfront Strand Café or in the guestrooms. Room service is available from the adjacent Good Stuff restaurant. *Directions*: Going south on the 405, exit at Redondo Beach Blvd. Go right to the Pacific Coast Highway, turn left, then right on Hermosa and left on 14th. Valet parking is $17 per day.

BEACH HOUSE
Manager: Kevin McCarthy
1300 The Strand
Hermosa Beach, CA 90254
Tel: (310) 374-3001, Fax: (310) 372-2115
96 rooms, Double: $249–$329
Open all year
Credit cards: all major
Room service from neighboring restaurant
Children welcome
Wheelchair friendly

We greatly appreciate the letters we often receive from readers sharing a particular favorite inn along with the unwritten implication that they are astounded that we could have missed such a gem. In the case of The Cedar Street Inn, I received a letter from the owner herself! My only defense is that I simply missed the inn, tucked just off North Circle Drive on a small quiet street of the same name. Within walking distance of the cute shops and restaurants at the heart of Idyllwild, The Cedar Street Inn offers quiet accommodation in cottagey rooms opening onto a central patio. The guestrooms, some of which are housed in private cabins, are individual in decor and offer their own special appointments and appeal. To name just a few of the rooms: the Victorian Suite enjoys a large Roman tub and fireplace; the Attic is accessed by its own private spiral staircase to an outside deck and boasts a bathroom which overlooks the treetops; the Captain's Quarters is decorated in a nautical decor and is warmed by a river-rock fireplace; the Carriage House is a tri-level suite with fireplace and a bathroom equipped with both tub and shower. Patty and Gary Tompkins are your gracious innkeepers, intent on making your stay at The Cedar Street Inn a special and memorable one. *Directions*: Turn off Route 243, turn east on North Circle Drive, and then turn right on Cedar Street.

THE CEDAR STREET INN
Owners: Patty & Gary Tompkins
25880 Cedar Street
P.O. Box 627
Idyllwild, CA 92549
Tel: (909) 659-4789
Fax: (909) 659-1049
8 rooms, 3 cabins, Double: $75–$165
Open all year, Credit cards: all major
No restaurant
Children welcome in cabins

Idyllwild is a mile-high village of some 3,000 residents and with its magnificent hiking trails affords a wonderful weekend getaway from the metropolitan areas of southern California. The Fern Valley Inn is a rustic country inn of 11 charming cabins nestled in the pines. Each cabin features charming antiques and handmade quilts with care taken to tastefully capture the beauty of the surroundings. The Fern Grotto cottage is charming and spacious with a large rock fireplace and a lush color scheme of whites and greens— ideal for honeymoons or special retreats. Warm cedar walls, quaint country decorations, and a kitchen make the Country Cottage an ideal choice for those that want a comfortable home away from home. Fireplaces enhance the ambiance and make for a warm and cozy setting during the cooler fall and winter nights. Several of the cottages feature a fully stocked kitchen. The grounds are serene—swept pathways wind amongst the cottages, leading to the heated pool and herb and lilac gardens. Homemade tea breads featuring seasonal fruits and vegetables are set in baskets in each cottage allowing each guest the convenience of a Continental breakfast at their leisure. The owners, Jamie and Theo Giannioses, personally manage the inn and cater to their guests. Private cabins are also available to accommodate groups, corporate retreats, and family reunions. *Directions:* Take Highway 10 west from Los Angeles to Banning and Highway 243 to Idyllwild. Turn left on North Circle, right on South Circle, and left on Fern Valley Road.

FERN VALLEY INN
Owners: Theo & Jamie Giannioses
25240 Fern Valley Road
P.O. Box 116, Idyllwild, CA 92549
Tel: (909) 659-2205 or (800) 659-7775
Fax: (909) 659-2630
Email: reservations@fernvalleyinn.com
11 cottages, Double: $85–$155
Open all year, Credit cards: all major
No restaurant
Children over 8 welcome
www.karenbrown.com/california/fernvalleyinn.html

Brigadoon Castle is spectacular. Tucked away on a private oasis of 86 acres and bounded by national forest, it is a magnificent property and a wonderfully romantic hideaway. The turreted entrance to the castle is through a handsome arched wooden door framed by ivy and wisteria. Inside, although impressive with its vaulted archways, dramatic stair, lofty ceilings, wide passageways, and regal decor, the ambiance is also welcoming and intimate. The two-tiered living room is magnificent with sofas set before its brick fireplace, which rises to the loft library, a lovely room looking out through towering windows to the surrounding greenery. Outside the living room a brick terrace stretches to the edge of the woods and a path beckons on up to the hot tub. Three guestrooms are found in the main castle. Fiona's Suite is especially attractive with its rich water-marked-taffeta wall coverings in beiges and creams, specially designed four-poster bed, fireplace, and sitting area whose windows frame the outdoor greenery. The gatekeeper's house, The Cottage, has its own living room, fireplace, loft bedroom, deck with hot tub, and a gorgeous setting next to the rushing creek. This is hostess Geri MacCallum's adventure of a lifetime, and she invites you to come to Brigadoon and let the magic stir your heart! *Directions*: A bit complicated! For a general orientation, Igo is located 15 miles southwest of Redding. Call for directions.

BRIGADOON CASTLE
Owner: Geri MacCallum
9036 Zogg Mine Road
P.O. Box 84, Igo, CA 96047
Tel: (530) 396-2785 or (888) 343-2836
Fax: (530) 396-2784
Email: inquiry@brigadooncastle.com
3 rooms, 1 cottage, Double: $195–$325
Open all year
Credit cards: all major
No restaurant
Children welcome in cottage
www.karenbrown.com/california/brigadooncastle.html

The Blackthorne Inn is the whimsical creation of Susan and Bill Wigert. They have built a Hansel and Gretel house tucked among the treetops, loaded with peaked roofs, dormer windows, funny little turrets, bay windows, and an octagonal tower. You wind up through the trees to the main entry level, which is wrapped by an enormous wooden deck, emphasizing the tree-house look. The living room is dominated by a floor-to-ceiling stone fireplace. Skylights, a stained-glass window, an Oriental carpet, wood-paneled walls, baskets of flowers, and walls of windows looking out into the trees make the room most appealing. The guestrooms, located on various levels, are not decorated in any particular period or style and because of the wooded setting vary in outlook and available sunlight. The favorite choice of many is the Eagle's Nest, located in the octagonal tower, where walls of glass give the impression one is sleeping under the stars—camping at its best. (Note: It is a bit rustic as the bathroom is outside, in the dressing room opposite the hot tub.) Each of the other guestrooms has its own personality, whether it is with stained-glass windows, a private entrance, a separate sitting room, or a bay window looking out into the trees. *Directions:* Take Sir Francis Drake Boulevard off Highway 1 to Olema. Turn right, go 2 miles, then left toward Inverness, go 1 mile, then left on Vallejo Avenue (at Debra's Bakery).

BLACKTHORNE INN
Owners: Susan & Bill Wigert
266 Vallejo Avenue
P.O. Box 712
Inverness, CA 94937
Tel: (415) 663-8621, Fax: (415) 663-8635
Email: susan@blackthorneinn.com
5 rooms, Double: $225–$350
Open all year
Credit cards: MC, VS
No restaurant
Inappropriate for children
www.karenbrown.com/california/blackthorneinn.html

Built as a hunting lodge by the Empire Club in 1917, this dark-shingled building highlighted with a white trim porch hung with greenery is a wonderful escape in the woods just up from Tomales Bay. Under the artistically brilliant direction of its owner, Manka's now offers intimate accommodation and a restaurant (open Thursday through Monday) whose menu is in keeping with the theme of a hunting lodge—much of the food is grilled over an open fire. Four guestrooms are found up a narrow flight of stairs above the restaurant. They occupy the four corners of the lodge and open onto a hallway hung with antlers and old paintings which creaks round the stairwell. Two of the rooms enjoy an expanse of deck looking out through the trees to the bay. Four rooms are located in a rambling annex at the back of the wooded property. Two cabins just below the lodge and two a short drive away, both nestled on the edge of the water enjoying their own acreage and private beach, offer the guest even more privacy and rustic seclusion. We love the wonderful four-poster beds made from rough-hewn Oregon fir, enhanced by warm flannel checks and plaids, and draped with heavy throw blankets. Manka's charm is its appealing, comfortable, rustic ambiance—a homey hideaway inviting you to nestle in with a good book and romantic company. Note: Breakfast is offered from a tempting menu at tables set in the lobby in front of the fire and is additional to the cost of the room. *Directions:* Manka's is at Argyle and Callendar Way.

MANKA'S INVERNESS LODGE
Owner: Margaret Grade
30 Callendar Way
P.O. Box 1110, Inverness, CA 94937
Tel: (415) 669-1034, Fax: (415) 669-1598
Email: mankas@best.com
11 rooms, 3 cabins, Double: $185–$465
Breakfast: $15 per person
Open all year, Credit cards: MC, VS
Restaurant open Thursday through Monday
Children welcome
www.karenbrown.com/california/mankasinvernesslodge.html

Sandy Cove Inn offers guests a spectacular setting of wilderness, beauty, and quiet. Its grounds boast a riding arena and stable, an expanse of well-tended garden, and, unbelievably, its own stretch of sand beach on Tomales Bay. Without venturing beyond the fenced compound one can picnic, swim, beachcomb, tidepool, kayak, or birdwatch. In addition to a parklike setting, the inn offers very private guest accommodation in cottages of weathered wood smartly trimmed in white, each with its own entrance. One feels ultimately pampered with every need anticipated: you are provided not only with the expected amenities, but with imaginative extras such as binoculars, first-aid kits, flashlights, backpacks, hats, walking sticks, insect repellent, beach maps, and slippers at the front door—an attention to detail I have seen nowhere else. A bountiful breakfast including a hot entree is served in your room. The handsome guestrooms are individual in decor and offerings. The North Suite has its own fire stove, a pine bed, a decor of rich cranberry with a nautical theme, and a deck overlooking the dressage arena, stables and Inverness Ridge; the South Suite, dressed with a subtle equestrian theme, enjoys a wood stove and a small sitting area overlooking the arena; and the West Suite has its own porch, a gas fireplace, and a decor of rich blues and burgundies. *Directions:* Drive north on Highway 101 from San Francisco. Head west on Sir Francis Drake Boulevard to Olema and continue west into the village of Inverness on the west shore of Tomales Bay. Continue past Inverness for 1 mile and look for Sandy Cove Inn on the right.

SANDY COVE INN
Owners: Kathy & Gerry Coles
12990 Sir Francis Drake Blvd
P.O. Box 869, Inverness, CA 94937
Tel: (415) 669-2683, Fax: (415) 669-7511
Email: innkeeper@sandycove.com
3 rooms, Double: $200–$350
Closed January to April, Credit cards: all major
No restaurant, Infants & children over 13 welcome
www.karenbrown.com/california/sandycoveinn.html

Ten Inverness Way is an attractive-looking inn—a cozy, redwood-shingled building originally built in 1904 as a family home. A flagstone path leads from the road up a slope, through the carefree, cheerful English garden to the front door. Inside, a staircase takes you to the second level and opens to the living room, which has an informal ambiance with a large stone fireplace and is decorated in blue and white with comfortable furniture slipcovered in denim and striped fabric. The room is inviting and homey. Guests relax and settle in here—playing games or snuggling up in a window seat with a good book. Teri, the owner and innkeeper, has converted what was once the breakfast room into a cozy library full of good books, and now small tables are set for breakfast along the windows of the living room. Simply decorated, the four small bedrooms are fresh and immaculately clean, with handmade quilts on the beds adding a special touch. A ground-level suite has a kitchen, French doors leading to its own garden, and a hand-painted mural surrounding the bed. Guests can reserve a hot tub in the back garden for a private soak. In the morning Teri serves a delicious full breakfast and is happy to pack a picnic lunch for your exploration of Point Reyes National Seashore. *Directions*: Drive into Inverness on the main road, Sir Francis Drake Boulevard, and watch for the sign pointing to your left to Ten Inverness Way.

TEN INVERNESS WAY
Owner: Teri Mattson Mowery
Ten Inverness Way
P.O. Box 63
Inverness, CA 94937
Tel: (415) 669-1648, Fax: (415) 669-7403
Email: inn@teninvernessway.com
5 rooms, Double: $145–$187
Open all year
Credit cards: MC, VS
No restaurant
Children over 12 welcome
www.karenbrown.com/california/teninvernessway.html

Built in 1859 and proudly claiming to be one of California's ten oldest hotels, the National Hotel is located on the main street of Jamestown, considered the gateway to the Gold Country. The first floor accommodates a wonderful restaurant where an extravagant breakfast buffet and morning newspapers are set out for resident guests and where lunch, dinner, and a Sunday champagne brunch are available to residents and non-residents. You can also opt to enjoy lunch or dinner at tables set on a side terrace under the shade of a vine-covered trellis. The handsome old redwood bar in the Gold Rush Saloon offers refreshment, possible entertainment, and local gossip. A steep stairway just off the entry leads to the nine guestrooms on the second floor. Wonderful old brass-and-iron beds decked with regal comforters, handsome trunks, lovely old armoires, antique washbasins, and lace curtains at the windows dominate the décor, which is pleasing and reminiscent of the Gold Rush era—but with modern comforts. All guestrooms enjoy private bathrooms and the hotel has a wonderful "soaking room," which accommodates an oversized claw-foot bathtub—available to all guests, who are supplied with bathrobe and slippers. The guestrooms are comfortable, air-conditioned, and all accessed off the one central hallway. The two front rooms overlook the balcony and the action of Main Street. *Directions*: Jamestown's Main Street intersects both Highways 108 and 49 on the east and west ends of town.

1859 HISTORIC NATIONAL HOTEL
Owner: Stephen Willey
18183 Main Street
P.O. Box 502
Jamestown, CA 95327
Tel: (209) 984-3446 or (800) 894-3446
Fax: (209) 984-5620
Email: info@national-hotel.com
9 rooms, Double: $90–$140
Open all year, Credit cards: all major
Restaurant, Children over 10 welcome
www.karenbrown.com/california/nationalhotel.html

Located in a residential area south of the old Gold Rush town of Julian is a miniature southern mansion, painted white with four stately columns accenting the front of the house. The style especially appealed to Alan whose family, many years ago, used to own a plantation, while the tranquil setting appealed to Mary. Inside, the home is lovely and inviting in its decor, with a definite sense of family and home. The living room opens onto a sunlit dining room with a wall of windows looking out to a sloping forest of trees. Guests gather in the dining room for a lavish, homemade breakfast served elegantly on family china and silver. Downstairs there are two bedrooms. The French Quarter room has a New Orleans theme and is wallpapered in muted shades of tan and dusty pink with a handsome Louis XVI antique bed. The Julian Suite is the largest room, with a king wrought-iron bed, gas-burning fireplace, whirlpool tub for two, and mountain view. Breakfast is served privately to this room in the dinette area. Upstairs, there are three guestrooms. The Honeymoon Suite is decorated in burgundy and tapestry. The East room is decorated in blues and whites. The Cotton Baron's room has just been redecorated in yellows and blues, has an arch over the bed, and is furnished with white hand-painted antiques. Gas fireplaces are available in the Honeymoon Suite and East Room. A spa is available in the rose garden area. *Directions:* One mile southwest of town on Highway 78/79. From Main Street make a left on Pine Hills Road. Proceed 2-3/10 miles and make a right on Blue Jay Drive.

THE JULIAN WHITE HOUSE
Owners: Mary & Alan Marvin
3014 Blue Jay Drive
P.O. Box 824, Julian, CA 92036
Tel: (760) 765-1764 or (800) 948-4687
Email: stay@julian-whitehouse-bnb.com
5 rooms, Double: $135–$195
Open all year, Credit cards: MC, VS
No restaurant, Inappropriate for children
www.karenbrown.com/california/julianwhitehouse.html

Just a block off Main Street on a Julian hillside sits a lovely property, open for just a few years, which already boasts a very loyal clientele. It is not surprising when you see the accommodation: guestrooms are lovely, with handsome country furnishings complemented by beautiful wallpapers and coordinating fabrics. The Yellow Bellflower, for example, is decorated in tones of soft blues and yellow, with a beautiful blue arch or faience hung over the bed, materials of a subtle pinstripe and blue check, and a multi-colored quilt draped at the foot of the bed. There is nothing country-cute in the decor—rather, rooms are spacious and subtle in their elegance. Cottage guestrooms, all with private entrances, are tucked in a garden setting along a wandering path and central courtyard. All rooms are equipped with TV and VCR (complimentary video library), all but one have a fireplace, and half have whirlpool tubs. Bathrooms are spacious, modern, and wonderfully appointed. At the top of the property, the handsome lodge offers more standard rooms in terms of size and price, a lovely large public room with high vaulted ceilings and river-stone fireplace, a dining room, and an upstairs common area with sofa, lounge chairs, and TV. Room prices include a full breakfast and evening hors d'oeuvres. In the intimacy of the lovely dining room a delicious menu is offered three evenings a week. *Directions*: Washington Street crosses Main Street at the north end of town.

ORCHARD HILL COUNTRY INN
Owners: Pat & Darrell Straube
2502 Washington Street
P.O. Box 2410, Julian, CA 92036-0425
Tel: (760) 765-1700 or (800) 71-ORCHARD
Fax: (760) 765-0290
Email: information@orchardhill.com
22 rooms, Double: $185–$285
Open all year, Credit cards: all major
Restaurant open for dinner Wednesday & Saturday only
Children over 12 welcome, Wheelchair friendly
www.karenbrown.com/california/orchardhillcountryinn.html

Just a block from the ocean and the hustle and bustle of La Jolla village, The La Jolla Bed & Breakfast Inn sits on a quiet, stylish suburban street. Originally built for George Kautz in 1913, the home's most famous occupant was the composer John Phillip Sousa, who lived here during the '20s. Behind its street-front façade you enter a grassy, flower-filled courtyard where the only sound is that of a tinkling fountain. Guests often take a breakfast tray out here on balmy mornings—alternatively, you can eat with your fellow guests round the breakfast table. Bedrooms vary from snug upstairs rooms in the original house to a spacious suite with a sitting room offering distant views of the ocean horizon. Beautiful furnishings, lovely fabrics, and fabulous antiques have been carefully selected by the decorator, who also serves as the inn's PR person. It's an excellent location for walking to the beach, shops, and restaurants of La Jolla village and it is just 200 yards from the Museum of Contemporary Art. I was pleased with the availability of on-street parking. *Directions:* From San Diego take Route 5 and exit right on La Jolla Village Drive. Turn left on Torrey Pines Road and proceed 2½ miles to Prospect Street. Turn right, drive through downtown La Jolla, and opposite the Museum of Contemporary Art turn right on Draper Avenue—the inn is the second building on the left.

THE LA JOLLA BED & BREAKFAST INN
Owner: Ron Shanks
7753 Draper Avenue
La Jolla, CA 92037
Tel: (858) 456-2066 or (800) 582-2466
Fax: (858) 456-1510
Email: bedbreakfast@innlajolla.com
15 rooms, Double: $159–$379
Open all year, Credit cards: all major
No restaurant, Children over 12 welcome
Wheelchair friendly
www.karenbrown.com/california/lajollabandb.html

La Valencia Hotel with her subtle-pink adobe-like walls, thick Spanish-tiled roof, and an interesting tower domed with blue-and-gold mosaics is a captivating hotel with much old-world charm. The hotel dates back to the 1920s: the essence and dream of the original hotel have been faithfully preserved, and even bettered by sensitive restoration and refurbishment. The reception opens onto a dramatic long parlor whose soft-buff-colored walls, wrought-iron chandeliers, subdued lighting, blue-and-yellow tiled planter, luscious displays of fresh flowers, and painted ceiling are dramatized by a wall of glass framing the sea. Guests gather in the evening in the Whalers Bar with its collection of scrimshaw before enjoying dinner in the La Rue Restaurant, or on the most special of occasions at the 12-table Sky Room Restaurant, which sits atop the hotel with dramatic 180-degree ocean views. While all the rooms are beautifully decorated, the most luxurious are those found in the Ocean Villas that terrace down behind the hotel toward La Jolla Cove— these spacious rooms and suites are exquisite. Within the main body of the hotel our favorite bedrooms are those that have the little balconies just large enough for a couple of chairs—some have ocean views while others overlook the bustle of the village. As an alternative to swimming in the ocean, La Valencia offers a tempting pool set on an ocean-view terrace amidst the perfectly tended gardens. *Directions:* Exit I-5 north at Ardath Road (5 south at La Jolla Village), travel to Torrey Pines Road, and turn right on Prospect Street to the hotel. Pull up in front of the hotel and the valet will park your car.

LA VALENCIA HOTEL
Director: Michael Ullman
1132 Prospect Street, La Jolla, CA 92037
Tel: (858) 454-0771 or (800) 451-0772
Fax: (858) 456-3921
Email: info@lavalencia.com
117 rooms, Double: $295–$4,000
Open all year, Credit cards: all major
Restaurants, Children welcome, Wheelchair friendly
www.karenbrown.com/california/lavalencia.html

The Scripps Inn enjoys an absolutely magnificent setting just steps away from the white sand of La Jolla's gorgeous cove and beach and expanse of sparkling blue water. You can walk or bike for miles along the pedestrian trail that contours along the bluff and it is also just a few short blocks up the hill to the heart of the village with its elegant shops and delightful restaurants. The location alone of this attractive two- and three-story tan building, trimmed in dark green and colored with bougainvillea warrants inclusion, but I was thrilled to find that the interior is as attractive as the location. Two wings of rooms wrap around the central car park and upstairs guestrooms are accessed off a covered walkway. The rooms are fresh and pretty—light and airy in their decor with tans, creams, and beiges in the fabrics complementing the light woods of the furnishings. All of the rooms have glimpses of the ocean, though for view none can rival the wonderful suite 14 where large sitting-room windows frame a 180-degree vista of La Jolla Cove. The two-bedroom suites and room 14 have a kitchenette and two rooms have fireplaces. In the evening it's a short walk into the village where you are spoilt for choice of restaurants. Muffins and pastries and a variety of juices (there are in-room coffee makers) are set out in the reception niche in the morning along with trays to take breakfast back to your room or to the lanai. *Directions:* From San Diego take Route 5 and exit right on La Jolla Village Drive. Turn left on Torrey Pines Road and proceed 2½ miles to Prospect Street. Turn right, drive through downtown La Jolla, and just after the Museum of Contemporary Art turn right on Cuvier, left on Coast, and immediately left into the inn's car park.

SCRIPPS INN
Innkeeper: Doris Rella
555 Coast Boulevard South
La Jolla, CA 92037
Tel: (858) 454-3391 or (800) 439-7529
Fax: (858) 456-0389
14 rooms, Double: $164–$415
Open all year, Credit cards: all major
No restaurant, Children welcome in first-floor rooms

Although Eagle's Landing is a bed and breakfast, it is run so professionally that guests have the feeling that they are in a miniature hotel. There are four guestrooms with private bathrooms and although each varies in decor, they all maintain a comfy-homey ambiance and are all meticulously kept—everything is "as neat as a new pin." One of the bedrooms, the Lake View Suite, is enormous, with its own fireplace and a spacious private deck with a view of the lake. However, my favorite room is the cozy Woods Room, tucked amongst the trees with its own little terrace and entrance. The living room has a large fireplace in the corner and a splendid long wooden trestle table, big enough for all the guests to gather and share their day's adventures. Just off the dining room is a cozy nook where guests enjoy breakfast. Speaking of breakfast, Dorothy prides herself on treating her guests to a full breakfast every morning and a special brunch on Sunday mornings, a hearty start for exploring the lake, which is just a short walk from Eagle's Landing. Since this is a private lake, public access is available only in the town of Arrowhead (about a five-minute drive or a thirty-minute lakeside walk away). *Directions:* Turn north from Highway 18 following signs for Blue Jay. Before you reach the lake, the road splits. Turn left on North Bay and watch for Cedarwood on your left—Eagle's Landing is on the corner of North Bay and Cedarwood.

EAGLE'S LANDING
Owners: Dorothy & Jack Stone
27406 Cedarwood
Lake Arrowhead, CA 92352
Mailing address:
 P.O. Box 1510, Blue Jay, CA 92317
Tel: (800) 835-5085, Tel & fax: (909) 336-2642
Email: eagleslanding498@cs.com
4 rooms, Double: $95–$195
Open all year
Credit cards: all major
No restaurant, Children over 10 welcome
www.karenbrown.com/california/eagleslanding.html

The Saddleback Inn is tucked into its own wooded oasis just a short stroll from Lake Arrowhead Village. Although the inn dates back about 70 years to when it was built in the style of an English tavern by two sisters from the Midwest, there is nothing "dated" about this intimate inn. Its present owners have completely renovated every nook and cranny, creating an elegant, yet charming hotel. Luckily, they have kept the old-world look with the use of a few antiques plus many reproductions in the decor. The reception area is located in the main lodge, which exudes a Victorian mood in its cozy bar and dining room. The original staircase leads off the lobby to ten guestrooms commemorating past guests like Howard Hughes, John Wayne, and Charles Lindburgh. Scattered throughout the 3½ acres are small cottages connected by pathways, which house the remaining guestrooms. All of the rooms are decorated with Laura Ashley fabrics and wallpapers, and most have double whirlpool tubs in the bathroom—a wonderful respite after a day of hiking or sightseeing. Enjoy fine dining in their award-winning restaurant. A pretty beach is within walking distance. *Directions:* From Highway 18 take the Lake Arrowhead turnoff. Drive 2 miles and the hotel is on the left at the entrance to Lake Arrowhead Village.

SADDLEBACK INN
Owners: Kurt & Bonnie Campbell
300 S. State Highway 173
P.O. Box 1890
Lake Arrowhead, CA 92352
Tel: (800) 858-3334, Fax: (909) 336-6111
Email: mtnrooms@aol.com
34 rooms, Double: $99–$230
Open all year
Credit cards: all major
Restaurant, Children welcome
www.karenbrown.com/california/saddlebackinn.html

Glendeven is a charming New England-style farmhouse built in 1867 by Isaiah Stevens for his bride, Rebecca. Today, this beautiful clapboard home, elegant in its simplicity, remains one of the most delightful inns on the Mendocino coast. Over the years the inn has been expanded to include four lovely guestrooms in Stevenscroft, a gabled, barn-sided building in the gardens, and a magnificent new suite in the nearby Carriage House. Most rooms at Glendeven have fireplaces and ocean views. The decor and details throughout are lovely in their proportion, style, and color. After enjoying a country breakfast in their room, guests usually stroll across to the gallery located on the ground floor of the Barn and Carriage House buildings. Across the highway a path leads through parkland to clifftops high above the ocean. Glendeven is adjacent to Van Damme State Park with its scenic walking paths. In 2000, owners Sharon and Higgins acquired La Bella Vista, a two-bedroom, two-bath vacation rental house across the meadow from Glendeven, with beautiful gardens, spectacular ocean views, hot tub, and kitchen—a great place for families or friends traveling together. *Directions*: From San Francisco take Highway 101 north, Highway 128 west, then Highway 1 north for 8-2/10 miles.

GLENDEVEN
Owners: Sharon & Higgins Williams
8205 North Highway 1
Little River, CA 95456
Tel: (707) 937-0083 or (800) 822-4536
Fax: (707) 937-6108
Email: innkeeper@glendeven.com
10 rooms, 1 cottage
Double: $125–$350
Open all year
Credit cards: all major
No restaurant, children welcome in cottage
www.karenbrown.com/california/glendeven.html

Vineyards are beginning to dress the foothills of the Livermore Valley as numerous wineries take up residence in the shadow of the windmills. With such giants as Wente, Ivan Tamas, Stony Ridge, Thomas Coyne, and Concannon as neighbors, the Purple Orchid Inn Resort and Spa is a convenient and luxurious retreat for exploring the wineries. A beautiful, sprawling log structure set against a backdrop of its own olive orchards, the inn is intended to be a destination in its own right. With a background in health care, owner Karen Hughes describes the inn as "a place of wellness, where guests can visit, relax, and make healthy life choices." Enjoy the expanded spa, a private building with its own reception and lunch. The spa staff is extensively trained in various massage methods, special body wraps, salt glows, and skin care. Definitely ask about the spa and golf packages. For dining, there are lots of local restaurants and on Friday evenings at the inn a delicious fondue repast (cheese, chicken, beef, and chocolate) is available. In the mornings, the chef will prepare whatever you crave for breakfast. The guestrooms, all with fireplaces, are attractive in their newness and bathrooms enjoy nice fixtures and Jacuzzi tubs (some for two). The newest patio suites are equipped with refrigerator, microwave and a stocked bar. Gorgeous hand-carved scenes on the guestroom doors depict the theme and decor for the rooms. *Directions:* Exit Highway 580 at Vasco Road to the south. At its end turn left on Tesla Road and then take a left on Cross Road to the inn.

PURPLE ORCHID INN
Owner: Karen Hughes
4549 Cross Road, Livermore, CA 94550
Tel: (925) 606-8855 or (800) 353-4549
Fax: (925) 606-8880
Email: info@purpleorchid.com
10 rooms, Double: $150–$360
Open all year, Credit cards: MC, VS
No restaurant, Children over 14 welcome
Wheelchair friendly
www.karenbrown.com/california/purpleorchid.html

Nestled in the Bel-Air hills of Los Angeles in a neighborhood of exclusive homes, the Hotel Bel-Air is exceptional—elegant and sophisticated, but unpretentious and extending a truly warm welcome. An awning-covered walkway leading to the hotel's reception area gives you your first glimpse of the lush 12 acres transected by babbling streams. Furnishings are gorgeous, with handsome antiques and dramatic flower arrangements. The one- or two-story buildings nestling in the greenery are painted in a soft pastel wash with white doors, creating a peaceful and soothing effect. There is an elegant interior restaurant and a terrace for dining under the shade of canopies and trees. Light meals are also available poolside as is a summertime grill. The setting is quiet, with the sound of fountains and a running stream breaking the natural silence. Most of the beautifully decorated guestrooms enjoy handsome tiled floors warmed by lovely needlepoint carpets, and a tea service is presented as a welcome to guests. Service is ever-present but subtle, with the wishes of guests seemingly anticipated, and nothing is too much of a problem or effort on the part of the staff. In my research I have seen some of the world's finest hotels and the Bel-Air made such an impression, it is one I am determined to return to as others do—on vacation as well as business! *Directions*: Take Sunset Boulevard west off Highway 405 and then turn north on Stone Canyon Road for about 1 mile. The hotel is on the left just past the intersection of Tortuosa Way.

HOTEL BEL-AIR
General Manager: Frank Bowling
701 Stone Canyon Road
Bel-Air, Los Angeles, CA 90077
Tel: (310) 472-1211 or (800) 648-4097
Fax: (310) 909-1606
92 rooms, Double: $435–$3,150
Open all year
Credit cards: all major
Restaurants
Children welcome, Wheelchair friendly

Elegant in its simplicity, Le Montrose is not an inn, but offers great value and exceptional accommodation in a safe neighborhood on the edge of Beverly Hills just up from the design center. Converted from an apartment complex, Le Montrose has a nondescript concrete square façade, which belies the charm of the interior. There are three sizes of guest suites: junior, executive, and one-bedroom. All have a sunken living room and come with welcome baskets of fruit, twice-daily maid service, color televisions equipped with VCRs and web TV, state-of-the-art multi-line phones, private Email, fax and copy machines, gas fireplaces, great mattresses, excellent lighting, and comfortable sitting areas. The decor in the rooms is handsomely elegant—tones of browns, beiges, golds, and blacks are used in the furnishings against the soft hues of the subtly elegant wallpapers and the classically framed art. The intimate, private library restaurant serves fine cuisine in a quiet ambiance or will provide 24-hour room service. A small but well-equipped fitness center is available to guests at no charge, lighted tennis courts are found on one level of the rooftop, and on a lower level a lovely large pool looks out to the rooftops of Los Angeles. Please request the Karen Brown bed and breakfast rates when making a reservation. *Directions*: Located one block east of Beverly Hills. Take a long journey east on Sunset Boulevard off the I-405, then turn right on Hammond Street, just past Doheny. Or from I-10 take La Cienega north, turn west on Sunset Boulevard (past Santa Monica Boulevard), and turn left on Hammond.

LE MONTROSE SUITE HOTEL
General Manager: John Douponce
900 Hammond Street
West Hollywood, CA 90069
Tel: (310) 855-1115 or (800) 776-0666
Fax: (310) 657-9192, Email: jdouponce@aol.com
132 suites, Double: $199–$575
Breakfast: $10 per person
Open all year, Credit cards: all major
Restaurant, Children welcome, Wheelchair friendly
www.karenbrown.com/california/lemontrosehotel.html

On a quiet shaded street of Los Olivos sits a distinguished, subtly elegant hotel, traditional in its ambiance. Beautiful in decor and lavish in its comfort, the inn is most definitely grand yet intimate in its number of guestrooms. Having just 21 rooms, the hotel gives guests personal and gracious attention. Each of the guestrooms, whether upstairs from the main lobby or in an attractive annex across the street, features wood moldings, brass fixtures, and French armoires, which create a romantic, turn-of-the-century ambiance. Guestroom amenities include a mini refrigerator, television, fireplace, beds topped with plump down comforters, and, in selected rooms, a Jacuzzi bathtub. A lovely heated swimming pool and Jacuzzi are a welcome treat for summer travelers as are the facilities at Spa Vigne. The award-winning Vintage Room restaurant is elegant with a French country ambiance and Le Saloon is an attractive full-service bar opening onto the gorgeous landscaped grounds of the hotel. We were pleased to learn that the hotel has just received approval to add in 2002 an additional 25 accommodations in the form of cottages and suites on a lot conveniently located just across from Spa Vigne. *Directions:* From Los Angeles, take Highway 101 north. Approximately 5 miles north of Buellton, exit onto Highway 154. Proceed 2 miles and turn right on Grand.

FESS PARKER'S WINE COUNTRY INN & SPA
General Manager: Karen Lindstrom
2860 Grand Avenue, P.O. Box 849
Los Olivos, CA 93441
Tel: (805) 688-7788 or (800) 446-2455
Fax: (805) 688-1942
Email: karen@fessparker.com
21 rooms, Double: $400–$600
Breakfast: $10 per person (included Sun through Thurs)
Open all year
Credit cards: all major
Restaurant
Children welcome, Wheelchair friendly
www.karenbrown.com/california/fessinn.html

The bland roadside exterior with its '50s motel sign is all that is left of the earlier version of this motel. Behind the façade is a simple, attractive entry dressed with fresh flowers opening onto the back central courtyard. The manicured back garden is beautifully landscaped and flows to a tiled patio, which extends out to a glass-enclosed bay-window alcove set with tables overlooking the ocean. A single-story wing of rooms sits right on the beach. Decorated in a simple, fresh look with wicker furniture, the beachfront rooms open onto a deck whose glass wall topped by a driftwood banister tempts one to climb right over and onto the sand. The new Malibu Suite has been completely remodeled with whitewashed open-beam ceilings, fireplace, Jacuzzi bath, and a private seaside deck. Other rooms are found in the building that fronts the Pacific Coast Highway, either on the first floor overlooking the lush interior courtyard or on the second floor enjoying views of the courtyard garden and glimpses of blue water. Some rooms are equipped with kitchenettes, some with gas fireplaces, and thoughtful touches such as bathroom amenities, in-room coffee makers, a soda and snack concession just off the courtyard, and the complimentary use of beach towels, chairs, and umbrellas are indicators of the caring owners. Continental breakfast featuring fresh-baked pastries from Wolfgang Pucks' restaurant, Granita, is offered each morning in the lobby and can enjoyed in your room or on the patio. Room service is available for lunch and dinner. *Directions*: Located south of town, on the Pacific Coast Highway between Cross Creek and Carbon Canyon roads.

CASA MALIBU
Owners: Joan & Richard Page
22752 Pacific Coast Highway
Malibu, CA 90265
Tel: (310) 456-2219 or (800) 831-085
Fax: (310) 456-5418
Email: casamalibu@earthlink.net
21 rooms, Double: $99–$349
Open all year, Credit cards: all major
No restaurant, Children welcome
www.karenbrown.com/california/casamalibu.html

Constructed in 1989, the Malibu Beach Inn resembles the type of small hotel you would find on the Mediterranean, washed in a soft peach and detailed with green awnings and door trim, with white doors and tile roof. Guestrooms at the back of the inn open up to magnificent ocean views and the sound of surf. The entrance sits opposite the parking lot and an attractive fountain set amongst a small ring of palm trees. The public area is open and lovely, handsome hand-painted tiles are found throughout, a fountain cascades, a fireplace dresses a sitting area, and an arched doorway opens out to a tiled deck set with tables. All rooms are a good value—in the heart of Santa Monica, the same ocean view would carry a price tag of $400. First-floor rooms have two-person Jacuzzis on the outside deck. One suite is found on each floor and enjoys a larger deck, Jacuzzi, and fireplace. Simple, clean decor is similar throughout. All rooms have a private oceanfront balcony, bamboo furniture and full amenities such as fully stocked wet bars and bathrobes. I liked room 318, a "pier room," which has a corner view of the beach and pier and a nice corner deck, and, as with all third-floor rooms, features a vaulted beamed ceiling. Most of the rooms have gas-log fireplaces. *Directions*: South of Malibu on the Pacific Coast Highway with Carbon Canyon Road as the closest cross street.

MALIBU BEACH INN
Owners: Vicky Cooper & Skip Miser
22878 Pacific Coast Highway
Malibu, CA 90265
Tel: (310) 456-6444 or (800) 4-MALIBU
Fax: (310) 456-1499
Email: reservations@malibubeachinn.com
47 rooms, Double: $199–$299
Open all year
Credit cards: all major
No restaurant
Children welcome, Wheelchair friendly
www.karenbrown.com/california/malibubeach.html

Set on 92 acres of meadow, woodland, and creek, Victorian Gardens, dating back to 1904, is a lovely two-story, four-bedroom classic Victorian. Decoration is respectful of the Victorian period and yet the furnishings are an artistic arrangement of both traditional and contemporary, with Pauline and Luciano's family heirlooms and art treasures on display. The kitchen, where breakfast is sometimes served, is definitely the "heart of the home" and Luciano's domain, a wonderful room warmed by a large open fireplace, which Luciano also uses for cooking. Dinner, by reservation only and open also to non-guests, is an elegant presentation of five courses featuring Italian regional dishes, with specially selected wines to complement the fixed menu, which changes daily. While Victorian Gardens has four guestrooms (two sharing a hall bath and two with private bath), only three rooms are rented out if all the guests are not together so that each room has its private bathroom. The Master Bedroom enjoys a sweeping view of meadow and the surrounding foothills; the Poppy Bedroom has an intimate reading nook; the Golden Bedroom is an inviting front corner room with a lovely nook enticing you to settle and enjoy glimpses of the ocean; and the handsome Northwest Bedroom is blessed with wonderful views and the most lavish bathroom. *Directions*: From San Francisco take 101 north to 128 west until it ends on Highway 1, then turn south. Travel 5 miles to Elk and then 8 miles to Victorian Gardens.

VICTORIAN GARDENS
Owners: Pauline & Luciano Zamboni
14409 South Highway 1
Manchester, CA 95459
Tel: (707) 882-3606
Fax: (707) 882-2718
4 rooms, 2 with private bathrooms
Double: $170–$250
Open all year
Credit cards: all major
Restaurant, Children over 6 welcome

The McCloud Guest House has a wonderful setting—in its own pretty little park, surrounded by green lawn and trees, with Mount Shasta, northern California's 14,162-foot giant, in the distance. It is very private and quiet, yet is only a two-block walk to downtown and the popular Shasta Street Sunset Dinner Train. The inn is not pretentious, but most attractive in its Craftsman-style simplicity. Built entirely of wood, the square building is wrapped with a spacious verandah whose supporting columns reach up to a steeply pitched roof from which little dormer windows peek out into the trees. Built in 1907, the inn was originally the estate of J. H. Queal, the president of the McCloud River Railroad Company. After extensive renovations, it reopened as a restaurant on the ground level with five bedrooms upstairs. Since then the restaurant has closed, but guests do enjoy a full breakfast. As you enter the foyer, the massive stone fireplace and wood-paneled walls set the country-lodge feeling. Upstairs, bedrooms, each with private bath, surround a guest parlor highlighted with an ornate pool table from the Hearst collection and a large stone fireplace. Each of the guestrooms has its own color scheme and personality, but all are decorated with period pieces such as antique dressers, white iron beds, and handmade quilts. Recent renovations include a new sauna, library, and game room. *Directions:* From Interstate 5 turn east on Highway 89 for 12 miles to McCloud. Before the village turn left on Colombero Drive.

McCLOUD GUEST HOUSE
Owner: Linda Baldwin
Innkeeper: Betty Stuart
606 West Colombero Drive
P.O. Box 1510
McCloud, CA 96057
Tel: (530) 964-3160 or (877) 964-3160
Fax: (530) 964-3202, Email: mcguesthouse@snowcrest.com
5 rooms, Double: $119–$182
Open all year, Credit cards: all major
No restaurant, Children over 12 welcome
www.karenbrown.com/california/mccloudguesthouse.html

With great determination, expenditure, and hard work, Lee and Marilyn Ogden renovated a long-abandoned historic building at the heart of the mountain town of McCloud and now the McCloud Hotel with its pretty yellow façade proudly dominates Main Street. Inside, the high, beamed ceiling and informal grouping of sofas and chairs set before a large fire give the feeling of a mountain lodge. Although the exterior of the hotel was in relatively good shape and required only cosmetic repairs, guestrooms benefit from the complete renovation and modernization of the interior. At the top of a wide, handsome staircase is an inviting upstairs parlor with access to the front expanse of porch. Rooms facing Main Street are a wonderful value, with a nice-size room, washbasin, toilet, and private bathroom. Rooms on the first and second floors at the back of the inn have four-poster beds and an additional but small sitting area. Four suites enjoy big Jacuzzi tubs, three of which are found in the room proper. The decor is similar in theme throughout, with the use of country patterns, old trunks, and washstands holding in-room washbasins. Breakfast and Saturday-afternoon tea are served at tables set in the lobby and guests staying in the suites have the extra option of having breakfast delivered to the room. *Directions*: From Interstate 5 take the McCloud-Reno exit and travel east on Highway 89 for 10 miles. Turn left on Colombero Drive and follow it into town, cross the tracks, and turn right on Main Street.

McCLOUD HOTEL
Owners: Marilyn & Lee Ogden
408 Main Street, P.O. Box 730, McCloud, CA 96057
Tel: (530) 964-2822 or (800) 964-2823
Fax: (530) 964-2844
Email: mchotel@snowcrest.net
17 rooms, Double: $103–$182
Open all year, Credit cards: all major
No restaurant, Children welcome only in first-floor rooms
Wheelchair friendly
www.karenbrown.com/california/mccloudhotel.html

The Agate Cove Inn is a beautiful property situated on a bluff across the coastal road from the ocean. The heart of the inn is a charming 1860s blue-trimmed, white clapboard farmhouse where you find the reception area and an appealing lounge with comfy chairs facing a brick fireplace where a cozy fire crackles on chilly days. Windows stretch across the entire west wall of the lounge, giving guests a spectacular view of the coast as they enjoy a scrumptious hot breakfast. Two of the bedrooms are in the main farmhouse, while the others are scattered about the property in little cottages painted a pretty country-blue with white trim. Most of the rooms have a gas fireplace, a deck, and a view of the sea. Even the least expensive rooms, although smaller and simpler, are sweet and pretty. All of the guestrooms are gradually undergoing total renovation. The inn was bought in 1999 by a charming young couple, Nancy and Dennis Freeze, who dreamed for years of opening their own inn. They visited many properties to experience first-hand what the finest had to offer, then set out on the lengthy "inn-hunting" process throughout all of California. When they discovered the Agate Cove Inn they knew they had found the perfect spot. It is no wonder they fell in love so quickly—the little houses are as cute as can be, and the setting superb. The view overlooking brilliantly colored flowers to the sparkling blue of the sea, framed by windswept cypress trees, is truly breathtaking. *Directions:* From Highway 1 take Little Lake left (west), then Lansing right (north).

AGATE COVE INN
Owners: Nancy & Dennis Freeze
11201 North Lansing Street
P.O. Box 1150, Mendocino, CA 95460
Tel: (707) 937-0551 or (800) 527-3111
Fax: (707) 937-0550
Email: info@agatecove.com
10 rooms, Double: $119–$269
Open all year, Credit cards: all major
No restaurant, Children over 12 welcome
www.karenbrown.com/california/agatecoveinn.html

The Blue Heron Inn is not the typical Mendocino Victorian, but a simple, New England-style house, painted white with blue trim, with a great red door. A white picket fence encloses the garden to each side, completing the adorable cottage look. The ground floor is a delightful restaurant (The Moosse Café) where daily specials (fresh fish and pasta dishes) are offered and complemented by a small wine list. Enjoy a Caesar salad for lunch and cioppino for dinner. In the morning a Continental breakfast with scones or muffins, fruit, and freshly squeezed orange juice is served here. Upstairs, you find three completely delightful bedrooms, each simply furnished with country antiques and containing a lovely queen-sized bed made with the most attractive linens. Sunset Room (in cool greens) captures ocean views across the rooftops and shares a modern bathroom with the adjacent Bay Room, which offers a tempting view of the ocean from its window. The Blue Heron Room has equally delightful decor, more space, and a pristine en-suite shower room. *Directions:* Follow Highway 1 north into Mendocino. Turn left at the Mendocino business district to Kasten Street, then turn right.

BLUE HERON INN
Owner: Linda Friedman
390 Kasten Street
Mendocino, CA 95460
Tel: (707) 937-4323, Fax: (707) 937-3611
Email: moosse@mcn.org
3 rooms, 1 with private bathroom
Double: $95–$115
Open all year
Credit cards: MC, VS
Restaurant
Children over 12 welcome
www.karenbrown.com/california/blueheroninn.html

The John Dougherty House has an unbeatable location, just steps from Mendocino's quaint shops and cute restaurants, yet only a few short blocks to the splendid headlands where you can stroll the bluffs with only the pounding of the surf, the cry of the seagulls, and the bark of the sea lions to disturb the silence. The heart of the inn is a beguiling blue cottage with perky white trim, dating back to 1867. Some of the guestrooms are in the main house, one in the adjacent wood-shingled water tower, another in the old carriage house, and others in cottages nestled in the beautifully kept garden. For the finest view, splurge on the Captain's Room, which has a spacious verandah looking out over the village to the bay. If this isn't available, choose either Raven or Osprey with their view balconies, king-sized four-poster beds, fireplaces, cable TVs, and jet tubs. The cozy "gathering" room has a breakfast table at one end and comfortable chairs grouped before a brick fireplace where a fire blazes on chilly days. When the weather is warm, most guests choose to enjoy the hearty breakfast outside on the terrace overlooking the garden and the sea. The country decor is fresh and uncluttered, with simple wood antiques set off to perfection by white walls enhanced by lovely stencils hand-painted by Marion. Everywhere you look, it is obvious that this small inn is lovingly managed by owners who take pride in caring for their guests. *Directions*: Coming north on 101, take the first street into Mendocino. Turn right on Kasten, then left on Ukiah.

THE JOHN DOUGHERTY HOUSE
Owners: Marion & David Wells
571 Ukiah Street
P.O. Box 817
Mendocino, CA 95460
Tel: (707) 937-5266 or (800) 486-2104
Email: jdhbmw@mcn.org
10 rooms, Double: $95–$115
Open all year, Credit cards: all major
No restaurant, Children over 12 welcome
www.karenbrown.com/california/johndougherty.html

The Joshua Grindle Inn, located just a short walk from the center of Mendocino, is surrounded by a 2-acre plot of land. A white picket fence encloses the front yard of this most attractive white clapboard farmhouse, which, although architecturally simple, has hints of the Victorian era in the fancy woodwork on the verandah. In the 1879 farmhouse you find the guest lounge, a sedate room with old paintings and portraits on the walls, a fireplace, white lace curtains, a trunk as a coffee table, and an antique pump organ. The light, airy guestrooms have a New-England country ambiance enhanced by the owner's early-American antiques and some have their own fireplace. Of the five guestrooms in the main building two overlook the town of Mendocino and the distant ocean, and all their bathrooms have been remodeled with luxurious enhancements such as marble counters and whirlpool and deep soaking tubs. A natural-wood cottage, Saltbox Cottage, has two intimate bedrooms, each with custom pine cabinets and luxurious cast-iron waterfall tubs and showers. Additional and very popular rooms are those tucked romantically into the age-weathered water tower in the rear garden. Especially attractive is Watertower II, a sunny, cozy room on the second floor with a glimpse of the ocean. All of the bedrooms are spotlessly maintained and immaculately decorated, and have well lighted, comfortably arranged sitting areas and private bathrooms. *Directions:* Follow Highway 1 north into Mendocino. After crossing the bridge into town, take the second left at the stop light onto Little Lake Road.

JOSHUA GRINDLE INN
Owners: Arlene & Jim Moorehead
Manager: Christine Wagner
44800 Little Lake Road, P.O. Box 647
Mendocino, CA 95460
Tel: (707) 937-4143 or (800) 474-6353
Email: stay@joshgrin.com
10 rooms, Double: $130–$245
Closed Christmas, Credit cards: MC, VS
No restaurant, Children over 10 welcome
www.karenbrown.com/california/joshuagrindleinn.html

Most of our selections for Mendocino feature the coastal splendor, but although not next to the ocean, the Mendocino Farmhouse has its own special qualities. It is located at the end of a narrow lane that weaves through a beautiful redwood glen, crosses a small creek, and then opens into a lovely meadow. There, amidst beds of flowers, next to a pond, and surrounded by a white picket fence, you will find an appealing farmhouse with white trim. Inside, the decor is fresh and pretty, with antique accents giving it an eclectic style. The breakfast tables capture the sunshine in a many-windowed niche overlooking the flower garden. Dining outside under redwoods is an option in good weather. A large family kitchen is located off the living room. There are four bedrooms in the farmhouse, each sparkling clean and with its own bathroom—two enjoy fireplaces. Our favorite rooms are Cedar and Pine, found in the converted barn surrounded by its own little garden. Each is rustic in mood with either cedar or bleached-pine paneling, a sitting area, and a large wood-burning fireplace. *Directions:* From Highway 1 take Comptche-Ukiah Road east of Mendocino. Go 1-7/10 miles to Olson Lane and turn left to the end of the road.

MENDOCINO FARMHOUSE
Owner: Margie Kamb
Olson Lane
P.O. Box 247
Mendocino, CA 95460
Tel: (707) 937-0241 or (800) 475-1536
Fax: none, Email: mkamb@mcn.org
6 rooms, Double: $95–$145
Open all year
Credit cards: MC, VS
No restaurant
Children over 10 welcome by prior arrangement
www.karenbrown.com/california/mendocinofarmhouse.html

At first glance The Stanford Inn by the Sea appears to be more like a motel than a country inn, but this is definitely untrue. Joan and Jeff Stanford have created a sophisticated little hotel within an attractive, but not unusual, two-story, natural-wood building. Today the inn consists of several buildings on the crest of a meadow overlooking their certified organic gardens and pastures where llamas graze. Each room has a view of the gardens and ocean and the guestrooms, many with four-poster beds, are snug little hideaways, with country antiques, color television with VCR (movies can be rented), telephone, vases of flowers, and either a wood-burning fireplace or stove with plenty of wood to warm you on nippy nights. Everything is fresh and pretty and immaculately clean. The entire operation seems extremely professional and yet has a very personal touch. The expansive lobbies are places where guests mingle during "Afternoons at the Inn." A wonderful bonus is the glass-enclosed sauna and "greenhouse" pool where guests can enjoy a swim, take a sauna, or soak in the spa, even on blustery days. For those who enjoy a workout, there is also an exercise room. Guests are encouraged to borrow the inn's mountain bikes to explore the coast or, if they would rather explore Big River, rent a kayak or canoe. Breakfast is taken in the inn's acclaimed vegetarian restaurant, which serves dinner nightly. *Directions:* A quarter of a mile south of the village of Mendocino at the intersection of Highway 1 and Comptche-Ukiah Road.

THE STANFORD INN BY THE SEA
Owners Innkeepers: Joan & Jeff Stanford
Highway 1 & Comptche-Ukiah Road
Mendocino, CA 95460
Tel: (707) 937-5615 or (800) 331-8884
Fax: (707) 937-0305
Email: stanford@stanfordinn.com
33 rooms, Double: $235–$425
Open all year, Credit cards: all major
Restaurant, Children welcome
Wheelchair friendly
www.karenbrown.com/california/stanfordinn.html

If you are looking for a place to stay in the heart of Mendocino that absolutely oozes Victorian charm, the Whitegate Inn is definitely for you. This adorable, white clapboard home, built in 1883, is set off from the sidewalk by a white picket fence and, of course, a *white gate*. Inside, you step into an elegant home of the 19th century brimming with antiques. To the right of the entry hall there is a nostalgic, old-fashioned parlor whose decor perfectly captures the Victorian era, with an Oriental carpet, crystal chandelier, dark wood furniture, gilt mirrors, ornate lamps, fancy drapes, knickknacks, bouquets of fresh flowers, and even an upright piano. The parlor opens to a formal dining room where a gourmet breakfast is presented each morning on a beautifully set table using English bone china and sterling silver. The guestrooms also capture the Victorian mood, with patterned carpets, many antique beds, fireplaces, and the clever use of old-fashioned wallpapers. However, except for the fireplaces, feather beds, and fine linens, the bedrooms have jumped into the 21st century with their modern bathrooms, cable television, telephones, cd/clock radios, and queen- or king-sized beds. Despite all these attributes, in my opinion, the inn's most outstanding feature is its gardens—here you find a terrace with lattice gazebo, lacy wrought-iron tables and chairs, and a cobblestone path that winds through a romantic display of gorgeous flowers. *Directions*: Take Highway 101 to Cloverdale, Highway 128 west to the coast, then go 9 miles north on Highway 1 to Mendocino. Turn west at the stoplight (Little Lake Road) then left on Howard Street and proceed two blocks.

WHITEGATE INN
Owners: Carol & George Bechtloff
Manager: Gi Gi Ebner
499 Howard Street, Mendocino, CA 95460
Tel: (707) 937-4892 or (800) 531-7282
Fax: (707) 937-1131
Email: staff@whitegateinn.com
6 rooms, Double: $169–$289
Open all year, Credit cards: all major
No restaurant, Children under 10 welcome in cottage
www.karenbrown.com/california/whitegateinn.html

Ann and Gene Swett converted their family home into what continues to be one of the very nicest country inns in California. Their home is a most attractive Tudor-style house shaded by giant oak trees in an acre of wooded gardens full of colorful begonias, fuchsias, rhododendrons, and lush ferns in a quiet Monterey suburb. Everything is beautifully tended, giving the grounds a parklike appearance. The inside of the house is an oasis of gentility and tranquillity where everything is done with the comfort of the guest in mind. All of the bedrooms in the main house, cottage, and carriage house have fireplaces, and all are beautifully decorated and thoughtfully appointed. The Library stands out as a particularly memorable bedroom with its book-lined walls, cozy fireplace, and private balcony overlooking the garden. A refrigerator is kept stocked with complimentary beverages, and juices and hot beverages are always available. In the evening the Swetts join their guests for wine and cheese in the living room. They are especially gracious hosts, adding great warmth and professionalism to their little inn. A full breakfast is served at the long oak table in the dining room or brought to your room. *Directions:* Traveling south on Highway 1, exit at Soledad/Munras, cross Munras Avenue, then go right on Pacific Street: Martin Street is on the left in a little over ½ mile.

OLD MONTEREY INN
Owners: Ann & Gene Swett
500 Martin Street
Monterey, CA 93940
Tel: (831) 375-8284 or (800) 350-2344
Fax: (831) 375-6730
Email: omi@oldmontereyinn.com
10 rooms, Double: $240–$450
Closed Christmas Day
Credit cards: MC, VS
No restaurant, Children over 12 welcome
www.karenbrown.com/california/oldmontereyinn.html

As an alternative to a bed and breakfast we recommend the Spindrift Inn, a lovely hotel with a great location overlooking the Monterey Bay. Just down the street from the fabulous Monterey Bay Aquarium, its rooms overlook either the bustle of Cannery Row or the serenity of the bay. We stayed in a front room overlooking Cannery Row and were pleasantly surprised to find that the deep-set windows and heavy drapes blocked out the noise of late-night revelers. Guestrooms on the bay side enjoy wonderful water views and corner rooms are spacious and have a lovely window seat. The Spindrift Inn offers 42 bedrooms, each handsomely decorated with rich European fabrics, all with wood-burning fireplaces, beds topped with down comforters and feather beds, and bathrooms finished in marble and brass. The feeling is European and the amenities are first-class. A Continental breakfast of Danish pastries or fresh-baked breads and a selection of fruit is served on a silver tray in the room and in the evening a buffet of wine and cheese is offered in the front lobby. Service is cordial. There is always someone at the front desk in the lobby to assist with information or reservations, but shifts change regularly. This is a hotel—efficient, attractive, and comfortable, with a premier location. *Directions:* Take the Pacific Grove/Del Monte exit off Highway 1. Follow signs to Cannery Row and the Aquarium. The Spindrift is on the right-hand side on Cannery Row.

SPINDRIFT INN
General Manager: Randy Venard
652 Cannery Row, Monterey, CA 93940
Tel: (831) 646-8900 or (800) 841-1879
Fax: (831) 646-5342
Email: reservations@innsofmonterey.com
42 rooms, Double: $199–$429
Open all year, Credit cards: all major
Children welcome (note that only 2 rooms
  accommodate more than 2 people)
Restaurant, Wheelchair friendly
www.karenbrown.com/california/spindriftinn.html

Karen (Brown) Herbert and her husband, Rick, have built their own romantic English manor-style hideaway, Seal Cove Inn. Located just half an hour's drive south of San Francisco, the inn is bordered by towering, windswept cypress trees and looks out over fields of wild flowers and acres of parkland to the ocean. You enter through a spacious entrance hall into an elegantly comfortable living room with a large fireplace centered between French doors. Adjoining the living room is a dining room and next to that, a small conference room—all with park and ocean views. Antiques are used throughout: grandfather clocks, cradles filled with flowers, handsome tables, antique beds, armoires, trunks, etc. Each of the large bedrooms has a wood-burning fireplace, comfortable reading chairs, television, VCR, hot towel rack, and a refrigerator stocked with complimentary soft drinks and wine. Best yet, each of the bedrooms has a view of the distant ocean and doors opening either to a private balcony or onto the terrace. From the inn you can walk to a secluded stretch of beach or stroll through the forest along a path that traces the ocean bluffs. Karen has already had the pleasure of welcoming many guests to Seal Cove Inn who are also readers of her travel guides. *Directions:* From San Francisco take Highway 1 south to Moss Beach (about 20 miles). Turn west on Cypress (at the Moss Beach Distillery sign). Seal Cove Inn is one block off the road on the right.

SEAL COVE INN
Owners: Karen & Rick Herbert
Manager: Dawn Grover
221 Cypress Avenue
Moss Beach, CA 94038
Tel: (650) 728-4114 or (800) 995-9987
Fax: (650) 728-4116
Email: sealcove@coastside.net
10 rooms, Double: $200–$300
Closed Christmas, Credit cards: all major
Children under 12 welcome in garden-level rooms
No restaurant, Wheelchair friendly
www.karenbrown.com/california/sealcoveinn.html

The Pelican Inn, nestled among pine trees, jasmine, and honeysuckle, is a wonderful re-creation of a cozy English tavern with a few attractive guestrooms tucked upstairs. Wide wood-planked floors, an appealing small bar (with dart board), low, beamed ceilings, a giant fireplace with priest hole (secret hiding place), a cozy little guest lounge, and a dining room with trestle tables complete the first-floor scene. Besides the large indoor dining room, there is also a trellised patio where guests can have snacks or dine (in the evenings the candlelit tables are set with linens). Lunch features such English treats as succulent bangers and mash and fish and chips; dinner includes prime rib and rack of lamb. (The restaurant is closed on Mondays from November to April.) Upstairs there are seven cozy bedrooms where the English motif is carried out with heavily draped half-tester beds, Oriental carpets, a decanter of sherry, and fresh flowers. Rooms are small but cozy and reminiscent of a wonderful old English inn. The location of the Pelican Inn is fabulous: only a few minutes' drive from the giant redwood grove at Muir Woods and a short walk to the ocean. Note: Reservations are needed six months in advance for weekends. Also be aware that the pub attracts hundreds of people on weekends and noise from the revelers can persist until the 11 pm closing time. *Directions:* From Highway 101 take the Stinson Beach/Highway 1 turnoff. At the Arco station, go left for 5 miles on Highway 1 to Muir Beach. Pelican Inn is on the left.

PELICAN INN
Owners: Ed & Susan Cunningham
Innkeeper: Katrinka McKay
10 Pacific Way
Muir Beach, CA 94965-9729
Tel: (415) 383-6000, Fax: (415) 383-3424
Email: innkeeper@pelicaninn.com
7 rooms, Double: $202–$240
Closed Christmas, Credit cards: MC, VS
Restaurant closed Monday Nov to Apr
Children welcome
www.karenbrown.com/california/pelicaninn.html

As the gold boom passed, Murphys was left to sleep under its locust and elm trees until tourists discovered its beauty and slower pace of life. A few old stone buildings survive, and one houses the Old Timers' Museum filled with pioneer and Gold Rush regalia. Dunbar House, 1880 is a handsome inn with a wraparound porch where guests can sit and sip Gold-Country wine or enjoy a refreshing glass of lemonade. Bob and Barbara's pride in their small inn is apparent—they have lavished their time and attention on making it extremely comfortable. Each of the cozy guestrooms has a fireplace, a small refrigerator with ice and a bottle of wine, and a TV with VCR hidden away in an armoire. The Sequoia Room has a king-size bed and a claw-foot tub set before a gas stove. The Cedar Room, just off the downstairs parlor, is a suite offering a luxurious Jacuzzi. Upstairs, the Ponderosa Room has a king bed, large claw-foot tub, and views of the garden, and the Sugar Pine Room is a two-room suite with a private balcony shaded by trees. Breakfast, served in the dining room by the fire, in the century-old garden, or in the privacy of your room, includes juice spritzer, fresh fruit, scones, turnovers, a main entree, and a hot beverage. An appetizer buffet is offered in the afternoon. *Directions:* From San Francisco take Highway 580 to Highway 99 north to Highway 4 east, then drive through Angels Camp towards Arnold. Murphys is 9 miles east of Angels Camp. Turn left off Highway 4 to Main Street, go two blocks, and turn left into Dunbar House's driveway.

DUNBAR HOUSE, 1880
Owners: Barbara & Bob Costa
271 Jones Street
Murphys, CA 95247
Tel: (209) 728-2897 or (800) 692-6006
Fax: (209) 728-1451
Email: innkeep@dunbarhouse.com
5 rooms, Double: $155–$215
Open all year, Credit cards: all major
No restaurant, Children over 10 welcome
www.karenbrown.com/california/dunbarhouse.html

La Residence is an inn that has grown around The Mansion—a beautiful Gothic-revival home built in the 1870s as a farmhouse to accommodate the large family of Harry Parker, a riverboat pilot from New Orleans. In later years, additions more Victorian in style changed the appearance of the home. Nine rooms, housed in the original mansion, are dramatic in their décor, which blends well with the grand feeling of the home. Rooms vary from cozy, top-floor rooms tucked under slanted ceilings to spacious and elegant accommodations with fireplaces on the first floor. The 11 rooms in Cabernet Hall, shingled and built in the style of a French barn, are beautifully designed and commodious, each enjoying a private bath, fireplace, and French doors opening onto a patio or balcony. These bedrooms are handsomely decorated with pine antiques imported from France and England and Laura Ashley prints. The gorgeous new suite, smartly decorated in muted shades of yellow with lovely floral fabric, has double French doors and many amenities. Breakfast is served in the Cabernet Hall's lovely dining room with tables set before a blazing fire. On the lovely grounds are two fountains, a heated swimming pool and Jacuzzi spa, and tall trees giving plenty of shade. The excellence of the inn reflects the expertise and talents of the partners who share in the management. *Directions*: Travel north on Highway 29 through Napa. Take the first right turn after the Salvador intersection onto a frontage road (no name) that winds back south to the inn.

LA RESIDENCE
Owners: David Jackson & Craig Claussen
4066 Saint Helena Highway
Napa, CA 94558
Tel: (707) 253-0337 or (800) 253-9203
Fax: (707) 253-0382,
20 rooms, Double: $225–$350
Open all year, Credit cards: all major
No restaurant
Children welcome
Wheelchair friendly
www.karenbrown.com/california/laresidence.html

With 600 acres of vineyards as its backdrop, the Oak Knoll Inn has one of the most idyllic settings in the Napa Valley. You find the entry and prettily decorated front sitting room in the original stone farmhouse. Another building was later added to each side to house guestrooms, each with a private entrance opening onto a wraparound deck overlooking the vineyards. Breakfast is a feast served on winter mornings in front of the stone fireplace and on warm mornings outside on the deck where you can often watch the graceful hot-air balloons as they drift silently over the vineyards in the early-morning sunshine. The guestrooms are luxurious in their size, magnified further by the high vaulted ceilings. My favorite, number 6 (a corner room at the end of the house), has an arched window that towers to the height of the ceiling and offers a splendid view of the vineyards. Each bedroom enjoys a king-size bed, a sitting area before a fireplace, and thick stone walls, which provide efficient insulation. The bedrooms have been individually redecorated with lovely, richly hued fabrics in a traditional style. The Oak Knoll Inn provides the perfect end to a perfect day of sightseeing. After sampling Napa Valley's many vineyards, you can sit poolside with a glass of wine and enjoy the quiet and beauty of a backdrop of vineyards and the valley's gorgeous hills. *Directions:* Go north on Highway 29 through Napa, then right on Oak Knoll Avenue, which has a left-right zigzag across Big Ranch Road. The inn is on the left side.

OAK KNOLL INN
Owners: Barbara Passino & John Kuhlmann
2200 E. Oak Knoll Avenue
Napa, CA 94558
Tel: (707) 255-2200, Fax: (707) 255-2296
4 rooms, Double: $315–$450
Open all year, Credit cards: MC, VS
No restaurant
Children over 14 welcome
www.karenbrown.com/california/oakknollinn.html

Chuck and Elaine Matroni are always ready to serve, spoil, and pamper guests in their three-story, soft-blue Queen Ann Victorian home, tiered on a hillside above gardens and lawn cascading down to the babbling Deer Creek. The parlors and dining room are typically Victorian with their formal furnishings and Oriental accents. The country kitchen is the heart of the home, where guests gather to chat to the innkeepers as they prepare their gourmet, multi-course breakfast, which is served either in the dining room or outside on the verandah. Deer Creek has five guestrooms, each named for the women who have owned the home since 1860. Sheryl's Room is a cheerful front corner room whose iron bed is set on an Oriental carpet. Lela's Room boasts a dramatic four-poster bed and a claw-foot tub framed in an alcove, romantically draped with lace curtains. Winifred's Room features a canopied bed, an in-room claw-foot tub, and a private deck. The antique oak furniture in Ida's Room is lovely against a floral backdrop and the trundle bed accompanying the white and brass day bed comfortably accommodates an additional person. Elaine's Room enjoys a lace-draped bed, a large Roman tub, and a private patio overlooking the grounds and the creek. *Directions*: Exit Highway 20/49 at Broad Street, traveling south across the creek. Turn left on Nevada Street. The inn is located just up the street on the right.

DEER CREEK INN
Owners: Elaine & Chuck Matroni
116 Nevada Street
Nevada City, CA 95959
Tel: (530) 265-0363 or (800) 655-0363
Fax: (530) 265-0980
Email: deercreek@gv.net
5 rooms, Double: $110–$170
Open all year
Credit cards: all major
No restaurant, Children over 13 welcome
www.karenbrown.com/california/deercreekinn.html

This lovely Victorian at the top of Broad Street, childhood home of 19th-century opera star Emma Nevada, is very charming with a soft-peach façade trimmed in white set behind a white picket fence bounded by roses. Guestrooms open off public areas that are central to the inn. The first guestroom off the entrance, Nightingale's Bower, was formerly the parlor and enjoys a bay window, gas fireplace, elegant Italian bedding, and Jacuzzi tub. Mignon's Boudoir, which has a fireplace, is luxurious in size but quite cozy with its French-country decor and Laura Ashley prints. A claw-foot tub in the bathroom is painted blue to cleverly match the decor and a sink is set in a beautiful antique cabinet. Laura's favorite is the ground-floor Empress's Chamber with its wealth of light streaming through a wall of windows and bath with Jacuzzi tub. At the top of the stairs are three additional cozy rooms—Mockingbird's Nest overlooking the front garden, Palmer's Loft whose ceilings and walls still have the handsome bead boarding original to the house, and Emma's Hideaway, a secluded room set under a steeply pitched roof. Public areas are also very attractive, with many windows. A full breakfast may be taken in the formal dining room, on the back deck under the shade of a 140-year-old cherry tree, or in the Sun Room with its interesting tower ceiling. *Directions*: Take the Broad Street exit off Highway 49, turn left and go up the hill. When the road splits, continue on Broad Street to the right.

EMMA NEVADA HOUSE
Owner: Laura Du Pée
528 E. Broad Street
Nevada City, CA 95959
Tel: (530) 265-4415 or (800) 916-3662 (EMMA)
Fax: (530) 265-4416
Email: mail@emmanevadahouse.com
6 rooms, Double: $110–$165
Open all year
Credit cards: all major
No restaurant, Children over 10 welcome
www.karenbrown.com/california/emmanevadahouse.html

When gold was discovered, Nevada City became an affluent boomtown. It remains prosperous-looking today, its beautifully restored downtown area full of tempting restaurants and inviting shops. Just beyond Broad Street's historic shopping district, enclosed within a mature garden of long rolling lawns, tidy bushes, and flowers, sits Grandmere's Inn, a stately Colonial Revival home built in 1856 for Aaron Sargent, a U.S. Senator, and his suffragette wife, Ellen, whose friend, Susan B. Anthony, often stayed here. Sargent authored the bill that eventually gave women the right to vote. Now Grandmere's is a lovely country inn decorated with flair, and each of the rooms has a very different personality. The Senator's Chambers is a delightful ground-floor suite with a lovely bedroom and a separate parlor with sofa drawn before the fireplace. The Diplomat's Suite is a spacious upstairs bedroom with a sitting area. Ellen's Garden Room, a romantic downstairs hideaway, has a private garden entry, light, airy decor, and lots of room. In the morning the aroma of coffee fills the air and at 9 o'clock the sideboard is loaded with breakfast goodies for the buffet breakfast. Enjoy the romance of Nevada City by taking a carriage ride round the town. You are spoilt for choice of places to eat in the evening and everything in town is within easy walking distance. *Directions*: From the San Francisco area, take the I-80 to 49 north 29 miles to Nevada City. Exit at Broad Street. Turn left and the inn is at the top of the street, on the left.

GRANDMERE'S INN
Managers: Sharon Rose & Stephano Woods
449 Broad Street
Nevada City, CA 95959
Tel: (530) 265-4660, Fax: (530) 265-4561
Email: grandmeresinn.com
6 rooms, Double: $125–$190
Open all year
Credit cards: all major
No restaurant
Children over 15 welcome
www.karenbrown.com/california/grandmeres.html

Heavy iron gates swing open magically, allowing you to enter a world far removed from the everyday activity of Oakhurst, a town just to the south of Yosemite National Park. You enter through the château's heavy doors, cross a cool, flagged limestone foyer, and step down into a stunning living room opening onto a circular tower room where a grand piano sits center stage beneath a whimsically frescoed ceiling. Doors open to reveal a sunny breakfast room and a tiny chapel. A spiraling stone staircase leads up to the individually decorated bedrooms named for herbs and flowers: Saffron has an enormous ebony bed and black-marble fireplace; Lavender is sunny in colors of periwinkle blue and lavender; and Elderberry is cool in blue and white. Each of the splendid bedrooms has a wood-burning fireplace (placed at just the right height to see it from the bed), goose-down duvet, hidden CD player, luxurious bathroom with a deep soaking tub (many large enough for two), the finest toiletries, thick towels, and the softest of robes. In the evening, walk across the garden, by the swimming pool, to the Elderberry House Restaurant where the château's owner, Erna Kubin-Clanin, presents a spectacular fixed-price six-course dinner. A beautiful new villa offers two luxurious bedrooms. *Directions:* From the center of Oakhurst take Highway 41 toward Fresno. As the road climbs the hill, turn right at Victoria Lane and drive in through the wrought-iron gates.

CHÂTEAU DU SUREAU
Owner: Erna Kubin-Clanin, Manager: Lucy Royse
48688 Victoria Lane
P.O. Box 577, Oakhurst, CA 93644
Tel: (559) 683-6860, Fax: (559) 683-0800
Email: chateau@chateausureau.com
10 rooms, 1 villa, Double: $325–$510,
  suite: $1,000–$1,500, villa: $2,500, 12% service charge
Closed first two weeks of January
Credit cards: all major, Restaurant
Children over 12 welcome, Wheelchair friendly
Relais & Châteaux Member
www.karenbrown.com/california/chateaudusureau.html

Occidental nestles between the rugged Sonoma coast and the vineyards of the Russian River valley. The Inn at Occidental, a block up from Main Street, dates from 1877. From the wraparound porch you enter the living room whose elegant furnishings are set in front of an inviting wood-burning fireplace. The dining room where breakfast is served is located in the wine cellar. Breakfast offerings include freshly baked pastries, seasonal fruit, and such tempting delights as orange-thyme pancakes. Beautiful fir floors accented with lovely Oriental carpets are found throughout the public rooms of the inn. The decor of each guestroom is taken from the colors in the original art displayed in the room and feather beds topped with European down comforters assure the guest of a wonderful night's sleep. Recently remodeled and with an addition of an entire new suite of rooms, the inn now has 16 rooms with appealing amenities such as a romantic fireplace, a hot tub in a private garden oasis, or a luxurious spa tub. A neighboring cottage is perfect for a family or long-term stay. Conference facilities are available in a downstairs room with antique pine furnishings and stone fireplace. Jack and his staff make this inn so very special. *Directions:* One hour north of San Francisco—take Highway 101 to Highway 116 west to Sebastopol. Then take the Bodega Highway west for 6 miles toward Bodega Bay to the Bohemian Highway to Occidental.

THE INN AT OCCIDENTAL
Owners: Jack, Bill & Jean Bullard
3657 Church Street, Occidental, CA 95465
Tel: (707) 874-1047 or (800) 522-6324
Fax: (707) 874-1078
Email: innkeeper@innatoccidental.com
16 rooms, 1 cottage, Double: $195–$320,
  cottage: $560–$600
Open all year, Credit cards: all major
No restaurant, but special wine-maker dinners
Children over 12 welcome
Wheelchair friendly
www.karenbrown.com/california/innatoccidental.html

Sandwiched between the busier resorts of Monterey and Carmel, Pacific Grove has managed to avoid much of their more touristy ambiance and retains the air of being an inviting Victorian summer retreat. The Gosby House Inn is a perfect place to retreat to, with certainly a lot more fun and frolic than in days gone by when it was the summer home of a stern Methodist family. While the decor is decidedly Victorian in flavor, it has been done with such whimsy and fun that all formal stuffiness has been dispelled: a glass-fronted cabinet in the dining room is filled with antique dolls and teddy bears are posed rakishly on each bed. The bedrooms are scattered upstairs and down, some have garden entrances and several occupy an adjacent clapboard house tucked behind the pretty garden. Over half the bedrooms have fireplaces and all but two have luxuriously appointed bathrooms. Each room is appealingly decorated in soft colors and many benefit from the romantic touch of antique beds. Before you venture out for dinner, enjoy hors d'oeuvres and wine in the living room. When you return, your bed will be turned down and chocolates placed on your pillow—such a sweet way to end the day. A full breakfast is set out downstairs between 8 and 10 every morning. *Directions:* Take Highway 1 to Highway 68 west to Pacific Grove. Continue on Forest Avenue to Lighthouse Avenue, turn left, and go three blocks to the inn.

GOSBY HOUSE INN
Innkeeper: Kalena Mittelman
643 Lighthouse Avenue
Pacific Grove, CA 93950
Tel: (831) 375-1287 or (800) 527-8828
Fax: (831) 655-9621,
22 rooms, 20 with private bathrooms
Double: $90–$170
Open all year
Credit cards: all major
No restaurant, Children welcome
www.karenbrown.com/california/gosbyhouse.html

The Green Gables Inn is sensationally positioned overlooking Monterey Bay. This romantic, half-timbered, Queen Anne-style mansion with many interesting dormers is as inviting inside as out. The living room and dining room have comfortable arrangements of sofas and chairs placed to maximize your enjoyment of the view. Upstairs many of the bedrooms, set under steeply slanting beamed ceilings with romantic diamond-paned casement windows, offer ocean views. While the Garret room does not have an ocean view, it is the coziest of hideaways. All but one of the upstairs bedrooms share bathrooms. The ground-floor suite has a sitting room and fireplace. The rooms in the adjacent carriage house all have fireplaces, sitting areas, and private bathrooms. While a guest at The Green Gables Inn you will certainly not perish from hunger or thirst—beverages are available all day, goodies are readily at hand in the cookie jar, and wine and hors d'oeuvres appear in the evening. Breakfast, too, is no disappointment: a hearty buffet of fruit, homemade breads, and a hot egg dish. *Directions:* From Highway 1 take the Pacific Grove-Del Monte exit. As you go through the tunnel, Del Monte becomes Lighthouse Avenue, which you follow into Pacific Grove. Go right one block and you are on Ocean View Boulevard—the inn is on the corner at Fifth Street.

THE GREEN GABLES INN
Innkeeper: Lucia Root
104 Fifth Street
Pacific Grove, CA 93950
Tel: (831) 375-2095 or (800) 722-1774
Fax: (831) 375-5437
11 rooms, 7 with private bathrooms
Double: $120–$260
Open all year, Credit cards: all major
No restaurant, Children welcome
Wheelchair friendly
www.karenbrown.com/california/greengablesinn.html

Casa Cody, a moderately priced hotel in the heart of Palm Springs, although quite simple, stands out like a gem. The one-story inn has three U-shaped garden courtyards, two with their own swimming pool. There is a nostalgic, old-fashioned comfort to this pink-stuccoed building with turquoise trim. Once owned by Wild Bill Cody's cousin, Casa Cody (the oldest continuously functioning hotel in Palm Springs) had fallen into a state of hopeless-looking disrepair until bought by Therese Hayes (who is French) and Frank Tysen (who is Dutch). After hard work, lots of imagination, and much love, the hotel once again blossomed into an appealing small hotel with a nice choice of accommodations ranging from a standard double to a spacious two-bedroom, two-bath suite. Many of the rooms have the added bonuses of kitchenettes and fireplaces. The interior decor exudes a fresh, clean "Santa Fe" look, with a southwest color scheme and handmade furniture. This friendly, comfortable inn is a remarkable value, especially the reasonably priced studio units such as 1, 2, 3, 4, 21, and 23, which have both fireplaces and well-equipped kitchens. We loved the 1920s doll-house-like, one-bedroom cottage (with kitchen) tucked in under the trees in the corner of the property. Our favorite is the two-bedroom Old Adobe House—where Charlie Chaplin used to stay. *Directions:* Drive south through Palm Springs on Palm Canyon Drive. Turn right on Tahquitz-McCallum Road, then left on Cahuilla Road, and Casa Cody is half a block along on the right.

CASA CODY
Owners: Therese Hayes & Frank Tysen
Innkeeper: Elissa Goforth
175 South Cahuilla Road
Palm Springs, CA 92262
Tel: (760) 320-9346, Fax: (760) 325-8610
Email: casacody@aol.com
22 rooms, 2 cottages, Double: $79–$349
Open all year, Credit cards: all major
No restaurant, Children welcome in most rooms
Wheelchair friendly
www.karenbrown.com/california/casacody.html

Stopping to chat with a delightful couple lounging by the pool, I was amazed to learn that this was their 36th season of vacationing at the Desert Hills Hotel. Actually, after a tour of the hotel I was not surprised to find the majority of guests return each year. Along with the scent of flowers, a gentle, friendly ambiance permeates the air, enhanced by the charming graciousness of your hostess, Joanne Petty, who built the hotel with her husband in 1956. The location is excellent—an easy walk to the heart of Old Palm Springs and yet snuggled up against the rugged San Jacinto Mountains. The hotel does not have an antique ambiance, but rather a timeless theme of restful, pleasing pastel desert colors. The spotlessly tidy guestrooms (most with kitchenettes) are attractive, with liberal use of rattan furniture, comfortable chairs, excellent lighting, and quality mattresses. The rooms face a lush lawn and well-tended gardens surrounding a pretty pool. From the outside the one-story Desert Hills looks like most of the other hotels of similar vintage on the street—you only realize its uniqueness when you see that every detail shows loving care. The Desert Hills is not a flashy, trendy hotel that would appeal to those looking for action, but rather the old-fashioned kind of tranquil oasis where you can settle in for an extended time, relaxing by the pool, hearing the wind whisper through the palm trees, and feeling like a friend of the family. Guests enjoy Continental breakfast, outdoor barbeques, a hot whirlpool, and bicycles. *Directions:* Turn west off Palm Canyon on Arenas and go six blocks—the hotel is on the northwest corner of Arenas.

DESERT HILLS HOTEL
Owners: Joanne & Alan Petty
601 West Arenas Road, Palm Springs, CA 92262
Tel: (760) 325-2777 or (800) 350-2527
Fax: (760) 325-6423
Email: deshils@aol.com
14 rooms, Double: $75–$180
Open all year, Credit cards: all major
No restaurant, Inappropriate for children
Wheelchair friendly
www.karenbrown.com/california/deserthillshotel.html

As you enter the large wrought-iron gates of the Ingleside Inn, you have the impression of being the guest on a private estate. This is not surprising, since the Ingleside Inn was once the home of the Humphrey Birge family, manufacturers of the Pierce Arrow automobile. Although the hotel is located in the heart of Palm Springs, it is an oasis of tranquillity. The parklike grounds are surrounded by a high adobe wall and the San Jacinto Mountains rise steeply behind the hotel, forming a dramatic backdrop. A pretty pool and gazebo highlight the front lawn. Some of the guestrooms open off an inner courtyard, while others are nestled in nearby cottages. Each room is individually decorated with antiques. All have whirlpool tubs, coffee makers, and refrigerators stocked with complimentary light snacks and juices. Many rooms have the added bonus of wood-burning fireplaces. Breakfast is served either on the verandah, poolside, or on your private patio. The owner of Ingleside Inn, Melvyn Haber, also owns one of the famous restaurants in Palm Springs, appropriately called "Melvyn's," which is located next to the lobby. In the evening the restaurant traffic intrudes somewhat upon the solitude, but it is wonderfully convenient to have such an excellent restaurant so close at hand. *Directions:* From Los Angeles on Highway 10 East exit to Highway 111 and proceed for 12 miles. Turn right on Ramon Road.

INGLESIDE INN
Owner: Melvyn Haber
200 West Ramon Road
Palm Springs, CA 92264
Tel: (760) 325-0046 or (800) 772-6655
Fax: (760) 325-0710
Email: ingleside@earthlink.net
29 rooms, Double: $95–$400
Open all year, Credit cards: all major
Restaurant
Inappropriate for children
Wheelchair friendly
www.karenbrown.com/california/inglesideinn.html

The magic of the desert can best be captured on balmy, starlit nights from the bougainvillea-shrouded patios of intimate hotels with the laid-back style and grace of yesterday. A rare example of such perfection is the Korakia Pensione, a 1920s Moorish-style villa just four blocks from the heart of Palm Springs, which was rescued from dilapidation by Doug Smith, an architect specializing in restoring historic buildings. With a backdrop of the San Jacinto Mountains, this delightful inn has the flavor of Morocco mingled with the romance of the Greek islands: simple whitewashed walls, Oriental carpets, handmade furniture, lovely natural fabrics, antiques, Moroccan fountains, fragrant fruit trees, torches blazing by the pools, and bougainvillea-draped archways create a stunning ambiance. Bedrooms mostly offer lots of privacy and are found around two swimming pools either in the original Moroccan-style pension or across the street in the Mediterranean-style villa. Know that you deserve the best and request our favorite rooms, the Nash House (part of a 1930s villa that belonged to movie star J. Carol Nash) or the Artist Studio (rumor has it Winston Churchill painted here). Private dinners created by Korakia's own chef are available Thursday through Sunday nights, served either in the room or poolside, and you can also enjoy old black-and-white movies outdoors on a Saturday night, a relaxing massage, Moroccan tea in the afternoon, and breakfast on the sun-drenched patio. *Directions:* Turn west off Palm Canyon on Arenas, go four blocks, and turn south on Patencio Road.

KORAKIA PENSIONE   New
Owner: Doug Smith
Manager: Melissa McDaniel
257 South Patencio Road
Palm Springs, CA 92262
Tel: (760) 864-6411, Fax: (760) 864-4147
22 rooms, Double: $119–$395
Open all year, Credit cards: MC, VS
No restaurant
Inappropriate for children, Wheelchair friendly
www.karenbrown.com/california/korakia.html

Once a sleepy desert town, Palm Springs was discovered in the 1920s by glamorous movie stars who made it their secret hideaway. This balmy paradise also captivated the heart of Samuel Untermyer, a New Yorker and famous anti-trust lawyer of the time, who bought a beautiful estate, The Willows, snuggled next to the mountains just a few blocks from the center of town, where in winter he entertained many distinguished friends. The home remained a private residence until opening in 1996 as a deluxe small hotel after total renovation, which returned it to its former elegance and successfully captured the ambiance of the 30s. The clay-colored building with wrought-iron trim and red-tiled roof is softened by a profusion of greenery and brightened by a cheerful array of colorful flowers. A pool nestles on the lower garden area—but an equally inviting nook for a refreshing drink is a beautiful flagstone terrace enclosed on one side by a wall of natural rock with a cascading waterfall. Every lovely guestroom has its own personality, with the price basically reflecting its size. The rates are expensive, but you will feel like guests in a private home displaying the opulence of a bygone era. *Directions:* Located in the heart of Palm Springs. From either Palm Canyon Drive or Indian Canyon Drive, take Tahquitz Canyon Way west. In a few blocks the street dead-ends. The Willows is at the end of the road on your right.

THE WILLOWS
Owners: Tracy Conrad & Paul Marut
412 West Tahquitz Canyon Way
Palm Springs, CA 92262
Tel: (760) 320-0771 or (800) 966-9597
Fax: (760) 320-0780
Email: innkeeper@thewillowspalmsprings.com
8 rooms, Double: $295–$550
Open all year
Credit cards: all major
No restaurant
Inappropriate for children
www.karenbrown.com/california/thewillows.html

When the last of Janet Marangi's four children left the nest, she fulfilled her dream of opening a small bed and breakfast. Just two blocks from the colorful center of South Pasadena, she found an 1895 Victorian-style farmhouse, built by a settler from Indiana for his family. The house is painted a pretty buttercup-yellow, accented by white trim. A white picket fence and old-fashioned swinging gate enclose a perfectly groomed front lawn. One hundred rose bushes line the fence and border the path leading to the spacious front porch. Janet's goal was to instill a totally comfortable, homey ambiance, re-creating happy memories of visits to grandmother's house. She has succeeded. The furnishings are mostly pieces lovingly collected over the years by Janet while browsing for antiques. The living room is painted a rich green, which sets off the traditional furniture and rich floral fabrics. The nine bedrooms are appealingly decorated, each representing an artistic period. Niceties such as fresh roses, water, port, European candy, and English towels are found in all rooms. The Eighteenth-Century English is a cheerful room with king-sized canopy bed, old-fashioned rose-patterned wallpaper, antique desk, and white lace curtains. Of the nine rooms, five are in the adjacent cottage: three are two-room suites with fireplaces, Jacuzzi tubs, and canopy beds. *Directions*: Fifteen minutes from downtown Los Angeles. Take Highway 110 (Pasadena Freeway), exiting at the Orange Grove off-ramp. Turn right on Orange Grove, go two blocks, and turn left on Magnolia.

THE ARTISTS' INN
Owner: Janet Marangi
Managers: Debi & Jeff Vine
1038 Magnolia Street
South Pasadena, CA 91030
Tel: (626) 799-5668 or (888) 799-5668
Fax: (626) 799-3678
Email: artistsinn@artistsinns.com
9 rooms, Double: $115–$205
Open all year, Credit cards: all major
No restaurant, Inappropriate for children
www.karenbrown.com/california/theartistsinn.html

Built in the 1880s for the renowned carpet-cleaner family, this is a lovely three-story home with dormer windows and wraparound porch set on a lush lawn shaded by mature trees, just 12 minutes from downtown Los Angeles. On one side of the entry you find the cozy library decorated in dark greens and plaids looking out onto the swimming pool and on the other side, through French doors, is the formal living room with its piano and sofas set in front of the fireplace. Central to the living room, the hand-carved wood fireplace opens up at the back so that it also warms the adjacent breakfast room. Just beyond the dining room it is fun to peek into the butler's pantry whose tin roof is original to the home and whose shelves display a lovely collection of Christmas Spode. The Prince Albert and English Holiday rooms are on the second floor and each has lovely old wooden floors, queen beds, and private bath. The third floor boasts three romantic accommodations tucked under the eaves. Thoughtful amenities like a communal refrigerator stocked with complimentary refreshments, cookies, and brownies as well as in-room touches such as large fluffy towels, robes, fresh flowers, and a basket of fruit make you feel very welcome and cared for. *Directions*: From either the 134, 210, or 110 freeways, take the Orange Grove Avenue exit. The Bissell House is located on Pasadena's historical Millionaires' Row on the southwest corner of Orange Grove and Columbia. The entrance is on Columbia.

THE BISSELL HOUSE
Owners: Russ, Leonore & Ivis Butcher
201 Orange Grove Avenue
South Pasadena, CA 91030
Tel: (626) 441-3535
Fax: (626) 441-3671
5 rooms, Double: $125–$175
Open all year
Credit cards: all major
No restaurant
Inappropriate for children

Justin Winery has a glorious setting, tucked in gently rolling hills 15 miles west of Paso Robles. The property is owned by Deborah and Justin Baldwin who left their banking careers in Southern California and moved to this secluded paradise with their two children, Evan and Morgane. The latest enhancement to their successful wine-growing venture is the addition of a very special inn. The complex (consisting of the tasting room, the Baldwins' home, reception, boutique, restaurant, and guestrooms) is beautiful and the setting is serene. The attractive wooden buildings are painted a dove gray, accented by white trim, and set off to perfection by lush lawn and well-tended gardens. The three suites (the Tuscany, the Provence, and the Sussex) combine the luxury and amenities of a five-star hotel with the friendliness of a family-run inn. The suites feature European antiques, fine fabrics, feather beds, imported linens, down comforters, frescoed ceilings, flower-filled windowboxes, marble bathrooms with hydro spas, and wood-burning fireplaces. The Sussex suite (the largest of the three) opens onto the garden while the Provence and Tuscany suites have balconies where you can sip a glass of wine while looking over the vineyards. Guests also have the use of the pretty swimming pool tucked in the garden. Amazingly for such a small inn, there is a restaurant, Deborah's Dining Room, which is open every night. In this cozy, elegantly decorated dining room a gourmet set dinner is served nightly. *Directions*: From Highway 101, at Paso Robles, exit at 24th Street. Turn right at Naciemiento Lake Road, then left on Chimney Rock Road.

JUST INN
Owners: Deborah & Justin Baldwin
11680 Chimney Rock Road
Paso Robles, CA 93446
Tel: (805) 238-6932 or (800) 226-0044
Fax: (805) 238-7382
Email: DeborahBaldwin@justinwine.com
3 suites: Double: $245–$295
Open all year, Credit cards: all major
Restaurant, Children over 12 welcome
www.karenbrown.com/california/justinn.html

As in the best bed and breakfasts, Deborah and Douglas Thomsen welcome guests with genuine hospitality and pamper them with individual attention. However, Orchard Hill Farm offers more elegance and professionalism than is often found in small bed and breakfasts. Instead of sharing the house with their hosts, guests have their own "home," a carriage house where they can come and go at leisure. The living room of the carriage house has a sophisticated California-western theme. One of the bedrooms has the same western motif while the other sports a Ralph Lauren look with bold-patterned floral fabrics and dark wicker furniture. Each room enjoys its own sitting area in addition to sharing the central living room. Everything looks decorator-perfect, which is not surprising as Deborah was a successful interior designer in Santa Ana before she and Douglas left the hectic Orange County lifestyle to build their dream home in these serenely beautiful rolling hills. You wind up the hill to the elegant main house crowning the knoll, with sweeping views of the unspoiled countryside. As you approach, a gate slowly swings open and you continue on up to a large, two-story, gabled manor constructed of wood, stucco, and stone. Just steps away is the guest house. Deborah not only prepares a full breakfast each morning, but also delights in assisting her guests plan their daily itinerary—with a selection of about 60 fascinating wineries in the area, you need a bit of help! *Directions*: From Highway 101, at Paso Robles take Highway 46 west for 8 miles. Turn right on Vineyard Drive for 2½ miles. The entrance is on your left.

ORCHARD HILL FARM
Owners: Deborah & Douglas Thomsen
5415 Vineyard Drive
Paso Robles, CA 93446
Tel: (805) 239-9680, Fax: (805) 239-9684
2 rooms, Double: $135–$175
Open all year
Credit cards: all major
No restaurant
Children over 12 welcome
www.karenbrown.com/california/orchardhillfarm.html

The newly built Summerwood Inn, with its nostalgic charm of a lovely country English-style home, makes an ideal choice if you want to stop en route between San Francisco and Southern California. Its setting is superb—nestled in a spectacularly beautiful area of gently rolling hills, either covered with vineyards or dotted with oak trees. You enter the long, low, white frame home with its old-fashioned wraparound porch and overhanging roof through large double doors into a spacious entry hall. To the left is a formal dining room, to the right is a sun-filled living room—bright and cheerful with sofas and chairs covered in colorful English-style fabrics. In the morning guests can choose from five items on the breakfast menu. Wine and cheese are served in the afternoon, and coffee or tea and a dessert at night. The guestrooms, all large and individually decorated, have a mood of comfortable elegance. Each bedroom has either a private terrace or balcony that looks out over the Summerwood vineyards (my personal favorites are the rooms in the rear that have the most expansive views) and a beautifully appointed bathroom. All of the rooms have their own gas log fireplaces. The adjacent Summerwood Winery has a gift shop and offers wine tasting. However, the Summerwood Inn is not only convenient for wine tasting, but also makes a good base for visiting Hearst Castle, which is just a short drive away by a scenic road. *Directions*: From Highway 101, at Paso Robles take Highway 46 west for 1¼ miles. Summerwood Inn is on your right.

SUMMERWOOD INN
Innkeeper: Andrea Boatman
2130 Arbor Road
Paso Robles, CA 93447
Tel: (805) 227-1111
Fax: (805) 227-1112
9 rooms, Double: $185–$285
Open all year, Credit cards: all major
No restaurant
Children over 12 welcome
Wheelchair friendly

Petaluma is a charming agricultural town situated on the Petaluma River, which feeds into San Francisco Bay. On a residential street, the Cavanagh Inn is within walking distance of the historic downtown area with its multitude of antique shops and the river. Accommodations are in two neighboring neoclassic Victorian homes sharing a lawn shaded by a large magnolia tree and enclosed by a white picket fence. The main home was built in 1902 as a family residence and the cottage added on in 1912. The main home is lovely, handsome, and rich, with redwood floors and walls. Just off the entry are the library and parlor with chairs set in front of an open fireplace and a dining room opening onto the back porch and garden. Climb a beautiful staircase to reach a stunning, octagonal, redwood-paneled landing. Four guestrooms open onto the landing where you will find a library of good books. The guestrooms in the house are very comfortable and homey, all with a private bath or shower. The three rooms in the cottage enjoy a welcoming sun porch and are smaller, with calico rather than Victorian decor. The twin-bedded room has a private bath, while the other two share a bath. A gourmet breakfast is offered to all in the dining room of the main house and each afternoon wine from one of the many Sonoma wineries is served. *Directions:* Heading north or south on Highway 101, exit at Washington Street West. On Washington Street, cross Petaluma Boulevard, then turn left on Keller Street. The inn is on the left side.

CAVANAGH INN
Owners: Jeanne & Ray Farris
10 Keller Street
Petaluma, CA 94952
Tel: (707) 765-4657 or (888) 765-4658
Fax: (707) 769-0466
Email: info@cavanaghinn.com
7 rooms, 5 with private bathrooms
Double: $100–$150
Open all year, Credit cards: all major
No restaurant, Children over 12 welcome
www.karenbrown.com/california/cavanaghinn.html

People simply driving by the Inn at Playa del Rey would probably not be drawn inside by the inn's exterior and location on a busy road. However, this newly constructed Cape Cod-style inn backs onto the Ballona Wetlands, a 350-acre bird sanctuary, and was beautifully designed to complement rather than compete with the setting and natural surroundings. Large picture windows frame a panorama of a grassy expanse of wetlands and distant marina. A narrow channel banded by an inviting bike path weaves a passage through the wetlands, often navigated by tall-masted boats charting a course to the ocean. The decor is light and airy, with pine furnishings matched with lovely fabrics and attractive wallpapers. The spacious guestrooms are each individual in style and floor plan, and maximize any opportunity to incorporate views. The choice rooms are, of course, those at the back of the inn with unobstructed views of the wetlands. These also have luxury baths stocked with Bulgari soaps. Rooms at the front are less expensive and enjoy the morning light while dual-glazed and shuttered windows minimize the noise of traffic. Public areas include a front, central outdoor courtyard and a lovely breakfast room and living room running the length of the back of the building, banked by handsome French doors. For the business traveler, there is also a computer center with Internet access, computer, printer, and fax. *Directions:* Exit off the San Diego Freeway (405) onto the Marina Freeway (90) and travel west toward Marina del Rey. The freeway ends at a stoplight at Culver Blvd. Turn left and proceed west for 2 miles to the inn.

INN AT PLAYA DEL REY
Owner: Susan Zolla
Innkeeper: Donna Donnelly
435 Culver Boulevard, Playa del Rey, CA 90293
Tel: (310) 574-1920, Fax: (310) 574-9920
Email: playainn@aol.com
21 rooms, Double: $160–$350
Open all year, Credit cards: all major
No restaurant, Children welcome
Wheelchair friendly
www.karenbrown.com/california/innatplayadelrey.html

The East Brother Light Station, sitting snugly on its own tiny island, dates back to 1873 when it was built to guide ships through a 2-mile-wide strait connecting San Francisco and San Pablo Bays. Adjoining the tower beacon, a small house with gingerbread trim was built for the lightkeepers and their families. This nostalgic lighthouse was doomed for destruction until a group of concerned citizens banded together in 1979, raised the funds, and rescued it. As a boy, one of the saviors, Walter Fanning, spent many happy hours at the East Brother Light Station, where his grandfather was the lighthouse keeper. Today, a few lucky guests enjoy the island in far more comfortable circumstances than the keepers of old. Guests are brought by boat in the afternoon, treated to a champagne tour and delicious four-course dinner with wines, then lulled to sleep by the sound of a foghorn. There are five pleasantly decorated guestrooms, all with a view of the bay. The innkeepers, Ann and Gary, live on the island, prepare the meals, and graciously tend to the needs of their guests. Because all the water is caught from rainfall and is limited, only guests staying more than one night may use the showers. *Directions:* The East Brother Light Station, located in San Pablo Bay, is reached by boat. When you call for reservations, ask for further information.

EAST BROTHER LIGHT STATION
Innkeepers: Captain Gary & First Mate Ann
117 Park Place
Point Richmond, CA 94801
Tel: (510) 233-2385 or (510) 812-1207
Fax: (510) 291-2243
Email: ebls@ricochet.net
5 rooms, 2 with private bathrooms
Double: $290–$390*
*Includes breakfast & dinner with wine
Open all year, Thursday to Sunday
Credit cards: all major, Restaurant for guests only
Children by special arrangement
www.karenbrown.com/california/eastbrother.html

The known history of the Rancho Santa Fe property dates back to 1845 when an 8,842-acre land grant was given to Juan Maria Osuna. In 1906 the Santa Fe Railroad purchased the land grant, changed the name to Rancho Santa Fe, and planted about three million eucalyptus seedlings with the idea of growing wood for railroad ties. The project failed: the wood was not appropriate, so the railroad decided instead to develop a planned community and built a lovely Spanish-style guesthouse for prospective home buyers. This became the nucleus for what is now the Inn at Rancho Santa Fe and houses the lounge, dining rooms, offices, and a few of the guestrooms. The lounge is extremely appealing, like a beautiful living room in a private home, with a large fireplace, comfortable seating, impressive floral arrangements, and a roaring fire. The dining rooms have a cozy atmosphere. The grounds are lovely, filled with flowers and shaded by fragrant eucalyptus trees. Here you find our favorite rooms tucked away in cottages, ranging in size from a snug queen-bedded room with private patio (a standard room) to a luxurious three-bedroom house. We especially loved the rooms with a private patio and fireplace, though have to admit we were smitten by room 133, a tiny little cottage. Slip away to the inn's beachhouse in nearby Del Mar or enjoy the pool and tennis courts on the property. Close by is the village of Rancho Santa Fe with its attractive shops and restaurants. *Directions:* From San Diego go north for 25 miles on I-5, take the Lomas Santa Fe Drive turnoff east, and travel 4-2/10 miles to the inn.

INN AT RANCHO SANTA FE
Owner: Duncan Royce Hadden
5951 Linea del Cielo at Paseo Delicias
P.O. Box 869, Rancho Santa Fe, CA 92067
Tel: (858) 756-1131 or (800) 843-4661
Fax: (858) 759-1604,
77 rooms, Double: $130–$700
Breakfast: $10–$15 per person
Open all year, Credit cards: all major
Restaurant, Children welcome, Wheelchair friendly
www.karenbrown.com/california/innatranchosantafe.html

Rancho Valencia Resort is a luxurious Relais & Châteaux hotel tucked away in the hills above Rancho Santa Fe minutes from the picturesque seaside town of Del Mar. This tranquil, secluded hideaway offers privacy, relaxation, and recreation on a very intimate scale. Sports enthusiasts love it here, for the resort has 18 tennis courts and privileges at exclusive private golf clubs. Garden paths bordered by an abundance of flowers wind through the grounds to the 20 *casitas* scattered throughout the property. One is a luxurious three-bedroom home while the rest are either spacious studios or suites. All have cathedral ceilings with exposed beams, lovely fireplaces, plantation-shuttered windows, and French doors leading to private garden patios. The heart of the property is the clubhouse with its central courtyard patios set with tables amidst terra-cotta pots overflowing with flowering plants. Rancho Valencia's signature restaurant offers casual, elegant dining inside and alfresco dining on the tiered terrace overlooking the tennis courts and the valley. *Directions*: From the Interstate 5 in Del Mar, take the Via de la Valley Road east to San Dieguito Road and follow signs to the resort.

RANCHO VALENCIA RESORT
Director: Michael Ullman
5921 Valencia Circle
P.O. Box 9126
Rancho Santa Fe, CA 92067
Tel: (858) 756-1123 or (800) 548-3664
Fax: (858) 756-0165
Email: reservations@ranchovalencia.com
*43 suites, Double: $450–$770**
**Breakfast not included*
Open all year
Credit cards: all major
Restaurant, Children welcome
Wheelchair friendly
Relais & Châteaux Member
www.karenbrown.com/california/ranchovalencia.html

Tiffany House is a pretty, dove-gray Victorian set back behind a white picket fence. From the formal parlor decorated in 1850s furniture and rich hues of dark blue, a staircase leads to three guestrooms in the main house. The Victorian Rose Room is dressed in colors of greens, mauves, and blacks, reminiscent of the Victorian period, and a claw-foot tub is staged dramatically in the alcove of the turret with distant but unobstructed views of Mount Lassen. Off the landing to the right is the attractive, light, and airy Oak Room whose colors of red, white, and blue complement the nostalgic Americana theme. This room, hung with 12 signed Wallace Nutting prints, has an inviting sitting area tucked under the eaves and overlooks the peaceful back garden. The Tierra Room is a pretty and restful room with its white iron bed and delicate blue-and-white prints all set under the delightful angles and eaves of the roofline. Accessed off the back garden patio with its own private entrance is Lavinia's Cottage, a light, airy, and spacious room with pine walls, a romantic, high iron bed, and an in-room Jacuzzi. From the corner sitting area an expanse of paned windows gives a lovely view of Mount Lassen. There is a charming garden, highlighted by a romantic gazebo, and on a lower terrace, a splendid large swimming pool. *Directions*: From Interstate 5, travel west on Lake Boulevard for 8/10 mile to Market Street. Go south on Market. Turn right at the first street, Benton Drive, then turn right again at the next street, Barbara Road.

TIFFANY HOUSE
Owners: Susan & Brady Stewart
1510 Barbara Road
Redding, CA 96003
Tel: (530) 244-3225, Fax: none
Email: tiffanyhse@aol.com
4 rooms, Double: $90–$140
Open all year
Credit cards: all major
No restaurant
Inappropriate for children
www.karenbrown.com/california/tiffanyhouse.html

The Swiss have returned to the Gold Rush Country! It was a surprise to me to learn that John Sutter, who discovered gold here, was Swiss and now Susanne and her brother, Hans Peter, whose family owns a charming farmhouse *auberge* in the Swiss countryside, have built a hotel in Rocklin. This is a larger property than we normally recommend, but its Swiss ties and theme make it an enjoyable place to stop either overnight or for a meal. Although close to and visible from the freeway, the hotel enjoys an expanse of woodland and garden at the back and has an absolutely beautiful rose garden with 200 roses in bloom year round. The grounds, understandably, have become a very popular setting for weddings. The focal point of the hotel is its wonderful bakery and restaurant where meals are offered in a large open room with views through big picture windows to the back garden and terrace. Tables are set on a mosaic of colored concrete tiles under high sienna-colored beams. Guestrooms all have the same attractive decor and enjoy the kinds of amenities found in the finest hotels: robes, safes, two-line phones, coffee makers, luxury soaps, and plush towels. Rooms have either a king or two queen beds and open onto either a small private deck or patio. The pool is a welcome spot to settle on hot days and there are a number of excellent public golf courses nearby. *Directions:* Leave I-80 east (to Reno) at Rocklin Road (the exit after Rocklin/Taylor Road) then turn right onto Aguilar Road. Turn right on China Garden Road and cross the bridge—the hotel is on the left.

ROCKLIN PARK HOTEL   **New**
Manager: Dirk Oldenburg
5450 China Garden Road, Rocklin, CA 95677
Tel: (916) 630-9400 or (888) 630-9400
Fax: (916) 630-0837
E-mail: hotel@rocklinpark.com
67 rooms, Double: $115–$225*
*Continental breakfast
Open all year, Credit cards: all major
Restaurant
Children welcome, Wheelchair friendly
www.karenbrown.com/california/rocklinpark.html

Built 117 years ago, The Ink House is a charming yellow and white Victorian accented with light-blue trim. Architecturally interesting, the house enjoys a verandah wrapped all the way around and a cupola that affords a 360-degree vista of the area. We immediately felt The Ink House's relaxing and comfortable atmosphere when we arrived to the laughter and conversation of guests—relative strangers—enjoying wine and hors d'oeuvres in the downstairs parlor. The guestrooms, on the second floor, vary in size—two share a bath, and some are rather small. The side and back rooms overlook vineyards and a large old barn that sits behind the house. Different in each room, the decor is fittingly traditional as it is in the public rooms downstairs. The accommodation can be described as homey, with Oriental carpets and family furnishings. A full breakfast is served in one of the two dining areas and guests are invited to take their coffee to the verandah. Although the house sits just off the principal road through the wine country, the double-paned windows help buffer the street noise, and the country setting is quiet and peaceful. Diane, with years of expertise, offers a genuine warmth of welcome to her guests. *Directions*: From San Francisco take Highway 80 north to Highway 37. Exit at Highway 29 north for Saint Helena and turn left at Whitehall Lane.

THE INK HOUSE
Owner: Diane DeFilipi
1575 St. Helena Highway at Whitehall Lane
Saint Helena, CA 94574-9775
Tel: (707) 963-3890, Fax: (707) 968-0739
Email: inkhousebb@aol.com
7 rooms, 5 with private bathrooms
Double: $115–$220
Closed Christmas Eve & Christmas Day
Credit cards: MC, VS
No restaurant, Children welcome in some rooms
www.karenbrown.com/california/inkhouse.html

Situated in a private 250-acre valley, Meadowood, an attractive complex of sand-gray gabled wooden buildings with crisp white trim, is a resort community in a secluded setting sheltered by towering Ponderosa pines and Douglas firs. Wooded areas open up to a nine-hole golf course, croquet lawns, tennis courts, and swimming pools. Centrally located, the clubhouse—a three-story structure overlooking the golf course—houses The Restaurant, featuring wine-country cuisine in an elegant setting, The Grill, offering meals in a less formal setting, a golf shop, and conference facilities. There are 13 guestrooms in the Croquet Lodge, which overlooks the perfectly manicured croquet lawn. Other bedrooms are found in clusters of lodges scattered about the property. The atmosphere, relaxed, informal, and unpretentious, is accurately described as "California casual." Although expensive, the accommodations are luxuriously appointed and attractively furnished, reflecting an incredible attention to detail. Concern for guests' comfort and satisfaction is foremost and service is presented with a friendly and professional air. Meadowood is a luxurious resort with every amenity, including a full-service, state-of-the-art health spa and a most caring staff. *Directions:* From San Francisco take Highway 80 north to Highway 37. Exit at Highway 29 north for Saint Helena. Turn left on the Silverado Trail and continue 2 miles to Pope Street. Turn right on Howell Mt. Road, go 500 feet and turn left on Meadowood Lane.

MEADOWOOD NAPA VALLEY
Managing Director: Ken Humes
900 Meadowood Lane, Saint Helena, CA 94574
Tel: (707) 963-3646 or (800) 458-8080
Fax: (707) 963-3532
Email: reservations@meadowood.com
85 rooms, Double: $470–$725*, *Breakfast not included
Open all year, Credit cards: all major
Restaurant, Children welcome
Wheelchair friendly (limited to only three rooms)
Relais & Châteaux Member
www.karenbrown.com/california/meadowood.html

Just off Highway 29 at the corner of El Bonita, on the outskirts of Saint Helena, the Vineyard Country Inn backs onto an expanse of vineyards. Constructed to resemble a French country manor, the inn's attention to detail and the quality of appointments are impressive. Handsome slate roofs dotted by whimsical brick chimneys top the complex of buildings. A path winds from the main building, which houses the lobby and attractive breakfast room, past the enclosed pool and Jacuzzi, through patches of flowering garden to the guestrooms. Accommodations are all suites enjoying a sitting area in front of a wood-burning fireplace, a game table or work area, and a bedroom furnished with either a four-poster king bed or two queen sleigh beds. The decor is clean and elegant in its simplicity. Bathrooms are lovely in their tile and wallpaper and are beautifully fresh and modern. Under beamed ceilings, the downstairs rooms (except for two) open onto patios; all the upstairs rooms open onto private decks. The Vineyard Country Inn offers guestrooms that are spacious and priced well in comparison to other luxury accommodation in the valley. A bountiful breakfast buffet is served. *Directions:* From San Francisco take Highway 101 north to Highway 37 east, then Highway 37 to Highway 121/129. Located on Highway 29 at El Bonita.

VINEYARD COUNTRY INN
Owners: Michael & Mary Ann Pietro
Innkeepers: Monika & Michael Wahlen
201 Main Street
Saint Helena, CA 94574
Tel: (707) 963-1000, Fax: (707) 963-1794
Email: eddbarrack@aol.com
21 suites, Double: $155–$230
Open all year
Credit cards: all major
No restaurant
Children welcome
Wheelchair friendly
www.karenbrown.com/california/vineyardcountry.html

The Wine Country Inn is a complex of buildings built of wood and stone, fashioned after the inns of New England, sitting on a low hillside and surrounded by acres of vineyards. The inn has twenty-four rooms and five cottages, which have been oriented to enjoy the tranquil and scenic setting: fourteen rooms are housed in the main building, six in the Brandy Barn, and four in the Hastings House. Many of the rooms have private patios, balconies, and fireplaces. Each room, unique in its appeal and character, has its own bath and is individually decorated with country furnishings. Many of the quilts were handmade by the owner. The setting is peaceful, the mood relaxing, and the staff knowledgeable and friendly. Public areas include a lovely lobby, which opens onto a large expanse of deck and a pool (heated all year) on the terraced hillside, bounded by a patio and colorful gardens. Room tariffs include a wonderful breakfast and an offering of wine and appetizers in the afternoon. *Directions:* Two miles north of Saint Helena on Highway 29 turn right onto Lodi Lane. The Wine Country Inn is in a quarter of a mile on the left.

THE WINE COUNTRY INN
Owner: Jim Smith
Manager: Deniese Steelman
1152 Lodi Lane
Saint Helena, CA 94574
Tel: (707) 963-7077 or (888) 465-4608
Fax: (707) 963-9018
Email: romance@winecountryinn.com
29 rooms, Double: $195–$395
Open all year
Credit cards: MC, VS
No restaurant
Children over 13 welcome
www.karenbrown.com/california/winecountryinn.html

This guide features small hotels with charm, so how could we even remotely consider including a resort hotel? Especially one with 681 rooms! The reason is quite simple: there is just nothing else in California to compare with the marvelously whimsical Hotel del Coronado—"The Del." If you are looking for a secluded hideaway or subdued elegance, this is not your cup of tea. But if you want a resort with boundless action, plenty of pizzazz, fabulous architecture, and an incredible creamy-white sandy beach, the Hotel del Coronado is tops. Its history dates back to 1887 when Elisha Babcock and H. L. Story purchased Coronado Island and reserved the prime 26 acres of real estate for their extravagant venture, then sold off the remainder of the land to finance the building of one of the world's largest wooden structures. Within a year, their dream came true. The Hotel del Coronado, a white Victorian, gingerbread hotel—a fantasy of turrets, wraparound porches, funny little towers, and perky gables—was ready to open. Over the years, two more buildings have been added and while the original Victorian structure remains on the outside much as it was over a hundred years ago, the interior has been restored to include classic design and air conditioning. If you want a contemporary beachfront room, opt for the Ocean Towers, but if you value nostalgia, ask to be in the Victorian building where accommodations range from intimate rooms to spacious suites. Dining choices range from oceanfront casual California cuisine to fine dining under the stars at The Prince of Wales. *Directions:* Take I-5 to the Coronado Bridge then turn left on Orange Avenue.

HOTEL DEL CORONADO
Manager: Michael Hardisty
1500 Orange Avenue
Coronado, CA 92118
Tel: (619) 435-6611 or (800) 468-3533
Fax: (619) 522-8262
681 rooms, Double: $250–$750*
*Breakfast not included
Open all year, Credit cards: all major
Restaurants, Children welcome
Wheelchair friendly

The slogan of the Crystal Pier Hotel & Cottages—"Sleep Over the Ocean"—aptly expresses what is unique and special about this property. Charming white clapboard cottages trimmed in blue and dressed with windowboxes cover the length of both sides of this private/public pier in colorful Pacific Beach. When the tide is in, the surf washes beneath the cottages and wooden slats of the pier. Cottages all enjoy an expanse of deck and unobstructed views of ocean, surfers, and beachcombers. It is easy to get to know your neighbors while watching the sunset over the ocean as only low white picket fences divide each cottage patio. The most private units are cottages towards the end of the pier for they are set at an angle and have private patios and the most spectacular ocean views. All the cottages enjoy a little kitchen (stocked with convenient utensils) and living room and are priced according to whether they are a spacious studio, one bedroom with bath, or two bedrooms with two baths. All but two have been remodeled within the last two years and all units are to be remodeled by the summer of 2002. We love to stay here with our children and friends. Be advised that the morning starts early on the pier with fishing at its end, the rumble of cars on the wooden slats as guests come and go, and the arrival of beachcombers, lifeguards, and surfers on the beach below. Although locked to the public in the evening with 24-hour security, the pier is open to the public by day. *Directions:* Exit I-5 at Balboa/Garnet Ave. The pier is located at the end of Garnet Avenue on Ocean Front walk.

CRYSTAL PIER HOTEL & COTTAGES
Manager: Jim Bostian
4500 Ocean Boulevard in Pacific Beach
San Diego, CA 92109
Tel: (858) 483-6983, Fax: (858) 483-6811
29 units, Double: $235–$350
Open all year, Credit cards: MC, VS
No restaurant, Children welcome
Wheelchair friendly
www.karenbrown.com/california/crystalpier.html

The Inn at Union Square has a convenient and strategic location, right in the heart of San Francisco—just steps from Union Square, theaters, and shopping. Owned by Nan and Norm Rosenblatt, this is a professionally managed, boutique hotel. The small lobby is entered from the street and appears to be the entryway of a country home. An elevator takes guests to the upper floors. As you step off the elevator, each floor has its own little sitting area with chairs grouped comfortably around a fireplace where complimentary wine and hors d'oeuvres are served in the evening from 5:30 to 8 pm. Newspapers are left outside each door in the morning. Guests can either go to the lounge for an expanded Continental breakfast or take a tray to their room. The decor in each of the rooms is most attractive, with a traditional mood created by the use of beautiful fabrics and fine furniture. Some of the rooms have their own fireplaces and the penthouse suite has a sauna and Jacuzzi tub. Every room, from the least expensive small rooms to the deluxe suites, is spotlessly maintained and appealing. (Half of the rooms and all of the bathrooms were redecorated in 1999.) All rooms are equipped with voice mail, dual-line phones, and modems. Room service is available. Complimentary massage is offered and the inn has membership to a full-service gym. *Directions*: Located one block off Union Square on Post Street, between Stockton and Powell.

THE INN AT UNION SQUARE
Owners: Norm & Nan Rosenblatt
Manager: Susan Platt
440 Post Street
San Francisco, CA 94102
Tel: (415) 397-3510 or (800) 288-4346
Fax: (415) 989-0529
Email: inn@unionsquare.com
30 rooms, Double: $195–$350
Open all year, Credit cards: all major
No restaurant, Children welcome
Wheelchair friendly
www.karenbrown.com/california/innatunionsquare.html

The Petite Auberge is a lovely little hotel on Bush Street sitting next to its sister "Four Sisters" hotel, the White Swan. Whereas the White Swan has an English flavor, the Petite Auberge is like a romantic French country inn snuggled at the heart of the city, just steps from the famous theater district and exclusive shopping and fine dining. The façade is most appealing—a slim, four-story building with a double column of bay windows bordered by narrow windows decorated with flowerboxes. An antique carousel horse, burnished woods, and soft pastel colors give a warm welcome to the cozy entry. Each guestroom is attractively decorated with delicate colors, all have private baths, and many have fireplaces. Downstairs there is a most inviting suite with a fireplace, Jacuzzi, and private outside entrance and deck. Wine, tea, and hors d'oeuvres are available from 4:30 to 6:30 pm for those guests who want a quiet moment after a busy day. A delicious breakfast is served buffet style in the delightful breakfast room with its French marketplace mural and sliding glass doors giving onto a pretty patio where you can sit in pleasant weather. Breakfast includes a selection of teas and coffee, homemade breads, fruit, a hot dish, cereals, and pastries. *Directions:* Take Van Ness Avenue north to Bush Street. Turn right on Bush and go about 1 mile. The inn is between Taylor and Mason.

PETITE AUBERGE
Innkeeper: Lin McMahan
863 Bush Street
San Francisco, CA 94108
Tel: (415) 928-6000 or (800) 365-3004
Fax: (415) 673-7214
26 rooms, Double: $145–$245
Open all year
Credit cards: all major
No restaurant
Children welcome
www.karenbrown.com/california/petiteauberge.html

The Sherman House is an oasis of luxury and provides San Francisco with some of its most exceptional accommodation and personalized and attentive service. This French-Italianate three-story mansion was built in 1876 for Leander Sherman, founder of the Sherman Clay Music Company and host to a number of famous musicians who performed within its walls. A soaring, three-story music hall is now a stunning salon for hotel guests. The main house contains 11 rooms or suites, while the carriage house, set in the middle of the gardens designed by Thomas Church, offers three spectacular suites. Armoires, mirrors, desks, chairs, paintings, and chandeliers have been carefully selected for each room. Each room, grand in decor but not necessarily grand in size, has an impressive canopy bed with feather-down mattress, sumptuously draped in luxurious fabrics, and a magnificent private bath finished in black granite (with the exception of one in Chinese slate). Wine is available in the sitting area each evening. The restaurant is open only to hotel residents and is spectacular when compared to any of the world's finest restaurants. The chef shops every day to obtain only the freshest and finest ingredients and plans his menu accordingly. Valet parking is available and is included in the room rate. *Directions:* From the south, take Highway 101 to Fell Street, bear left onto Fell for one block, then turn right on Webster. After about 35 blocks turn left off Webster onto Green Street. The Sherman House will be in the middle of the block on the right-hand side, between Webster and Fillmore.

SHERMAN HOUSE
Owner: Manou Mobedshahi
2160 Green Street
San Francisco, CA 94123
Tel: (415) 563-3600 or (800) 424-5777
Fax: (415) 563-1882
14 rooms, Double: $460–$1,200
Open all year, Credit cards: all major
Restaurant for guests only, closed Wednesday for dinner
Children welcome
Relais & Châteaux Member

For those familiar with San Francisco, Union Street is always a favorite place to dine, shop, and play. The several blocks of Union Street stretching out at the foot of exclusive Pacific Heights offer charming restaurants and pretty boutiques in quaint Victorian houses. Right in the heart of this attractive area, snuggled into a pretty, light-yellow Victorian house with green trim, is The Union Street Inn. Steps on the left side of the building lead up to the front door, which opens into a small reception foyer. To the left is an old-fashioned parlor, comfortably furnished with antiques. Doors from the parlor lead out to the most special feature of the inn—an exceptionally attractive, English-style garden where a brick path meanders through a medley of shrubs, flowers, and shade trees. At the end of the garden, behind a white picket fence, is a cute cottage converted into a guest suite. In the house itself are five more guestrooms, each individually decorated in a traditional style. My favorite is the English Garden Room, which has its own small deck overlooking the garden. All of the rooms have a welcome basket of fresh fruit. Continuing the mood of hospitality, refreshments are set out for guests each afternoon, and in the morning a full breakfast is served. Your hosts are Jane Bertorelli, who is English, and David Coyle, who is Irish. They oversee every detail of the inn and personally welcome guests. *Directions:* From Highway 101 north, take Lombard Street, turn right on Steiner, then left on Union. The inn is between Fillmore and Steiner.

THE UNION STREET INN
Owners: Jane Bertorelli & David Coyle
Manager: Katie Edison
2229 Union Street
San Francisco, CA 94123
Tel: (415) 346-0424, Fax: (415) 922-8046
Email: innkeeper@unionstreetinn.com
6 rooms, Double: $159–$269
Open all year, Credit cards: all major
No restaurant
Children welcome
www.karenbrown.com/california/unionstreetinn.html

The Washington Square Inn has a great location in the North Beach area, facing historic Washington Square. Within easy strolling distance you find a wealth of wonderful little places to eat and a bit farther, but an interesting walk through Chinatown, are the theaters and shops of the Union Square area. From the moment you enter, the ambiance of the French countryside surrounds you—an antique dining table, mellowed with age and surrounded by country chairs, stretches in front of large windows framed with tie-back drapes. Large gilt mirrors, pots of orchids, and a fireplace with an antique wooden mantel add to the country appeal. In the afternoon guests have tea or wine and hors d'oeuvres in front of the fire and in the morning an expanded Continental breakfast of juice, fruit, muffins, breads, croissants, and hot and cold cereals is served here (if guests prefer, breakfast will be brought to their room). Two staircases lead to the guestrooms, each individually decorated. From the simplest room to the most luxurious suite, each of the rooms, dressed with beautiful coordinating fabrics, exudes a lovely country charm. A couple of rooms have cozy bay windows accented with inviting sitting nooks. The restaurant next door, Moose's, serves fine cuisine. *Directions:* In North Beach, on Washington Square, between Union and Filbert.

WASHINGTON SQUARE INN
Innkeeper: David A. Norwitt
1660 Stockton Street
San Francisco, CA 94133
Tel: (415) 981-4220 or (800) 388-0220
Fax: (415) 397-7242
Email: david@wsisf.com
15 rooms, Double: $155–$250
Open all year
Credit cards: all major
No restaurant
Children welcome
Wheelchair friendly
www.karenbrown.com/california/washingtonsquareinn.html

The White Swan Inn, a small, London-style hotel with English-country decor, has a splendid location just steps from a wide selection of quaint restaurants and a five-minute walk from San Francisco's fabulous Union Square shopping and theater district. But the appeal of the White Swan is far greater than its setting: From the moment you enter, you will know immediately that this is not a standard commercial hotel. Off the entry a small sitting area and a reception desk greet you, but the heart of the inn is down a flight of stairs where a spacious lounge awaits with one section set up with tables and chairs for a full buffet breakfast—a hearty meal of coffee, muffins, a hot entree, juices, and cereals. Tea and hors d'oeuvres are set out between 4:30 and 6:30 pm. Beyond the eating area is a pretty living room with a fireplace and comfortable lounge chairs. Next door is the library, with a cricket bat mounted on the wall, another cozy area for relaxing, and a small exercise room. Although the inn is in the center of the city, French doors open out from a conference room at the back onto a deck and small English-style garden. The bedrooms are beautifully decorated with pretty coordinating fabrics. Each room has a separate sitting area, fireplace (which can be turned on by a bedside switch), small refrigerator, wet bar, direct-dial telephone, and color television. This hotel is an absolute delight. *Directions:* Take Van Ness Avenue north, turn right on Bush and go about 1 mile. The inn is between Taylor and Mason.

WHITE SWAN INN
Innkeeper: Lin McMahan
845 Bush Street
San Francisco, CA 94108
Tel: (415) 775-1755 or (800) 999-9570
Fax: (415) 775-5717
26 rooms, Double: $180–$275
Open all year, Credit cards: all major
No restaurant
Children welcome
www.karenbrown.com/california/whiteswaninn.html

The Gerstle Park Inn, a rambling, wood-shingled home on 1½ acres, is a beautiful inn set in a residential district of San Rafael, catering mostly to business travelers and local families, as well as tourists. The inn carries an air of sophistication wonderfully complemented by a homey and welcoming ambiance. Just off the entry are the formal living room with its Asian-inspired decor and the enclosed wraparound porch, which serves as an intimate and elegant breakfast room where a full, cooked-to-order breakfast is served each morning. Upstairs, rooms range from the Redwood Suite, cozy and romantic with a pine-planked, low-angled ceiling and wooded views afforded by a row of windows at ceiling height, to the San Rafael Suite, spanning the length of one end of the building, with its twin beds and large deck facing the surrounding hills. The separate carriage house has two suites complete with well-stocked kitchens, breakfast nooks, living rooms, and private patios. Two stand-alone cottages also have kitchens and provide wonderful privacy. All the rooms enjoy amenities and conveniences such as two-line telephones with voice mail, televisions, VCRs, hairdryers, and robes. For Judy and Jim Dowling, your gracious and talented hosts, running Gerstle Park Inn is a dream fulfilled. *Directions*: Exit Highway 101 at San Rafael Central exit. Go west on 3rd Street, then left on D Street, right on San Rafael Avenue, and left on Grove Street.

GERSTLE PARK INN
Owners: Judy & Jim Dowling
Manager: Barbara Searles
34 Grove Street
San Rafael, CA 94901
Tel: (415) 721-7611 or (800) 726-7611
Fax: (415) 721-7600
Email: innkeeper@gerstleparkinn.com
12 rooms, Double: $179–$250
Open all year, Credit cards: all major
No restaurant, Children welcome
www.karenbrown.com/california/gerstleparkinn.html

The Cheshire Cat is comprised of two lovely beige and white Victorians sitting side by side and connected by a tranquil bricked patio (where breakfast is served on all but grim days), and a third building, the James House, located across the street. In the foyer of the main house a grouping of *Alice in Wonderland* figurines sets the whimsical theme of the inn. Many of the rooms are named for an *Alice in Wonderland* character. Each guestroom is unique in appeal although consistent in the Laura Ashley coordinated prints and wallpapers that are used in the decor, from plums and creams in the Mad Hatter Room to smoke-blue and cream in the Dormouse's Room. Two wonderful suites, Tweedle Dum and Tweedle Dee, are located above the garage and enjoy the luxury of space, fireplace, Jacuzzi, and their own entrance off the back garden. Named after the prettiest villages in Cheshire, three two-bedroom cottages, Woodford, Prestbury, and Mobberly, are elegant in their furnishings and afford the decadence of a fully stocked kitchen, living room, fireplaces, and a large private redwood deck with a hot tub for luxuriating under the stars. James House, a lovely peach and white-trimmed building houses four beautiful new guest accommodations: The Lion, on the ground floor, and White King, White Queen, and Unicorn on the first floor. White King is an especially appealing room with a large king bed set on pine flooring and seating in a pretty bay-window alcove. Its bathroom is large and luxurious with a Jacuzzi tub. *Directions:* Exit Highway 101 at Mission Street, go east on Mission for five blocks, right on State Street for three blocks, and right on Valerio.

THE CHESHIRE CAT
Owner: Christine Dunstan
36 West Valerio Street
Santa Barbara, CA 93101
Tel: (805) 569-1610, Fax: (805) 682-1876
Email: cheshire@cheshirecat.com
21 rooms, Double: $165–$400
Open all year, Credit cards: all major
No restaurant, Children welcome in cottages
Wheelchair friendly
www.karenbrown.com/california/thecheshirecat.html

Having always admired State Street in downtown Santa Barbara for its whitewashed Spanish-style buildings, we were delighted to discover the Hotel Santa Barbara, situated in the heart of the plaza just one block from the town's open-air malls and quaint boutiques. There has been a hotel on this site since 1876, with the present concrete structure being built in 1925 and recently restored and updated at a cost of $4 million. This family-managed hotel reminds you of the 1920s Hollywood movie era—in fact, it used to be a getaway for stars such as Clark Gable and Carol Lombard. With cool, tiled floors in the foyer and colors of sand and rust, the atmosphere is that of a Moroccan arched marketplace. There are comfy pillow-filled sofas and café-style seating in the area where your Continental breakfast is served. This is a four-storied, mission-style building with the guestrooms, some with Juliet balconies, facing onto a U-shaped court. Rooms, all air-conditioned, are furnished in bold colors of blues and yellows and have elegant, stark-white bathrooms. The large, well-appointed suites are extremely comfortable. There is some noise from the street, so request a room away from the activity. A great bonus for families—there is no charge for children under 16 staying with a parent. Room service from the restaurant next door and valet parking are available. *Directions*: From Highway 101 exit at Carrillo, drive for several blocks, then turn right on Chapala. Turn left on Cota—the hotel is on the right half a block down at the corner of Cota and State streets.

HOTEL SANTA BARBARA
Manager: Bill Evans
533 State Street
Santa Barbara, CA 93101
Tel: (805) 957-9300 or (888) 259-7700
Fax: (805) 962-2412
75 rooms, Double: $159–$189
Open all year
Credit cards: all major
No restaurant, Children welcome
Wheelchair friendly

The Secret Garden Inn is a charming complex of cottages shaded by trees and banded by a beautiful garden. Dominique Hannaux, the current owner, hails from France and the Secret Garden Inn looks absolutely beautiful as a result of her focused attention and charming decor. Since she bought the inn a couple of years ago, Dominique has not made dramatic changes, but rather subtle ones to the decor that surprisingly make a huge difference to the appeal and ambiance of the inn. The main building houses an inviting living room, a lovely country dining room, and two of the guest accommodations. The other guestrooms are extremely private, located in individual cottages with their own entrance—very romantic, peaceful, and restful. Each room has its own decor and special appeal, such as Hummingbird with a private deck and hot tub and Nightingale with a spacious living room, fireplace, and private deck with hot tub. Central to the cottages at the back of the main house is a lovely, lush garden, which surrounds a patio shaded by persimmon, avocado, and mock orange trees. On mornings blessed with sunshine, tables are set here for breakfast. *Directions*: Take Highway 101 to the Mission Street exit then go east on Mission for one block to Castillo Street. Turn right on Castillo, then left on Pedegossa, and left again on Bath Street. The Secret Garden Inn is on the right.

THE SECRET GARDEN INN
Owner: Dominique Hannaux
1908 Bath Street
Santa Barbara, CA 93101
Tel: (805) 687-2300 or (800) 676-1622
Fax: (805) 687-4576
Email: garden@secretgarden.com
11 rooms, Double: $120–$250
Open all year, Credit cards: all major
No restaurant
Children welcome
www.karenbrown.com/california/secretgardeninn.html

The Simpson House Inn, a handsome, rosy-beige Victorian landmark with white and smoke-blue trim, is located on a quiet residential street only a five-minute walk from the historic downtown shopping attractions of State Street. The lush surrounding gardens of the inn include an acre of lawn banded by beautiful flowerbeds and mature shade trees. An irresistible feature of the inn is a cheerful back porch under an arbor of draping wisteria with white wicker chairs and comfy pillows: a perfect niche to enjoy the garden. In the main house the sitting room and dining room are quite formal. However, the formality disappears upstairs in the charming guest chambers, each individually decorated with hand-printed Victorian wallpapers to suit different tastes—from feminine to a more tailored look. Three cottages in the back garden are beautifully decorated in rich fabrics and intimate with a Jacuzzi tub nestled right into a bay window. The barn also offers spacious accommodations, light and airy, whose pine furnishings are perfect against the exposed beams of the original barn. Each room enjoys niceties such as robes, fresh flowers, and bottled water. In the evenings sherry and local wine are offered with an extensive Mediterranean hors d'oeuvres buffet. An efficient and capable staff assists Dixie Budke with the duties of the inn. *Directions:* From downtown take Santa Barbara Street northeast toward Mission, then turn left onto Arrellaga.

SIMPSON HOUSE INN
Owners: Linda & Glyn Davies
Manager: Dixie Budke
121 East Arrellaga Street
Santa Barbara, CA 93101
Tel: (805) 963-7067 or (800) 676-1280
Fax: (805) 564-4811
Email: reservations@simpsonhouseinn.com
15 rooms, Double: $215–$550
Open all year, Credit cards: all major
No restaurant
Children over 12 welcome, Wheelchair friendly
www.karenbrown.com/california/simpsonhouseinn.html

The foundations of The Babbling Brook Inn date back to the 1790s when padres from the Santa Cruz Mission built a grist mill on the property, taking advantage of the small stream to grind corn. In the late 19th century a tannery powered by a huge water wheel was constructed. A rustic log cabin remains today as the "heart" of the inn with a homey living room where guests congregate around a roaring fire with tea and coffee and homemade cookies. The historic wheel was recently returned to the brook pond. Most of the 13 guestrooms are in shingled chalets nestled in the garden surrounded by pines and redwoods and overlooking the idyllic little meandering brook. The rooms are decorated in French-country style with pretty fabrics and colors. Each has a private bathroom, telephone, radio with alarm, television, a cozy fireplace, and an outside entrance. Most rooms have a private deck and some even have soaking jet bathtubs for two. The two spacious suites, which can be adjoining, are tastefully decorated and quite private on the top floor. One suite has a private outdoor hot tub recessed into the deck, which overlooks the entire garden. A full buffet breakfast including one hot entree is served in the dining room, but guests are welcome to retreat to their rooms with breakfast. *Directions:* From San Jose or San Francisco take Highway 17 to Santa Cruz. Turn north on Highway 1, which becomes Mission Street, then left on Laurel for one and a half blocks to the inn, which is on the right-hand side.

THE BABBLING BROOK INN
Innkeeper: Jennifer Stanger
1025 Laurel Street
Santa Cruz, CA 95060
Tel: (831) 427-2437 or (800) 866-1131
Fax: (831) 427-2457
Email: lodging@babblingbrookinn.com
13 rooms, Double: $170–$235
Open all year
Credit cards: all major, No restaurant
Children welcome, Wheelchair friendly
www.karenbrown.com/california/babblingbrook.html

The Channel Road Inn dates back to 1910 when Thomas McCall built an elaborate wood-shingled home for his family of six daughters. Although the house was large to begin with, a third story was later added, giving plenty of space for 14 guestrooms it now offers. The house has an interesting location: just on the fringe of the elegant suburb of Pacific Palisades yet on a busy street that leads through a somewhat honky-tonk neighborhood to the beach. But oh, what a beach! The wide, sandy stretch of the Santa Monica beach is a wonderful playground. The downstairs lounge and dining areas of the inn are sedately decorated, beautifully in keeping with the style of the home. The guestrooms, tucked throughout the large house, are all individually decorated and each has its own delightful personality. My favorite room was number 1, one of the less expensive rooms but delightful with a fresh white-and-blue color scheme and sharing a large, quiet rooftop terrace with the adjacent room 5. When making reservations, keep in mind that the rooms vary in size and decide whether you want a patio, soaking tub, or the relative quiet of an inside-facing room. A ground-floor handicap room has ramp access direct from its parking space. Bikes are available for excursions along the strand, a 30-mile-long bike path that skirts the beach from Santa Monica south. Recover from your exertions with a soak in the hot tub nestled on a terrace behind the inn. *Directions:* From Highway 405 take 10 west, then Pacific Coast Highway (Route 1) north 2 miles. Make a hard right on West Channel Road, continue 1 block, and the inn is on the left.

CHANNEL ROAD INN
Owner: Susan Zolla, Manager: Heather Suskin
219 West Channel Road
Santa Monica, CA 90402
Tel: (310) 459-1920, Fax: (310) 454-9920
Email: channelinn@aol.com
14 rooms, Double: $175–$375
Open all year, Credit cards: all major
No restaurant, Children welcome
Wheelchair friendly
www.karenbrown.com/california/channelroadinn.html

With the opening in 1993 of Shutters on the Beach, a stunning, deluxe, and expensive hotel emerged in the Los Angeles area. The property fronts directly onto the superb Santa Monica beach and although it is of new construction, the hotel has a delightfully nostalgic mood. The attractive, Cape Cod-like, whisper-gray, wood-shingled building is enhanced by white gingerbread trim. I am not sure how it is accomplished, but there is an engaging, homelike ambiance throughout—perhaps it is the wood-beam ceiling or the cozy groupings of plump, comfy sofas, or the fireplaces. The designer's goal was to create an inn where guests would feel that they were staying at a friend's beach house rather than a commercial hotel: that goal has certainly been achieved. My favorite rooms are in the three-story building that fronts the sea. A garden terrace (where white lounge chairs are grouped around an attractive swimming pool) spans a small street to connect the beach house with a more traditional-looking hotel section. All of the guestrooms are attractive: pastel blues, aquas, beiges, and peach colors accent a predominantly white color scheme. An uncluttered, simple, yet elegant mood prevails, enhanced by fine linens and furniture of excellent quality. Every room has heavy, wooden, white louvered shutters, which give the hotel its name. *Directions*: Go west on Highway 10 (Santa Monica Expressway) to Santa Monica. Take the 4th Street exit south to Pico Boulevard. Shutters on the Beach is located where Pico Boulevard meets the beach.

SHUTTERS ON THE BEACH
General Manager: Armella Stepan
One Pico Boulevard
Santa Monica, CA 90405
Tel: (310) 458-0030, Fax: (310) 458-4589
Email: information@shuttersonthebeach.com
198 rooms, Double: $360–$595*
*Breakfast not included, plus 17% service charge
Open all year, Credit cards: all major
Restaurants, Children welcome
Wheelchair friendly
www.karenbrown.com/california/shutters.html

The Gables Wine Country Inn is a fine example of a bed and breakfast whose owners' love, dedication, and caring enhance the comfort and welcome and make it a very special place to stay. Judy and Mike selected The Gables Wine Country Inn, an aristocratic Victorian home on the outskirts of Santa Rosa, with a dream of opening a bed and breakfast. Although the Gables enjoys an expanse of 3 acres at the back, with a wonderful old barn that creaks with age, the home sits just off Petaluma Hill Road. A little traffic can be heard from the front guestrooms, but the back rooms overlooking the garden enjoy the quiet of the country meadow setting. The decor throughout the inn is in keeping with the grandeur of the home. Guestrooms are spacious and pretty with a country-Victorian theme. Accommodation is also offered in a dear side cottage with its own little sitting area, fireplace, wet bar, Jacuzzi tub, TV, VCR, and video library, and cozy upstairs sleeping loft. Judy is an accomplished cook and her casual afternoon tea features homemade cookies and brownies. Breakfasts are quite a repast with freshly squeezed juice, fruit, and a main course—a bounty that will take you right through to dinner. Mike is a talented craftsman and he is responsible for many of the fine finishes throughout the inn, most notably a lovely birdcage that sits on the back deck. *Directions:* From San Francisco take Highway 101 north, exiting at Rohnert Park Expressway. Turn right off the exit ramp and go 2½ miles, turning left on Petaluma Hill Road.

THE GABLES WINE COUNTRY INN
Owners: Judy & Mike Ogne
4257 Petaluma Hill Road
Santa Rosa, CA 95404
Tel: (707) 585-7777 or (800) 422-5376
Fax: (707) 584-5634
Email: innkeeper@thegablesinn.com
8 rooms, Double: $175–$250
Open all year, Credit cards: all major
No restaurant, Children over 10 welcome
Wheelchair friendly
www.karenbrown.com/california/thegables.html

For those who would rather stay in a hotel with all the attendant amenities than in a bed and breakfast, the Vintners Inn is a natural choice, centrally located for visiting the Napa, Sonoma, or Russian River areas. Just off the freeway, the Mediterranean-style building is set amid 90 acres of vineyards (be sure to request a room that faces the vineyards). The 44 spacious rooms are housed in 3 buildings that encircle a fountain in the bricked courtyard. The guestroom decor is French country with antique pine furniture, and all the rooms offer oversized tubs, small refrigerators, robes, televisions, data ports, and patios or balconies. Junior suites with vineyard views have fireplaces, wet bars, and sitting areas. Guests enjoy a deluxe, lavish buffet breakfast in the Fireside Dining Room or, in warm weather, on the adjacent wisteria-covered terrace. Added bonuses are the outdoor Jacuzzi and use of a luxury health club five minutes from the inn. There is also a restaurant, John Ash & Co, on the property. Vintners Inn is a comfortable, well-appointed accommodation at the crossroads of the Wine Country. *Directions*: From San Francisco travel Highway 101 north to Santa Rosa. Exit at River Road, turn left over the freeway, and take the first left onto Barnes Road. Turn left into the first driveway.

VINTNERS INN
Owners: Don & Rhonda Carano
4350 Barnes Road
Santa Rosa, CA 95403
Tel: (707) 575-7350 or (800) 421-2584
Fax: (707) 575-1426
Email: info@vintnersinn.com
44 rooms, Double: $193–$298
Open all year
Credit cards: all major
Restaurant
Children welcome
Wheelchair friendly
www.karenbrown.com/california/vintners.html

The Hotel Sausalito boasts a colorful past. Its early days saw activity as a bordello, and as a speakeasy during Prohibition—with its location next to the docks, liquor from the trucks that rumbled past its doors conveniently found its way into its parlor. It is now home to a delightful family that hails from Scotland. The Purdies' Scottish brogue will charm you, but it is their warm, professional approach to innkeeping that impresses. A steep flight of stairs (there is an elevator) leads up to guestrooms from the small street-side entry. With a backdrop of walls washed in warm pastel tones, the furnishings are handsome—custom-designed and handcrafted by local artisans—and have been selected to enhance the individuality of each guestroom. The size, outlook, and bathroom appointments determine the room tariff. Some of the rooms are snug, yet greatly appreciated by the traveler looking for value. Regardless of the guestroom's location or size, its appointments, such as furnishings, art, the finest linens, desktop phones with data port, voice mail, and cable television, are luxurious and provided to pamper the guest. We enjoyed one of the larger rooms that overlooked the activity of Sausalito's main street, but was buffered from the noise by well-insulated windows. A lovely second-floor roof garden is a tranquil place to relax. A complimentary morning newspaper is delivered to your doorstep and although breakfast is not served in the hotel, coupons are provided for coffee and pastries next door at Café Tutti. *Directions:* Refer to directions for The Inn Above Tide—they are neighboring hotels.

HOTEL SAUSALITO
Owners: Josephine & Billy Purdie
16 El Portal (at Bridgeway)
Sausalito, CA 94965
Tel: (415) 332-0700 or (888) 442-0700
Fax: (415) 332-8788
Email: hotelsaus@aol.com
16 rooms, Double: $145–$270
Open all year, Credit cards: all major
No restaurant, Children welcome
www.karenbrown.com/california/hotelsausalito.html

Just beyond Sausalito's yacht club and only steps away from the ferry dock, right on the water's edge, sits The Inn Above Tide, very cleverly converted to an inn from what was originally an apartment complex and then most recently an office building. All of its 30 rooms enjoy million-dollar views of the San Francisco Bay and skyline and are appropriately stocked with binoculars. Twenty-four of the rooms have wonderful little decks whose partitioning wall is of glass, creating the illusion of being right on the water, almost boatside. The remaining six rooms, although without a deck, benefit from being a little more spacious. The rooms, many of which have fireplaces, are attractive—light and airy so as not to compete with the view. The decor plays on a nautical theme with porthole windows and soft green-and-white prints with little fish. The two suites are both spectacular, spacious rooms with private decks and magnificent views of the city. The buffet in the drawing room is set in the evenings with a selection of wine and cheese, and in the mornings with a Continental breakfast. (Trays are also available should you prefer to enjoy breakfast in the privacy of your guestroom.) If you want to use Sausalito as a base for exploring San Francisco, you can easily journey back and forth by ferry, avoiding the hassle and cost of a car. *Directions*: From San Francisco cross the Golden Gate Bridge and exit on Alexander Avenue. Alexander becomes Bridgeway. Turn right towards the water after the first stop light, on El Portal.

THE INN ABOVE TIDE
Owner: William McDevitt
Manager: Mark Flaherty
30 El Portal, Sausalito, CA 94965
Tel: (415) 332-9535 or (800) 893-8433
Fax: (415) 332-6714
Email: inntide@ix.netcom.com
30 rooms, Double: $245–$650
Open all year, Credit cards: all major
No restaurant, Children welcome
Wheelchair friendly
www.karenbrown.com/california/innabovetide.html

More New Orleans French Quarter than Southern California beach, The Seal Beach Inn dates back to the 1920s when the little town of Seal Beach was the playground of Los Angeles and a wild party town of dance halls, offshore gambling ships, and bath houses. Today the only hint of the inn's glitzy past is its vintage neon sign, which blends in very nicely with owner Marjorie Bettenhausen-Schmaehl's collection of bygones, from old street lamps and ornate, wrought-iron railings to an 8-foot-tall Parisian frescoed fountain bubbling on the patio beside the pool. Every nook and cranny is filled with a profusion of colorful flowers, vines, shrubs, and trees. Not only are the guestrooms named after flowers, but the gardens contain all the namesake species—wisteria, honeysuckle, bougainvillea, zinnia. Several rooms have fireplaces, kitchens, Jacuzzi baths, and Roman soaking tubs. All have thick towels, fine linens, and grand furnishings that range from an old Persian mural and carved pre-Civil-War headboards to sumptuous Victorian pieces. A lavish breakfast buffet of Belgian waffles, a selection of quiches, granola, fruit, bread, and yogurt is laid out in the dining room each morning and coffee and teas are available all day in the adjacent library. You can walk to over 20 restaurants and the beach. Just down the road is Long Beach with its famous aquarium and the *Queen Mary. Directions:* Going south on the 405, exit at Seal Beach Boulevard. Go left to Pacific Coast Highway, turn right then left on 5th street. The inn is two blocks down on the left.

THE SEAL BEACH INN
Owner: Marjorie Bettenhausen-Schmaehl
212 5th Street
Seal Beach, CA 90740
Tel: (562) 493-2416 or (800) 443-3292
Fax: (562) 799-0483
Email: hideaway@sealbeachinn.com
23 rooms, Double: $169–$399
Open all year, Credit cards: all major
No restaurant, Inappropriate for children
Wheelchair friendly
www.karenbrown.com/california/sealbeachinn.html

Located on the western outskirts of Shingletown 19 miles from Mount Lassen National Park, Weston House offers a private oasis nestled on 5½ mountaintop acres with million-dollar views of meadows, valleys, and mountains stretching for miles below. The setting and views are breathtaking and the handsome complex of wood-shingled houses complement rather than compete with the setting. Running the length of the main house is a magnificent lap pool banded by an expanse of deck whose various levels afford intimate settings from which to enjoy the sweeping panorama. There are just five guestrooms. Anna's Room and Evan's Room are accessed off the pool deck on the ground floor and share a spectacular bath. Climb the stair in the tower to Vanessa's Room, my favorite, with a wood stove and lovely queen bed angled in the corner to maximize the view through the sliding glass door across the small private balcony to some fabulous scenery. Just up from the pool and off a meadow of glorious wildflowers are Helen's and Laura's rooms, two rooms very popular with guests. There are three dogs and two cats on the property. Note: As restaurant options are limited, you might want to consider packing a picnic dinner. A full breakfast is provided. *Directions*: Take Shingletown Ridge Road (on the west side of town) off Highway 44 and then turn left on Red Rock Road. Signs encourage you along as the road winds, narrows, and changes from asphalt to loose gravel.

WESTON HOUSE
Owner: Angela Weston
Red Rock Road
P.O. Box 276
Shingletown, CA 96088
Tel: (530) 474-3738, Fax: (530) 244-9494
5 rooms, 3 with private bathrooms
Double: $95–$165
Closed January & February
Credit cards: MC, VS
No restaurant, Children welcome

The Alisal Guest Ranch, a quintessential family resort located in the bucolic Santa Ynez Valley in the town of Solvang, appeals to the child of any age with its horseback riding, golf, tennis, country dancing, and western barbecues. Originally a land grant in the 1700s to a Spanish conquistador, Alisal has been a working cattle ranch and secluded hideaway since 1946. Its 73 cottages, ranging from studios to large suites, are all extremely comfortable and tastefully decorated and have wood-burning fireplaces. The "California ranch" decor is very inviting, with high beamed ceilings, Spanish tile, and fine western art. Each cottage is its own private retreat with garden views and covered porches—a home away from home. If quiet and privacy are your desires, visit the ranch during the week off season and stay in the cottages nearest the golf course—these are farthest from the main activities. Breakfast and dinner, which are included in the price, are taken in the large Ranch Room where you are assigned a table for the duration of your stay. We have heard about Alisal for years from friends who enjoy it as a family retreat to which they return again and again, generation after generation. *Directions*: Take Highway 101 to Buellton and exit at Highway 246 (Solvang/Lompoc). Coming from the north, turn left from the off ramp; from the south, turn right. Follow signs to Solvang and turn right on Alisal Road, past the golf courses, to the main entrance.

THE ALISAL GUEST RANCH & RESORT   **New**
General Manager: David Loutensack
1054 Alisal Road
Solvang, CA 93463
Tel: (805) 688-6411 or (800) 425-4725
Fax: (805) 688-2510
Email: sales@alisal.com
73 cottages, Double: $385–$475*
*Includes breakfast & dinner
Open all year, Credit cards: all major
Restaurant, Children welcome
Wheelchair friendly
www.karenbrown.com/california/alisalguestranch

The name of the inn, "Storybook," represents the theme that runs from its whimsical architecture to the decor of the guestrooms. Though a bit cutesy, the inn seems fitting in cobbled Solvang, which might itself be described as a storybook version of Denmark. Timbered at the front and with a pretty band of flowers coloring the walkway, the inn is newly constructed. The entry of the inn is set up as the reception area. Just off the entry are a small sitting room with a television and a lovely large breakfast room. Rates include a full breakfast, which varies daily with tempting selections, and afternoon wine and cheese. A main staircase winds up from the entry to staggered levels and guestrooms opening onto a central corridor. Each room is named for various Hans Christian Anderson fairy tales such as *The Ugly Duckling*, *The Little Mermaid*, *The Princess and the Pea*, *Thumbelina*, and *The Emperor's New Clothes*. The decor is individual to each room and complements its theme. All the guestrooms are furnished with a mix of European antiques and reproduction furnishings, attractive canopy, sleigh, or four-poster beds, and fresh, pretty fabrics, wallpapers, and hand-painted murals. This inn has the feeling of a home, and it definitely is a family operation—we were fortunate to meet Liz, the Ortons' daughter, who was manning the front desk on the day of our visit. *Directions*: Highway 246 off Highway 101 becomes Mission Drive, the main street of Solvang. Turn east off Mission onto First Street.

THE STORYBOOK INN
Owners: Carol & Chip Orton
409 First Street
Solvang, CA 93463
Tel: (805) 688-1703, Fax: (805) 686-0953
9 rooms, Double: $142–$214
Open all year
Credit cards: MC, VS
No restaurant
Children over 12 welcome
Wheelchair friendly

Just a short walk from the bustling historic plaza, MacArthur Place, one of Sonoma's oldest and grandest Victorian homes, has been restored and transformed into the most luxurious of country inns. Within the white picket fence the grounds boast perfectly manicured box hedges, flourishing rose gardens, majestic trees, ponds, water fountains, and a charming gazebo. The original manor houses ten lovely guestrooms, one of which is a large suite with its own verandah and an original claw-foot tub. Fifteen more cottages with fifty-four guestrooms have been added to the property and are tucked around the gardens and fruit orchards. The Caretaker's Cottage, a spacious suite, enjoys a Jacuzzi tub and a lovely private porch. There are twenty-nine new suites, each featuring a wood-burning fireplace, jet hydrotherapy tub, wet bar, original art, and verandah or balcony overlooking the gardens. All rooms have splendid garden views, modern bathrooms with oversized showers, walk-in closets, down comforters, monogrammed robes, DVD and CD players, and dual-line telephones with data port and voice mail. The Garden Spa at MacArthur Place offers an array of body treatments, massages, and facials based around elements found in the garden. An outdoor swimming pool and whirlpool are located next to the spa. In the restored barn, decorated with equestrian artifacts, is Saddles Restaurant, a casual yet intimate traditional steakhouse featuring an extensive wine list. Breakfast is served each morning in the barn. *Directions:* From the Sonoma plaza, turn right on Broadway. Turn left at the first stoplight, MacArthur Street

MACARTHUR PLACE
Owner: Suzanne Brangham
General Manager: Bill Blum
29 E. MacArthur Street
Sonoma, CA 95476
Tel: (707) 938-2929 or (800) 722-1866
Fax: (707) 933-9833
64 rooms, Double: $195–$475
Open all year, Credit cards: all major
Restaurant, Children welcome
Wheelchair friendly

On a full hilltop acre above the town of Sonora, the attractive Barretta Gardens Inn, built around 1895, sits off the road in the shade of its own mature and lush landscaped garden. Barretta Gardens benefits from the enthusiasm, dedication, and graciousness of its proprietors, Sally and Bruno Trial, who have thoughtfully refurbished the inn to give it its present fresh and tastefully elegant appearance. On one side of the living room with its array of family pictures is the dining room whose custom table is original to the home. Two guestrooms are found on the entry level. The Odette, off the living room with windows overlooking the front porch and a private entrance, is set under 10-foot-high ceilings and a crystal chandelier, and enjoys an appealing plant-filled sitting room furnished with white wicker furniture. Beautiful Italian beds have been converted to accommodate a queen mattress. The attached bathroom with whirlpool spa for two has lace-covered windows overlooking the rose garden and foothills. The Isabelle room, with its wall of windows looking out to the Sonora hills, is dressed in greens and maroons and enjoys a large Jacuzzi tub for two. Upstairs, the Chantal room is pretty in a wash of rose, while the Liliane room has a brass king-size bed. A small parlor sits between the Liliane room and the pretty Janine room, which together can be rented as a two-room suite or as a one-room suite with just the Janine. Bruno, a French baker, bakes fresh pastries in his on-site *boulangerie*, which are added to the full gourmet breakfast served each morning. *Directions*: Take Highway 108 to Washington. Make a right on Restano Way, a right at Mono Way, and a left on Barretta.

BARRETTA GARDENS INN
Owners: Sally & Bruno Trial
700 South Barretta Street
Sonora, CA 95370
Tel: (209) 532-6039 or (800) 206-3333
Fax: (209) 532-8257
5 rooms, Double: $130–$235
Open all year, Credit cards: all major
No restaurant, Children welcome

The Casa del Mar, a Mediterranean-style villa crowning a maze of lovely terraced gardens, is a pastel-peach, three-story stucco building with a red-tile roof. Refreshingly different from most California bed and breakfasts, Casa del Mar has no fussy frills in its decor: it has fresh white interior walls, furnishings of light pine and wicker, terra-cotta tiled floors, and colorful fabrics. For accent, the owner, Rick Klein, has selected bright, dramatic paintings and sculptures from local talent. The guestrooms are modest in size, with just enough space to accommodate a queen mattress set upon a custom-made wood platform and a corner chair or two. The closet is a functional alcove with a freestanding chest of drawers. Six guestrooms (Passion Flower, Shell, Hummingbird, Penthouse, Garden, and Heron) have subtle decorative touches to match their name and balconies where chairs are set for you to enjoy the view—the decor is fitting for a beach and park setting. You can enjoy evening hors d'oeuvres and linger over an incredible morning feast with the sound of waves in the distance. Just steps from this bed and breakfast is an entrance to the park which accesses hundreds of miles of trails, while two blocks down the road is the justifiably famous white sandy stretch of Stinson Beach. *Directions:* As you drive into town from the south, the first building on the right is a small firehouse. Turn right at the firehouse onto Belvedere Avenue. Casa del Mar is located 100 yards up the street, on the left.

CASA DEL MAR
Owner: Rick Klein
37 Belvedere Avenue
P.O. Box 238, Stinson Beach, CA 94970
Tel: (415) 868-2124 or (800) 552-2124
Fax: (415) 868-2305
Email: inn@stinsonbeach.com
6 rooms, Double: $180–$300
Open all year, Credit cards: all major
No restaurant, 1 room suitable for children
www.karenbrown.com/california/casadelmar.html

Sutter Creek is a charming Gold Country town whose main street is bordered at either end by New England-style residences surrounded by green lawns and neatly clipped hedges. Occupying one of these attractive homes is The Foxes, an idyllic hideaway put together with great flair and taste by Min and Pete Fox. The symbol of the inn is the fox and the perky little fellow pops up everywhere, yet this is not an inn with a cutesy theme, but an unpretentious, sophisticated inn where everything has been done with exquisite flair. Four suites are found in the main house and there are three suites to the rear. The lovely Victorian and Anniversary Suites upstairs in the main house have a service area for cold drinks and coffee between them. The Honeymoon Suite, very spacious, is a most elegant bedchamber where a large brick fireplace overlooks a magnificent bed and gorgeous Austrian armoire. Sparkling crystal chandeliers light the enormous bathroom. Each suite has a sitting area with a table for breakfast. Min and Pete discuss with you what you would like for breakfast, and then it is brought to your room with silver service accompanied by a large pot of coffee or tea. The Foxes definitely pamper their guests. *Directions:* From Sacramento take Highway 50 toward Placerville and Lake Tahoe. At the Watt Avenue exit, drive south to Jackson Highway (Highway 16). Drive east on Highway 16 and continue to the junction with Highway 49 where you turn south to Sutter Creek. The Foxes is located on the north end of Main Street (Highway 49) on the west side.

THE FOXES
Owners: Min & Pete Fox
77 Main Street
P.O. Box 159, Sutter Creek, CA 95685
Tel: (209) 267-5882 or (800) 987-3344
Fax: (209) 267-0712
Email: foxes@cdepot.net
7 suites, Double: $140–$205
Closed Christmas Eve & Day
Credit cards: MC, VS
No restaurant, Inappropriate for children
www.karenbrown.com/california/thefoxes.html

Grey Gables Inn is a pretty, soft-gray-blue house detailed with white trim sitting appealingly behind an English boxwood hedge within easy walking distance of the wonderful array of shops and restaurants in Sutter Creek. A red-brick pathway winds to the front entrance and weaves its way through a lovely back garden with fountains, vine-covered arbors, and a patchwork of flowers. Inside this renovated inn (the original part of the house dates back to 1897), the ambiance reflects the owners' heritage—Roger and Sue Garlick hail originally from the Cotswolds, and they have brought a touch of the English countryside to the Mother Lode. Seven of the eight guestrooms are named for an English poet. Browning, Byron, Wordsworth, and Shelley are located on the main floor, just off the entry, while Keats, Brontë, and Tennyson are found on the lower garden level. Garden-level rooms have fewer windows. Secluded away on the top floor is the Victorian Suite. All the rooms are decorated with floral spreads that complement the decor in hues of greens, rose, and mauve. All rooms have fireplaces, most have garden views, and some enjoy claw-foot tubs. Guests settle in the formal dining room and parlor to enjoy an informal afternoon tea with cake and scones, wine and hors d'oeuvres in the evening, and a bountiful breakfast served on fine English china. *Directions*: From Sacramento, take Highway 16 east to Highway 49 south for 6 miles to Sutter Creek. Grey Gables Inn is located on the west side of Highway 49, one block to the north of the downtown area.

GREY GABLES INN
Owners: Sue & Roger Garlick
161 Hanford Street
P.O. Box 1687, Sutter Creek, CA 95685
Tel: (209) 267-1039 or (800) 473-9422
Fax: (209) 267-0998
Email: reservations@greygables.com
8 rooms, Double: $110–$195
Open all year, Credit cards: all major
No restaurant, Children over 12 welcome
Wheelchair friendly
www.karenbrown.com/california/greygablesinn.html

The Cottage Inn, built as a resort in 1938, offers a number of storybook cottages nestled under the trees on the edge of Lake Tahoe. Parking is limited, so unfortunately the drive that weaves through the grounds is hampered by guests' cars. The lovely cottages, all with individual themes, capture the mountain-cabin atmosphere with their exposed knotty-pine walls, rich fabrics, Swedish pine furniture, and a variety of beds (brass, willow, or pine). The Fireplace Room has the added attraction of a wood-burning fireplace. The Pomin House, the original home on the property, contains a reception area, a breakfast room, and a large sitting room with games, books, local restaurant menus, and a small sitting area where wine and cheese are set out in the afternoons before the blazing log fire. In summer you can happily wile away the hours sunning yourself on the dock and swimming in Lake Tahoe's cool, clear waters—the inn has access to a private beach. The more energetic can take advantage of the lovely bicycle trail that passes in front of the inn and travels the lakeshore drive. Vikingsholm, Emerald Bay, and D.L. Bliss Park are a short car ride south. Ski resorts are between a five-minute and twenty-minute drive. *Directions*: From the Bay Area take Highway 80 to 89, Tahoe City exit. Follow the river to Tahoe City and continue south on 89 following West Lake Boulevard: the inn is 2 miles along on your left.

THE COTTAGE INN
Owner: Susanne Muhr
1690 West Lake Boulevard
P.O. Box 66
Tahoe City, CA 96145
Tel: (530) 581-4073
Fax: (530) 581-0226
Email: cottage@sierra.net
15 rooms, Double: $155–$255
Open all year, Credit cards: MC, VS
No restaurant, Inappropriate for children
Wheelchair friendly
www.karenbrown.com/california/cottageinn.html

Lake Tahoe is an exquisite, crystal-clear blue lake ringed by pines and backed by high mountains. The only outlet for this enormous body of water is the Truckee River, and standing at one of its broad bends some 3 miles downstream is River Ranch. This historic lodge enjoys a marvelous setting, best enjoyed from the circular bar with its picture windows and expanse of outdoor patio opening onto the river. Four of the five bedrooms in the lodge itself have sliding glass doors opening to small balconies and the rushing river. These lodge rooms are decorated with traditional antiques. The remaining bedrooms are decorated in a mountain-lodge style with lodgepole-pine beds (usually king-size)—be sure to request one with a balcony and/or a river view. (There are several rooms without the view that are less expensive.) In the mornings a Continental breakfast is served in a part of the dining room that is cantilevered over the river. The restaurant offers California-style cuisine and specializes in steaks, fresh seafood, and wild game. In winter Squaw Valley (5 miles) and Alpine Meadows (3 miles) operate shuttle buses to and from the lodge. In warm weather lunch or a cocktail on the spacious deck over the river is a wonderful way to end a raft trip, walk, or bicycle tour of the area. In spring and fall room rates are discounted. *Directions:* From the Bay Area take Highway 80 to Truckee. At Truckee take Highway 89 south and exit toward Tahoe City. River Ranch is 11 miles south of the freeway on Highway 89 at Alpine Meadows Road.

RIVER RANCH LODGE
General Manager: Bric Haley
Innkeeper: Jane Glynn
2285 River Road
P.O. Box 197, Tahoe City, CA 96145
Tel: (530) 583-4264 or (800) 535-9900
Fax: (530) 583-7237
Email: info@riverranchlodge.com
19 rooms, Double: $75–$150
Open all year, Credit cards: all major
Restaurant, Children welcome
www.karenbrown.com/california/riverranch.html

From the deck of this comfortable mountain lodge you can look over the crystal-clear blue waters of Lake Tahoe to pines and high mountains—an exquisite view at any time and magnificent when the mountains are capped with snow and pink and purple hues paint a spectacular sunset. Lake Tahoe has long been one of our favorite spots in California and since we found Sunnyside we have a base from which to go skiing in winter, water skiing, sailing, and hiking in the High Sierra in summer, and revel in the beauty of the area year round. A meal at Sunnyside is a real pleasure for not only do the dining room and deck have magnificent lake views but the food is most enjoyable, with the menu offering fresh seafood, prime rib, chicken dishes, and pasta, followed by a tempting array of desserts. It would be a shame to stay in such a lovely spot and not have a view of the lake, which Sunnyside's rooms offer you. Several bedrooms have wonderful river-stone fireplaces—what could be more romantic on a winter evening? Sunnyside has its own marina offering sailboat rentals and water skiing during the summer. In winter discount tickets for nearby major ski resorts are available. If you are unable to bring your own mountain bike, you'll find no shortage of places to rent one. Nevada casinos with their gambling opportunities and super-star entertainment are less than an hour's drive away. *Directions*: From Truckee take Highway 89 to Tahoe City. Turn right at the traffic lights and follow the lake shore south for 2 miles to Sunnyside.

SUNNYSIDE RESTAURANT & LODGE
Lodge Manager: Janet Gregor
1850 West Lake Blvd
P.O. Box 5969
Tahoe City, CA 96145
Tel: (530) 583-7200 or (800) 822-2754
Fax: (530) 583-2551,
24 rooms, Double: $90–$225
Open all year
Credit cards: all major, Restaurant
Children welcome, Wheelchair friendly

Tiburon is an enchanting waterfront community that enjoys million-dollar views across the bay to Angel Island and San Francisco. Surprisingly, it has never drawn the crowds that its famous neighbor, Sausalito, does—but that is definitely part of its charm. It is a relatively undiscovered jewel and its network of small streets that navigate to the water's edge are home to some enticing shops, boutiques, restaurants, and a small theater. Sandwiched between two great restaurants, Sam's and Guaymas, this hotel is located right on the dock at the water's edge. Appropriately named, Waters Edge Hotel is a narrow, two-story building spanning the distance between Main Street and the dock. Two guestrooms wide, the filtered water views from the guestrooms (many of which enjoy snug, private balconies) gets better as the location of the rooms gets closer to the back. The two Grand King rooms are the choice end rooms and enjoy the magnificent and only truly unobstructed views. Guestrooms, cozy in size, all have fireplaces and a similar, clean and corporate decor with beds topped with white feather duvets and comfortable seating by the windows. If you want to mingle with other guests, enjoy the wine and cheese service from 5 to 7 pm. A Continental breakfast is served in the rooms. *Directions:* Located to the north of San Francisco and the Golden Gate Bridge. From Highway 101 north or south, take the Tiburon exit east. Follow it into town and take a right onto Main Street. The hotel is located on Main Street just before you get to the Corinthian Yacht Club.

WATERS EDGE HOTEL
Owners: Joie de Vivre Hospitality
General Manager: Karlene Holloman
25 Main Street
Tiburon, CA 94920
Tel: (415) 789-5999 or (877) 789-5999
Fax: (415) 789-5888
23 rooms, Double: $195–$350
Open all year, Credit cards: all major
No restaurant, Children welcome, Wheelchair friendly

The Lost Whale, a gray-wash Cape-Cod house with blue trim set on 5 acres of windswept Northern Californian coast, was designed by Susanne and Lee Miller who manage it with a refreshing, bountiful enthusiasm. The mood is set by the living room with its fir floors warmed by throw rugs and comfortable sofas arranged to enjoy not only the fireplace but also the magnificent view across the garden, through the towering pine trees to the ocean. Five rooms capture this same glorious view while three overlook the northern gardens. Whichever room you select, you will find it decorated in a light, airy style. Several rooms have an extra bed to accommodate a child and two have a sleeping loft. Whereas most inns discourage children, here at The Lost Whale they are made genuinely welcome. Relax on the deck or well-placed chairs in a quiet corner of the garden and listen to the crashing waves and the distant barking of sea lions. Stroll down the cliff path to the 2-mile private beach or pop into your car for the short drive up the road to Patrick's Point State Park with its miles of beaches, walking paths along rocky headlands, and the opportunity to explore a re-created Indian village. The Lost Whale is a homey inn in a spectacular setting. *Directions:* North from Trinidad take the Seawood Drive exit, turn right on Patrick's Point Drive, drive 1-1/8 mile north. South from Oregon, exit at Patrick's Point Drive, continue south 1 mile.

THE LOST WHALE
Owners: Susanne Lakin & Lee Miller
3452 Patrick's Point Drive
Trinidad, CA 95570
Tel: (800) 677-7859, Fax: (707) 677-0284
Email: lmiller@lostwhaleinn.com
8 rooms, Double: $138–$198
Open all year
Credit cards: all major
No restaurant
Children welcome
www.karenbrown.com/california/lostwhale.html

The charming Carrville Inn, located in the splendid Trinity Alps, dates back to the mid-1800s when it was a popular stop for stagecoaches on their way to Oregon. You cannot help falling in love with this inn, an appealing wooden home with a romantic, two-tiered porch stretching across the front where guests relax in comfy, old-fashioned wicker chairs to soak in the idyllic view. A dark-green, densely wooded hill rises behind the hotel, setting off to perfection the pristine white of the building. In front, a meadow sweeps toward distant hills and farm animals graze in the pasture. On hot days, a swimming pool enclosed by a picket fence is a welcome sight, or you might prefer just to laze in the hammock and dream. The decor throughout is appropriately Victorian with many antiques of the period. The dining room is especially cheerful, with large windows opening onto the rose garden. Upstairs there are five individually decorated bedrooms, three with private bathrooms and two sharing a large bathroom. Your charming hosts, Sheri and Dave Overly, had never even stayed in a bed and breakfast before buying the inn in 1998, but the art of innkeeping comes naturally to them. In the evening your bed linens are turned down, the lamps softly lit, a pitcher of iced water is placed beside the bed, and chocolates are set on the pillow. *Directions*: Take Highway 3 north from Weaverville and continue 6 miles past Trinity Center to the Carrville Loop Road (the first paved road on your left after passing the lake).

CARRVILLE INN
Owners: Sheri & Dave Overly
Carrville Loop Road
Rt. 2, Box 3536
Trinity Center, CA 96091
Tel: (530) 266-3511, Fax: (530) 266-3778
5 bedrooms, 3 with private bathrooms
Double: $120–$155
Open April to late October
Credit cards: none
No restaurant, Children over 16 welcome

The McCaffrey House B&B Inn is a lovely country home nestled in a grove of giant oak, pine, and cedar trees. In 1996, Michael and Stephanie built this three-story house on the lot where Stephanie's family cabin sat for 35 years. The living room and other common areas are tastefully decorated and inviting for visiting with other guests or reading a book. You will also find over 500 videos for watching in your room. The warmth of the owners is apparent throughout the inn by the family photos hung on the walls and by their love of their two dogs. Because the McCaffreys designed the house as a bed and breakfast, its seven rooms are spacious, comfortable, and well appointed, each with an iron firestove with a self-timer so that you can doze off in front of the fire, and a bathroom with tub and shower. A handmade Amish quilt sets the color scheme for each room, and robes and extra towels are provided for jaunts to the hot tub. Most rooms have a balcony or patio, and some have views down to a creek. The McCaffreys serve a complete breakfast at 9, but are happy to accommodate schedules by serving earlier. Thoughtful appointments, charming owners, and a picturesque setting make this a winner. *Directions*: From San Francisco take Highway 580 east to 205, go east to 120, then east to 108. When you reach Sonora, travel east for 11 miles, and ½ mile above the East Twain Harte exit, make a right turn off the highway just beyond the 4,000-feet elevation marker.

McCAFFREY HOUSE B&B INN
Owners: Stephanie & Michael McCaffrey
P.O. Box 67
23251 Highway 108
Twain Harte, CA 95383
Tel: (888) 586-0757, Fax: (209) 586-3689
Email: innkeeper@mccaffreyhouse.com
7 rooms, Double: $125–$180
Open all year, Credit cards: all major
No restaurant
Inappropriate for infants
www.karenbrown.com/california/mccaffreyhouse.html

Immediately south of Santa Monica, Venice Beach is one of Los Angeles's most popular stretches of sand and its Oceanfront Walk draws a colorful crowd. Just a block from the bustle of Oceanfront Walk the Venice Beach House is a lovely California Craftsman House that is on the National Register of Historic Places. Sheltered behind its own fence and large expanse of lovely gardens, the Beach House is inviting, with a lived-in ambiance and comfort. You enter from the front porch into an open, pretty sitting room where iced tea and cookies are set out in the afternoons and a Continental breakfast is served each morning. Fresh flowers dress the room, which is warmed on cooler days by a wood-burning fireplace. The welcome by the innkeeper is casual and relaxed, yet gracious and warm. The home has nine guestrooms of varying sizes, five of which enjoy a private bathroom, and all are decorated like bedrooms in a private home. Just off the front room the Olympic Suite, which commemorates the 1932 Olympic games hosted by Venice Beach, is lovely, with a large bay window which seems to bring the garden into the room. Favorite rooms upstairs are the Abbott Kinney, small but cozy with its own porch and decorated in a tartan of blues and greens, and the Pier Suite, which has a distant ocean view and a wood-burning fireplace. *Directions:* Exit the 405 at Washington Street, travel west on Pacific, turn right and then left on 29th. The Venice Beach House is located off Speedway between 29th and 30th. (The inn has parking spaces on 29th Avenue.)

VENICE BEACH HOUSE
Owners: Vivian & Phillip Boesch
15 Thirtieth Avenue
Venice, CA 90291
Tel: (310) 823-1966
Fax: (310) 823-1842
9 rooms, 5 with private bathrooms
Double: $95–$165
Open all year
Credit cards: all major
No restaurant
Children welcome

While the attractions of staying in Yosemite Valley cannot be denied, a more serene, country atmosphere pervades the Wawona Hotel, located within Yosemite Park about a 30-mile drive south of the valley. With its shaded verandahs overlooking broad, rolling lawns and a nine-hole golf course, the hotel presents a welcoming picture that invites one to wile away the afternoon beside the pool, fondly referred to as the swimming tank. Bedrooms are in several scattered buildings and private bathrooms are at a premium. Hotel rooms without private baths have bathroom and shower facilities located at the end of each building's verandah. The Annex building was completely refurbished in 1996, and the main dining room renovated in 1997—both in a gracious turn-of-the-century style. This is the kind of wonderful old hotel that attracts lots of families. In the summer rangers give interpretive presentations on such topics as bears, climbing, and photography and there are carriage rides, wonderful Sunday brunches, Saturday-night barbecues, and barn dances. Ask about the Wawona's "discounted lodging packages," which are very good value for money. Accommodation and golf packages are available in the spring and fall. *Directions:* Wawona is in Yosemite National Park, 30 miles south of Yosemite Valley on Highway 41.

WAWONA HOTEL
Manager: Al Gonzalez
Yosemite National Park, CA 95389
Tel: (559) 252-4848, Fax: (559) 456-0542
104 rooms, 50 with private bathrooms
Double: $99–$158*
*Breakfast not included
Open mid-Mar to Dec, weekends only Jan to mid-Mar
Credit cards: all major
Restaurant
Children welcome
Wheelchair friendly

The Ahwahnee with its 123 bedrooms hardly qualifies for inclusion in a country inn guide. It is a large, bustling resort with a level of activity in its lobby that is comparable to that at many airports, yet it merits inclusion because it is the most individual of hotels, with all the sophistication of a grand European castle, surrounded by the awesome beauty of Yosemite Valley. The lofty vastness of the lounge dwarfs the sofas and chairs and its huge windows frame magnificent views of the outdoors. The dining room has to be the largest in the United States: it is gorgeous with its massive floor-to-ceiling windows framing towering granite walls, cascading waterfalls, and giant sugar pines. In contrast to the surrounding wilderness, the dining room wears an air of sophistication in the evening when guests dress for dinner and flickering candlelight casts its magical spell. Bedrooms are in the main building or in little cottages in a nearby woodland grove. There is a small swimming pool just off the back patio and it is not unusual to see deer grazing on the lawn. This is undeniably a grand old hotel but if the price tag is a little rich for your blood, less expensive accommodations in Yosemite Valley are briefly outlined on page 53. *Directions:* The Ahwahnee is located in Yosemite Valley just east of Yosemite Village.

THE AHWAHNEE
Manager: Larry Ross
Yosemite National Park, CA 95389
Tel: (559) 252-4848, Fax: (559) 456-0542
123 rooms & cottages
Double: $318.75–$662.85*
*Breakfast not included
Open all year
Credit cards: all major
Restaurant
Children welcome
Wheelchair friendly

Lavender, which opened in the fall of 1999, is the youngest addition to the Four Sisters' family of small, charming hotels. The location is superb—in the quaint town of Yountville, just a short stroll to the boutiques and restaurants. The house was built in the 1850s by the Grigsby family, early pioneers who came across the continent by covered wagon. The two-story, gray building, which exudes the flavor of a country farmhouse, is charming in its simplicity. The house was totally renovated and completely modernized inside, but great care was taken to retain the shell of the building, which still maintains its authentic historic character. On the old-fashioned verandah that wraps around two sides of the home you will find an inviting porch swing where guests can sit back and relax. Behind and to the side of the main house are three individual cottages providing eight elegant guestrooms, all with fireplaces, direct-dial telephones with data ports, individual air conditioning, imported tiles, and custom-made "old-world" furniture. The vibrant colors used throughout are reminiscent of Provence, a theme enhanced by nearly 200 feet of fragrant lavender planted in the garden, forming a seasonal garland of purple around the inn. The room price includes a scrumptious full gourmet breakfast, afternoon tea, hors d'oeuvres, and the use of the inn's bicycles to explore the surrounding countryside. *Directions*: Coming north on Highway 29, take the Yountville exit. Turn right at the bottom of the exit, then quickly left on Washington Street. Go to Webber Avenue and turn right. Lavender is on the corner of Webber and Jefferson, marked by a giant oak.

LAVENDER
Innkeeper: Jessica Anderegg
2020 Webber Avenue
Yountville, CA 94599
Tel: (707) 944-1388 or (800) 522-4140
Fax: (707) 944-1579
8 rooms, Double: $200–$250
Open all year, Credit cards: all major
No restaurant, Children welcome
Wheelchair friendly
www.karenbrown.com/california/lavenderinn.html

The location of the Maison Fleurie is superb—right in the heart of the quaint town of Yountville, within walking distance of great shopping and a selection of restaurants. The inn (with a look of the French countryside) is a romantic cluster of thick stone and brick buildings, entrancingly draped with ivy. From the moment you enter, the mood is conducive to a carefree holiday. You come into a parlor-like foyer with a corner fireplace, sofa, and chairs. When you begin to wonder if this is a hotel, you notice a discreet reception desk in the room beyond. To the right, a few steps lead down to an inviting lounge where two comfortable sofas (slipcovered with a pretty floral fabric) flank a brick fireplace. The price of the bedrooms depends upon size—the larger are more expensive. None are especially spacious, but all are appealingly decorated and well priced for the value received. The friendly, well-managed Maison Fleurie offers many extras: not only is a hearty breakfast served in the morning, but also wine and hors d'oeuvres in the late afternoon. Cold and hot drinks are available all day, along with cookies. The morning paper, bathrobes, turn-down service, and the complimentary use of bicycles are additional amenities. Tucked into the courtyards behind the inn are a swimming pool and a hot tub. *Directions:* Coming north from Napa on Highway 29, turn right into Yountville onto Washington Street. When the road splits, keep to the right onto Yount Street. You will see the inn on your left.

MAISON FLEURIE
Innkeeper: Jessica Anderegg
6529 Yount Street
Yountville, CA 94599
Tel: (707) 944-2056 or (800) 788-0369
Fax: (707) 944-9342
13 rooms, Double: $110–$260
Open all year
Credit cards: all major
No restaurant, Children welcome
Wheelchair friendly
www.karenbrown.com/california/maisonfleurie.html

The Vintage Inn is a large hotel complex nestled between Highway 29 and the main street of Yountville. The 80 rooms are housed in an attractive mix of two-story green and blue, wood-sided and red-brick buildings, which are connected by meandering paths. We recommend the Vintage Inn as an alternative to bed and breakfast accommodation if you seek a bit more anonymity, privacy, and the full services of a luxury hotel. A concierge is present for assistance, a limited menu is offered poolside and through room service, and the stretch limousine parked at the front entry is available for hire. Guestrooms are very attractive in their decor, spacious, and comfortable, equipped with television, fireplace (duraflame logs), coffee maker, a complimentary bottle of wine, tub-shower with Jacuzzi jets, and terrycloth robes. Turn-down service is offered each evening and appreciated touches such as a fresh supply of towels and bedside chocolates are thoughtfully provided. In the mornings, an appetizing champagne breakfast buffet with juice, hot beverages, fresh-baked pastries, cereals, yogurt, and fruit is set out in the front lobby and you can sit either inside or at tables on the patio. The Vintage Inn has a capable management team, which extends a courteous welcome and strives to please. *Directions:* Take the Yountville exit off Highway 29, turn right at the bottom of the exit, then quickly left on Washington Street. The inn is just off Washington Street beyond Vintage 1870.

VINTAGE INN
Manager: David Shipman
6541 Washington Street
Yountville, CA 94599
Tel: (707) 944-1112 or (800) 351-1133
Fax: (707) 944-1617
80 rooms, Double: $275–$450
Open all year
Credit cards: all major
No restaurant
Children welcome
Wheelchair friendly

Index

Travel Your Dreams • Order Your Karen Brown Guides Today

Please ask in your local bookstore for Karen Brown's Guides. If the books you want are unavailable, you may order directly from the publisher. Books will be shipped immediately.

_____ *Austria: Charming Inns & Itineraries* $19.95

_____ *California: Charming Inns & Itineraries* $19.95

_____ *England: Charming Bed & Breakfasts* $18.95

_____ *England, Wales & Scotland: Charming Hotels & Itineraries* $19.95

_____ *France: Charming Bed & Breakfasts* $18.95

_____ *France: Charming Inns & Itineraries* $19.95

_____ *Germany: Charming Inns & Itineraries* $19.95

_____ *Ireland: Charming Inns & Itineraries* $19.95

_____ *Italy: Charming Bed & Breakfasts* $18.95

_____ *Italy: Charming Inns & Itineraries* $19.95

_____ *Mid-Atlantic: Charming Inns & Itineraries* $19.95

_____ *New England: Charming Inns & Itineraries* $19.95

_____ *Portugal: Charming Inns & Itineraries* $19.95

_____ *Spain: Charming Inns & Itineraries* $19.95

_____ *Switzerland: Charming Inns & Itineraries* $19.95

Name _____ Street _____

Town _____ State_____ Zip _____ Tel _____

Credit Card (MasterCard or Visa) _____ Expires: _____

For orders in the USA, add $5 for the first book and $1 for each additional book for shipment. Overseas shipping(airmail) is $10 for 1 to 2 books, $20 for 3 to 4 books etc. CA residents add 8% sales tax. Fax or mail form with check or credit card information to:

KAREN BROWN'S GUIDES
Post Office Box 70 • San Mateo • California • 94401 • USA
tel: (650) 342-9117, fax: (650) 342-9153, e-mail: karen@karenbrown.com

Become a Karen Brown Member

Why become a Karen Brown Member? **Savings**! In no time at all KB Members earn back their membership fee. In most cases, when they use just **one** of our packaged discounts! Introductory memberships are special-priced through 2001. Visit the Karen Brown website: www.karenbown.com for the most current details.

Karen Brown online store discount
A members-only discount worth an **additional 20%** off all orders in our store.

First Access to new discoveries
Receive early access to our newly discovered properties. If you cannot find a room in one of our currently recommended properties, these yet-to-be-published gems might be able to offer you alternative accommodation—a priceless benefit!

Discounts negotiated through our travel partners
Partners include participating recommended properties, such as Karen's own Seal Cove Inn. Benefits include condo rental upgrades in Mexico, airline discounts, auto rental discounts and more!

A complete listing of member benefits can be found on our website:
www.karenbrown.com

<u>Become a Member Today</u>

KB Travel Service

❖ **KB Travel Service** offers travel planning assistance using itineraries designed by *Karen Brown* and published in her guidebooks. We will customize any itinerary to fit your personal interests.

❖ We will plan your itinerary with you, help you decide how long to stay and what to do once you arrive, and work out the details.

❖ We will book your airline tickets and your rental car, arrange rail travel, reserve accommodations recommended in *Karen Brown's Guides,* and supply you with point-to-point information and consultation.

Contact us to start planning your travel!

800.782.2128 or e-mail: info@kbtravelservice.com

Service fees do apply

KB Travel Service
16 East Third Avenue
San Mateo, CA 94401 USA
www.kbtravelservice.com

Independently owned and operated by Town & Country Travel
CST 2001543-10

auto ✲ europe.

Karen Brown's

Preferred Car Rental Service Provider

When Traveling to Europe
for

International Car Rental Services
Chauffeur & Transfer Services
Prestige & Sports Cars
Motor Home Rentals

800-223-5555

Be sure to identify yourself as a Karen Brown Traveler.
For special offers and discounts use your
Karen Brown ID number 99006187.

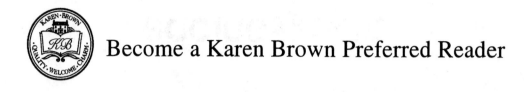

Become a Karen Brown Preferred Reader

We'd love to welcome you as a Karen Brown Preferred Reader. Send us your name and address and you will be entered in our monthly drawing to receive a free Karen Brown guide. As a Preferred Reader, you will receive special promotions and be the first to know when new editions of Karen Brown's guides go to press.

Name: _____

Street: _____

Town: _____

State: _____ Zip: _____ Country: _____

Tel: _____ Fax: _____

Email: _____

Please send to:
Karen Brown's Guides
Post Office Box 70
San Mateo, California 94401, USA
tel: (650) 342-9117
fax: (650) 342-9153

e-mail: karen@karenbrown.com,   website: www: karenbrown.com

Let's do something monumental.

Italians make even the simplest pleasures feel larger than life. And only Alitalia delivers that feeling to every journey you make.

As Italy's premier airline, Alitalia offers the most nonstop flights to Italy from New York's JFK, Newark, Boston, Chicago, Los Angeles, San Francisco and Miami.

And when you choose to continue your journey Alitalia flies to over 57 countries worldwide, connecting to cities in Europe, Africa, Australia, the Middle and Far East.

Fly Magnifica Class or economy and enjoy global travel coupled with attentive service and wide-body comfort. Relax with world-class wines, the finest cuisine and designer shopping on board. It's everything you'd expect from a culture that has turned living into an art form.

Discover Italy with Karen Brown's guides and Alitalia!
Book online or call 800.223.5730.

Let's fly **Alitalia**

alitaliausa.com

CRITIQUE PLACES IN OUR BOOK

We greatly appreciate first-hand evaluations of places in our guides so your critiques are invaluable to us. To stay current on the properties in our guides, we keep a database of readers' comments. To keep our readers up to date, we also sometimes share feedback with them via our website.

Please list your comments on properties that you have visited. We welcome accolades, as well as criticisms.

Name of Hotel or B&B _____

Town _____ Country _____

Comments:

Your name _____ Street _____

Town _____ State _____ Zip _____ Country _____

Tel _____ E-mail _____ Date _____

Do we have your permission to electronically publish your comments on our website? Yes _____ No _____

If yes, would you like to remain anonymous? Yes ___No ___, or may we use your name? Yes___ No___

Please send report to: Karen Brown's Guides, Post Office Box 70, San Mateo, California 94401, USA
tel: (650) 342-9117, fax: (650) 342-9153, e-mail: karen@karenbrown.com, www.karenbrown.com

SHARE YOUR DISCOVERIES WITH US

Outstanding properties often come from readers' discoveries. We would love to hear from you.

Please list below any hotel or bed & breakfast you discover. Tell us what you liked about the property and, if possible, please include a brochure or photographs so we can share your enthusiasm. We keep a permanent database of all of your recommendations for future use. Note: we regret we cannot return photos.

Owner _____ Hotel or B&B _____

Address _____ Town _____ Country _____

Comments:

Your name _____ Street _____

Town _____ State _____ Zip _____ Country _____

Tel _____ E-mail _____ Date _____

Do we have your permission to electronically publish your comments on our website? Yes _____ No _____

If yes, would you like to remain anonymous? Yes ___No ___, or may we use your name? Yes___ No___

Please send report to: Karen Brown's Guides, Post Office Box 70, San Mateo, California 94401, USA
tel: (650) 342-9117, fax: (650) 342-9153, e-mail: karen@karenbrown.com, www.karenbrown.com

KAREN BROWN wrote her first travel guide in 1976. Her personalized travel series has grown to fourteen titles which Karen and her small staff work diligently to keep updated. Karen, her husband, Rick, and their children, Alexandra and Richard, live in Moss Beach, a small town on the coast south of San Francisco. They settled here in 1991 when they opened Seal Cove Inn. Karen is frequently traveling, but when she is home, in her role as innkeeper, enjoys welcoming Karen Brown readers.

CLARE BROWN was a travel consultant for many years, specializing in planning itineraries to Europe using charming small hotels in the countryside. The focus of her job remains unchanged, but now her expertise is available to a larger audience—the readers of her daughter Karen's country inn guides. When Clare and her husband, Bill, are not traveling, they live either in Hillsborough, California, or at their home in Vail, Colorado, where family and friends frequently join them for skiing.

JUNE BROWN'S love of travel was inspired by the *National Geographic* magazines that she read as a girl in her dentist's office—so far she has visited over 40 countries. June hails from Sheffield, England and lived in Zambia and Canada before moving to northern California where she lives in San Mateo with her husband, Tony, their daughter Clare, their German Shepherd, and a Siamese cat.

BARBARA TAPP, the talented artist who produces all of the hotel sketches and delightful illustrations in this guide, was raised in Australia where she studied in Sydney at the School of Interior Design. Although Barbara continues with freelance projects, she devotes much of her time to illustrating the Karen Brown guides. Barbara lives in Kensington, California, with her husband, Richard, their two sons, Jonothan and Alexander, and daughter, Georgia.

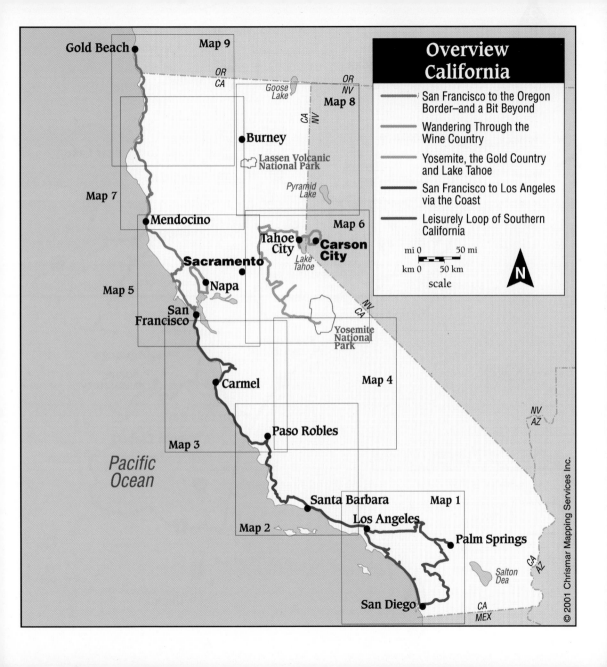

Gold Beach

Map 9

OR
CA

Goose
Lake

OR
NV

Map 8

CA
NV

Burney

Lassen Volcanic
National Park

Pyramid
Lake

Map 7

Mendocino

Sacramento

Napa

Map 6

Tahoe
City

Carson
City

Lake
Tahoe

Map 5

San
Francisco

NV
CA

Yosemite
National
Park

Map 4

Carmel

Map 3

Paso Robles

Pacific
Ocean

NV
AZ

Santa Barbara

Map 1

Map 2

Los Angeles

Palm Springs

Salton
Dea

CA
AZ

San Diego

CA
MEX

Overview
California

— San Francisco to the Oregon
  Border–and a Bit Beyond
— Wandering Through the
  Wine Country
— Yosemite, the Gold Country
  and Lake Tahoe
— San Francisco to Los Angeles
  via the Coast
— Leisurely Loop of Southern
  California

mi 0   50 mi

km 0   50 km

scale

N

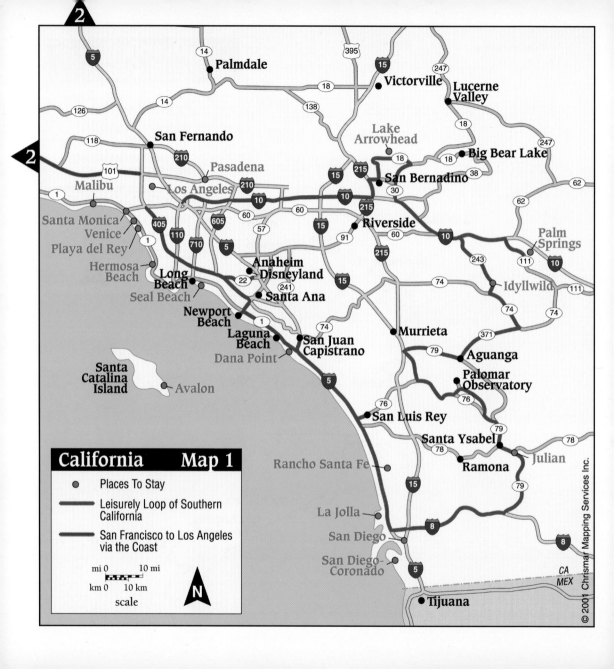

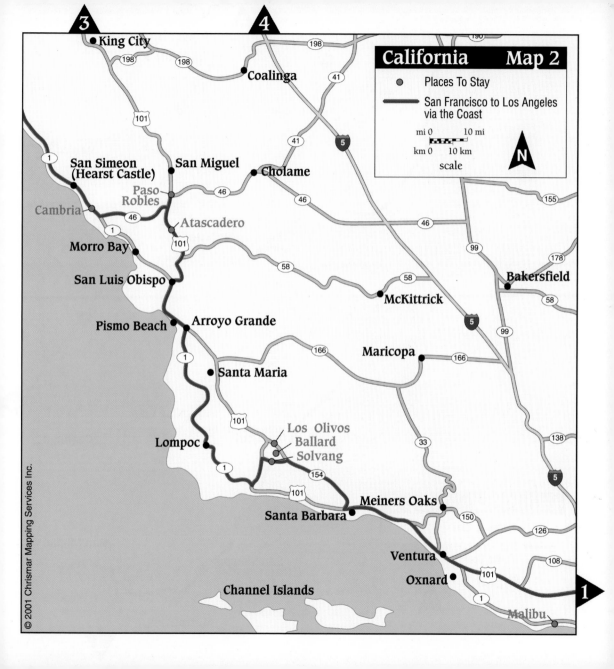

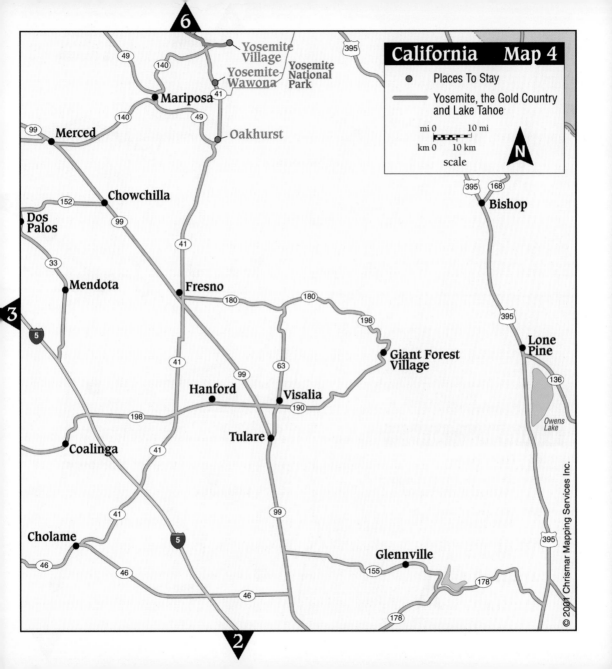

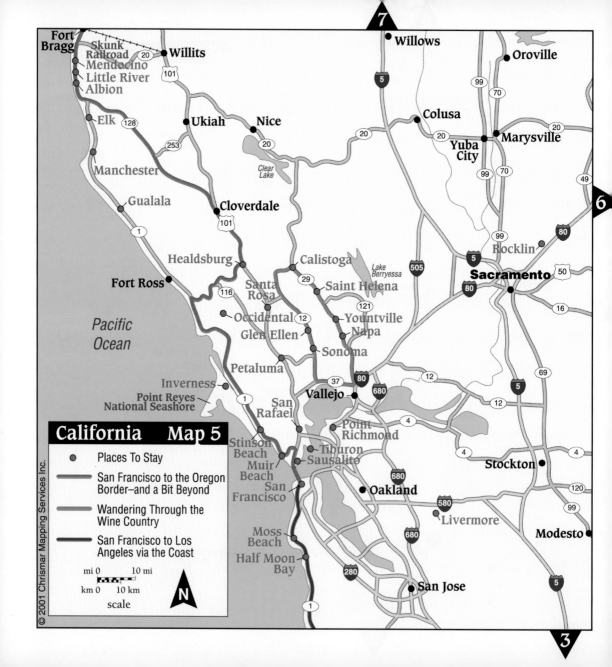

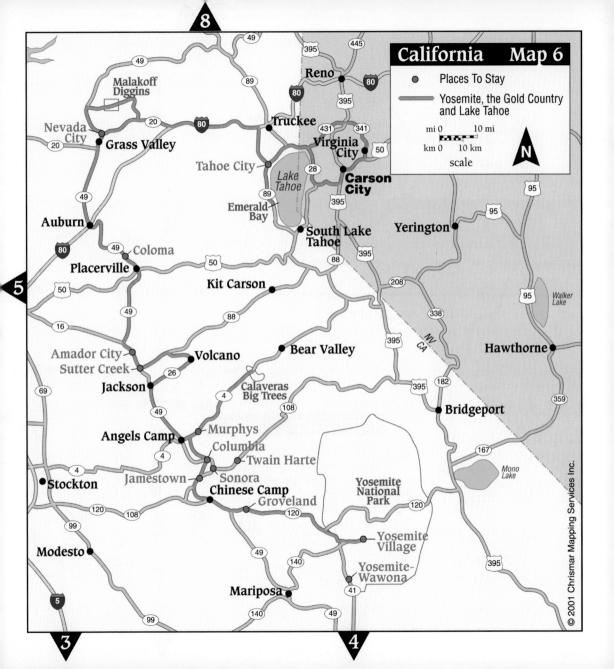

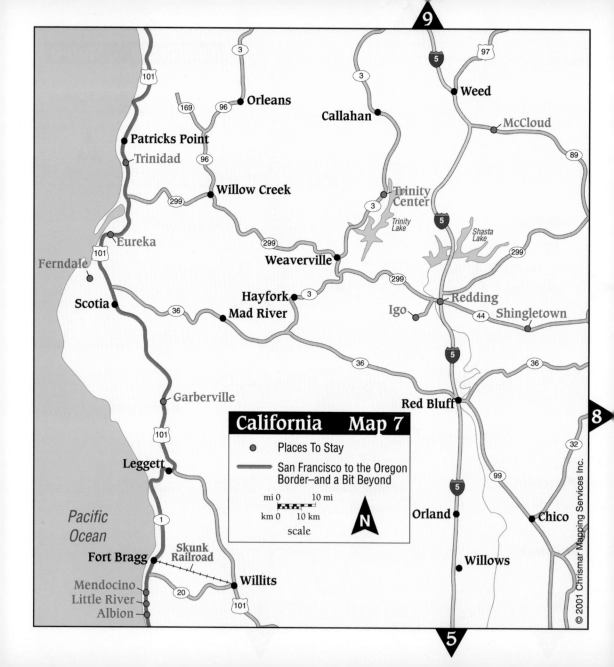

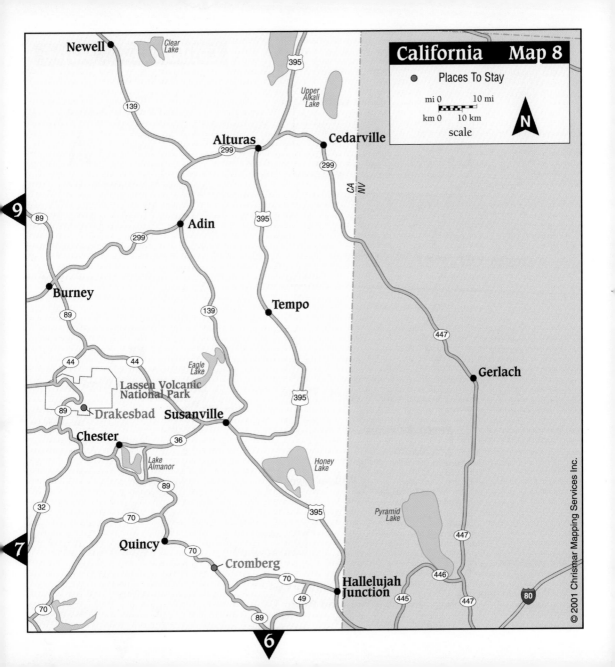

Newell

Clear
Lake

395

Upper
Alkali
Lake

139

Alturas
299

Cedarville

299

CA
NV

395

Adin

299

89

89

Burney

139

Tempo

89

447

44

44

Eagle
Lake

Gerlach

Lassen Volcanic
National Park

89

Drakesbad

Susanville

Chester

36

Lake
Almanor

Honey
Lake

89

395

32

70

Pyramid
Lake

Quincy

70

Cromberg

70

447

Hallelujah
Junction

70

49

446

445

447

89

70

80

California   Map 8

Places To Stay

mi 0   10 mi

km 0   10 km
scale

N

9

7

6

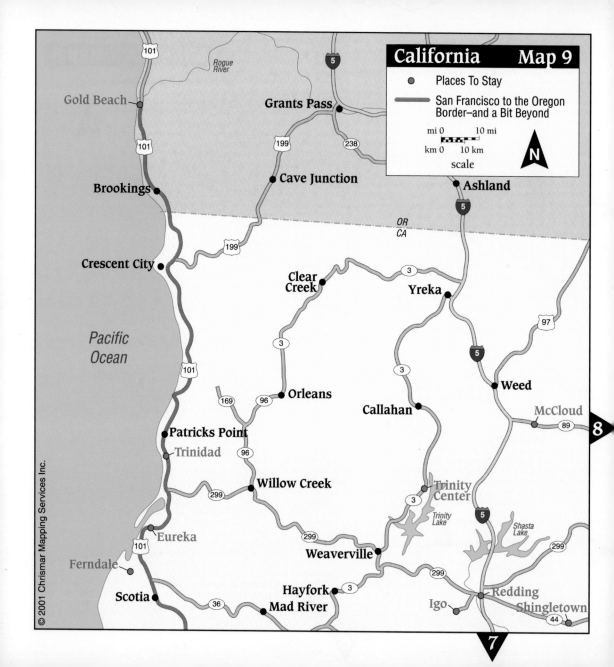

California   Map 9

Places To Stay

San Francisco to the Oregon Border–and a Bit Beyond

mi 0   10 mi
km 0   10 km
scale

N

101

Rogue River

5

Gold Beach

Grants Pass

101

199

238

Cave Junction

Ashland

5

Brookings

OR
CA

199

Crescent City

Clear Creek

Yreka

3

97

Pacific Ocean

3

5

101

3

Weed

McCloud

169   96

Orleans

Callahan

89

8

Patricks Point

Trinidad

96

Willow Creek

Trinity Center

299

3

Trinity Lake

5

Shasta Lake

Eureka

101

299

Weaverville

299

299

Ferndale

Hayfork

3

Igo

Redding

Scotia

36

Mad River

Shingletown

44

7

© 2001 Chrismar Mapping Services Inc.

California

Mid-Atlantic

New England

Austria

Enhance Your Guides
www.karenbrown.com

England

- Hotels
- Itineraries
- Color photos
- Coordinated Maps
- Edits, updates and specials
- Direct email links for ease of reservations
- Direct web links for additional documentation
- Visit our online store for discounts & specials
- Be the first to learn about our newest discoveries
- Benefit from our research before our books go to press
- Enjoy benefits and privileges as a Karen Brown Member

France

Germany

Ireland

Switzerland

Spain

Portugal

Italy

Karen Brown's

Seal Cove Inn

Located on the coastside, south of San Francisco

Seal Cove Inn, 221 Cypress Avenue, Moss Beach, Ca. 94038

Tel: (650) 728-4114, Fax: (650) 728-4116, E-mail: sealcove@coastside.net

www.sealcoveinn.com